Life and
Times
in
Colonial
Philadelphia

(Pa. Hist. & Museum Comm., Harrisburg; original in Hist. Society of Penna., Phila.)

WILLIAM PENN—Age 22
Uneasy in armor amid apocolyptic flashes

Life and Times in
Colonial
Philadelphia

Joseph J. Kelley, Jr.

Stackpole Books

LIFE AND TIMES IN COLONIAL PHILADELPHIA

Copyright © 1973 by
The Stackpole Company

Published by
Stackpole Books
Cameron and Kelker Streets
Harrisburg, Pa. 17105

917.4811
K29l
1973

All rights reserved, including the right to reproduce this book or portions thereof in any form or by any means, electronic or mechanical, including photocopying, recording, or by any information storage and retrieval system, without permission in writing from the publisher. All inquiries should be addressed to Stackpole Books, Cameron and Kelker Streets, Harrisburg, Pennsylvania 17105.

Printed in the U.S.A.

Library of Congress Cataloging in Publication Data

Kelley, Joseph J
    Life and times in colonial Philadelphia.

    Bibliography: p.
    1. Philadelphia—History—Colonial period.
2. Philadelphia—Social life and customs.
I. Title.
F158.4.K44   917.48'11'032   73-3409
ISBN 0-8117-0949-3

H. F. Davis Memorial Library
Colby Community Junior College
Colby, Kansas 67701

26137

To the Memory of my Parents
JOSEPH J. and KATHRYNE HOOKEY KELLEY
from whom I inherited my
love for Philadelphia

CONTENTS

Under the banner of the intriguing Queen Christina the Swedes come to the Delaware Valley, and the 400 lb. Governor Printz leaves heavy footprints in the vicinity of future Philadelphia as he tries to establish a society. Indians, Dutchmen and Finns add complications, and Printz's imperious daughter, Armegot, makes a lasting impression. Steam baths and life styles become firmly fixed before the English inherit the earth, by conquest.

William Penn's social and spiritual philosophy takes shape through confrontations with the British Government which lead to pamphlets and prison, and ultimately into his "Holy Experiment." The intensity with which he pursues his dream of a city founded on peace and love embraces the Indians whose lineage he believes stems from one of the lost tribes of Israel. Difficulties and dilemmas created by those he thought "friends" obstruct the way, but his theories and powerful prose foreshadow ideas of the present. Young Benjamin Franklin comes to Philadelphia as Penn dies embittered in England a few years earlier, and inadvertently provides the city with a continuity of individualistic personality.

A planned city from the beginning, Philadelphia emerges from the outlines of Penn's vision, with admirable docking facilities but streets that have problems in the form of mud, underground streams and a surplus of dogs. Two of the four squares, ultimately to be called Washington and Franklin, serve purposes Penn never planned.

eardrums of the performers, while chamber music eventually makes its appearance in the homes of the affluent, and music clubs magnetize diversified talents. The pioneer concert producer goes insane but in his lamentable death leaves a determined coterie of afficiandos who eventually give the art the lift to professionalism.

The Painter's Brush Found Fertile Ground in Penn's Model City

Prosperous Quakers compromised their precept against graven images to give posterity a limited glimpse of their faces and forms (fully dressed). Prosperity and vanity thus create a market for artists. West, Peale and Stuart are, of course, here, along with lesser known colleagues. Captain John Andre, Robert Fulton—more famous for other things—are talented with pen and brush—and miniatures are carried as symbols of love.

The Battle Between Good and Evil was Well Fought in Philadelphia

Colonial Philadelphia is a microcosm of Christian soldiers at war with each other, as sects fight among themselves and get involved in politics, too. George Whitefield comes to preach and draws thousands with his evangelism, momentarily diverting the populace from the flesh and the devil, while Franklin is fascinated by the range of his voice, measures it and the mood of the audience. Of all the major denominations only the Jews escape intramural strife, proving themselves better Christians than the Christians. Jemima Wilkenson, a beautiful brunette "Free Quaker", draws bedazzled males to hear her sermons, and invites tired housewives to forget the bonds of matrimony and join her New Jerusalem where men do the chores and women reign as synthetic angels. Penn's doctrine of "religious toleration" is an invitation to curious creeds.

Pleasure Was Where They Found It, and Often in a Noggin

A guided tour of grogshops, inns and taverns from the Blue Anchor in 1681 to the Three Jolly Irishmen a century later features among other things Franklin's drinking songs, brawls and beefsteaks and Reverend Israel Acrelius who undertakes an odd survey of the variety of drinks served in 18th century America. Philadelphia gives the "mint julep" to the South—the Paxtang Boys shoot the weathervanes on the Indian Queen's stables—visitors like John Adams rate different inns, and visiting sailors prefer the "Helltown" pubs, descendants of the tippling houses that plagued Penn and early lawmen. The City Tavern is "the" place to be seen during meetings of the Continental Congress and the British occupation, and is succeeded by the French hotel, Oeller's.

Despite Quaker frowns love found its inevitable way, and as Philadelphia increased in stature, its people acquired more sophistication. The Swedes took a broad view of marriage and divorce, as did their Dutch neighbors, but 18th century Philadelphians find themselves wrestling with stricter English standards. The British Army, with the carefree attitude troops across the centuries have adopted toward sex, broadened horizons for many maidens, and after them came the French. Manners and morals are more scintillating than the minuet and hoop skirts suggest, and brothels make their own curious contribution to the city's culture.

"Brass knuckle" politics had its inception in Penn's day and developed nicely. The press has a hard time breaking into the act as the politicians close ranks to put down printers like William Bradford. Franklin, as both politician and printer, eases the way. By 1750 newspapers gain their niche as commentators and critics on governmental affairs, and the power of the press grows apace. No journalistic fraternity yet existed, for the objective was to drive rivals out of business—a technique which Franklin perfected in several different models. Andrew Hamilton, the attorney who gave impetus to the phrase of praise, "Philadelphia lawyer" argues the Zenger case in New York and establishes a landmark, on a theory advanced by a beleagured Bradford in Philadelphia some years before. Good, bad or indifferent, newspapers afford a picture of the years and the people, and between the lines of clashing opinions truth sometimes emerges.

Federal, State and city governments converge on Philadelphia as a troika in the last quarter of the 18th century—Washington meets the press and loses his temper—crusty William Cobbett comes to his rescue, as Secretary of State Jefferson's newspaper cuts at the Administration's anti-French policies—Stuart comes to town to paint portraits of Washington and plans to make copies he calls his "$100 bills"—violence breaks out among editors—Abigail Adams is shocked by the low-cut dresses that make Philadelphia women look like "nursing mothers"—John Adams becomes President and the press gets so vehement Congress passes the Alien and Sedition Acts to curb the influx of democratic Irish immigrants and opposition newspapers—Anne Bingham presides over the social sector—the New Theatre in Chestnut Street opens and Rickett's Circus burns down—and both Congress and the State Government leave town as the 19th century begins.

AN INTRODUCTORY WORD

Philadelphia summers are notoriously hot. A visiting Frenchman in 1781 thought walking in the streets "intolerably inconvenient; the houses and footpaths being generally of brick, are not even cooled until some hours after sunset." Yet it was in two such summers—1776 and 1787—that a single generation produced the Declaration of Independence and the Constitution of the United States. It is remarkable enough that any deliberative bodies could move so swiftly on matters of such magnitude. That they could, in the process, draft and adopt two immortal documents is almost miraculous. But I have often wondered how much they were prodded by the oppressive heat, and the pesky horseflies from nearby livery stables who swarmed through the open windows of the State House.

We tend to overlook such seeming trivia, forgetting that major events often pivot on tiny things. Homespun philosophers of the 18th century, however, stressed the importance of trifles, and "Poor Richard's Almanack" is replete with such axioms.

The moral of the story is this: we cannot be content to view colonial Philadelphia through the windows of an "elegant country seat" from the comfort of a Chippendale chair. That is just one dimension of the

11

scene. Yet somehow, in the romantic 19th century the notion prevailed that except for polite and deferential servants and tradesmen, the greater Philadelphians were genteel people who lived strictly by the Ten Commandments, and punctuated sprightly minuets with discreet sips of Madeira.

For the sake of our forebears I hope this book dispels such myths. Their Philadelphia was an exciting and exuberant town which, between 1681 and 1776, they transformed from a few scattered Swedish farms into one of the largest cities in the British Empire, surpassed only by London. They accomplished this with style, and tempered driving ambition with a cosmopolitan air. Even the hard-bitten sailors who patronized the waterfront brothels caught a bit of the grace and charm, and delightfully dubbed the doxies, "the frail ladies."

I have tried to bottle some of the flavor of this Philadelphia in thirteen essays, bolstered by a fourteenth on sources and suggestions for deeper explorations by those so inclined. As a lawyer I feel a bit naked without footnotes, but take comfort in the realization these are conversation pieces, designed for easy reading. To keep this from being too big a book, I have had to confine myself to the 18th century city limits, although occasionally I wander a bit beyond. For the same reason I have had to be selective in my choice of topics.

In a subsequent volume I plan to touch other facets, including a definitive look at 18th century lawyers—crime and punishment—and the social issues of the day. Germantown, Frankford, and communities along the present Main Line will come in for deserved recognition.

But for now I trust this will give the reader a panoramic perspective of a vibrant city.

JOSEPH J. KELLEY, Jr.

1

"IN THIS MIRROR":

The Swedes Come Before Penn

*   *   *   *   *

I look at least a hundred times a day in this mirror, God knows with what meditation, for I am here alone and there are hardly thirty men, of all that are here, upon whom I can rely . . .

                          —Governor Johann Printz, 1644

*   *   *   *   *

Life and Times in Colonial Philadelphia

I n 1643, a year before Admiral Sir William Penn's son William was born, a band of Swedes established the first permanent foothold in the future colony which would bear his name. A number of touchstones still furnish proof. Queen Christina, endlessly fascinating, keeps a tryst with Philadelphia through Queen's Village and Christian Street; Swanson Street recalls a pioneer family; remnants of ancient log houses and relics of mill traces along Cobbs Creek form a frame. The exquisite Gloria Dei church—eight blocks south of Independence Hall—is their most precious monument, guarded by the shades of early settlers who sleep beneath worn headstones. Within, models of the *Key of Kalmar* and *Flying Griffin*, the two ships which brought the first Swedes to the Delaware Valley, hang suspended from the ceiling. The baptismal font and altar carvings were brought from Gothenburg in 1642, and from under the organ loft two wide-eyed cherubims' wooden faces have looked out since 1700 upon the worshippers. Their startled expressions may have been a portent, for an early pastor thought the congregation "very irregular and lax," needing reform "especially among the rising generation." Built on the site of a small 1669 chapel, the picturesque trim brick edifice was Lutheran—the State Church of Sweden—until 1845 when it became affiliated with the Episcopal Diocese of Philadelphia. Whether or not the transition helped attendance is of no immediate moment, but we have vignettes of other Swedes making their way in the late seventeenth and early eighteenth centuries along the Schuylkill to crude log chapels—the men in canoes, the women in buckskin "outer petticoats" riding double on horseback— and once arrived, hanging their riding outfits on a line while they attended services. "We have good reason to thank the Almighty for daily support," they wrote in 1693, urging Sweden to send them clergymen. That year Penn's officials took a census and recorded 188 families with 942 persons as the Swedish population in and about Philadelphia.

Fifty years earlier there were less than a hundred, all concentrated in the vicinity of Christiana (Wilmington) until Governor Johann Printz arrived. Most of them were convicts transported to the remote outpost, because the law-abiding Swedes preferred to stay home. Printz brought more, including two found guilty of having "committed adultery three times and one of them, in addition, shot some elks." With him there were also some Finns, rounded up by the paternalistic Swedish government under whose dominion they then happened to live. Hardy hunters and woodsmen, the Finns were a happy group, ardent believers in the black arts, and heralded the "hex" phenomenon that has long been a part of Pennsylvania lore. No one could overshadow Printz, "a man of brave size, who weighed over four hundred pounds," sent to New Sweden to organize the small colony Peter Minuit began in 1638. The friendly Indians

14

who watched with astonishment as he disembarked called him "Big Belly," while his unenthusiastic countrymen dubbed him "The Tub."

He had attended three universities, served as a lieutenant colonel in the cavalry, and was knighted by Christina in 1642 despite the loss of his command after surrendering the city of Chemitz in 1640. Now, at fifty, he was expected to keep the Dutch trading post at Gloucester across the river under a vigilant eye, build more forts, promote agriculture, administer justice, convert the Indians, increase fur shipments, and bring New Sweden to the status of a major colony.

Printz did not linger. After constructing a small defensive work twelve miles south of Christiana on the eastern shore, he moved upriver to Tinicum Island, six miles below the mouth of the Schuylkill. There he drove his men relentlessly until they finished Fort New Gothenburg, a bastion of round hemlock logs with four small copper cannon. Then they built a two-story house for him, laying the hemlock logs one upon the other and mortising at the corners, introducing to the country a technique that displaced the "straight-up" style favored by the French and English. Its interior featured glazed windows, fireplaces and chimneys of imported brick, and reasonably finished woodwork. A fortified storehouse, a bathhouse, a "pleasure house" or pergola, an orchard and gardens gave the place the baronial setting the governor wanted to accommodate his wife, five daughters, and a son. His next request was for a "yacht," which his carpenters produced. This was appreciated by much later generations who established the Essington Yacht Club on Tinicum, more than by the poor, overworked hands that somehow met the seemingly impossible demands. Twenty-five Swedes died the first year; nineteen deaths Printz cryptically ascribed to "hard work and little food."

Over on the mainland a small settlement grew up in the shadow of the governor's residence, and acquired the name Optland, or Upland—eventually under Penn to be renamed Chester. The contrast between the crude dwellings, with vents for chimneys, heated by oblong fireplaces reminiscent of the "long fires" of the Viking era, and the comparative opulence of his home "Printzhof" contributed to the simmering resentment against the governor.

In March 1644, the *Fama* arrived with a complement of colonists and a cargo which included grindstones, millstones, saws, tools, 250 copper kettles, 200 barrels of flour, 20 barrels of salt, 10 hogsheads of French wine, one of brandy, 6,000 bricks along with flag-cloth, shoes, clothing, and ten gilded flagpole knobs.

But on November 25, 1645, Printz reported,

> . . . between ten and eleven o'clock, the gunner Swen Wass set Fort New Gothenburg on fire; in a short time all was lamentably burnt down, and not the least thing saved, except the barn. The people escaped naked and destitute. The winter immediately set in, bitterly cold; the river and the creeks froze up; and nobody was able to get near us. The sharpness of the winter lasted far into the month of March; so that, if some rye and corn had not been unthreshed, I myself and all the people with me on the island would have starved to death. . . . The above-mentioned Swen Wass who caused the fire, I have brought to court, and caused him to be tried and sentenced; so I have sent him home in irons. . . .

Distance gave him room for exaggeration, and there is some evidence Swen Wass was trying to keep warm with a watch-fire that managed on the wings of a November wind to get out of control. Certainly Printz was not in danger of isolation, and if the inventory of his losses submitted for reimbursement were accurate he must have had a substantial library, but Madame Printz's dresses, jewels, and "underwear" were valued at eight times the books. The larder had contained 3,000 pounds of smoked ham and bacon, 80 pounds of cheese, and 200 pounds of lard. Malt and hops to brew Dutch beer and 100 pounds of candles were also destroyed. In the wake of the fire, Printz rebuilt the storehouse and also "caused a church to be built . . . decorating it according to our Swedish fashion, so far as our resources and means allow." Near Upland his construction crew went to work raising a splendid new house which he christened Printzdorp.

In most of his assignments Printz apparently performed well, but he was singularly unenthusiastic about trying to bring the Indians to Christianity. He got a few of them as far as the church, but they were not impressed with the ceremony, asking "why one man stood alone and talked so long and had so much to say, while all the rest were listening in silence?" The governor thought the gentle Delawares a pretty useless lot, and dreamed about importing 200 soldiers from Sweden "to break the necks of everyone on the River." Then, suddenly conscious of his missionary role, he amended the idea to dispatch only those unwilling to accept "the one true religion." Authorities at home soon quashed that suggestion, and the Queen herself was having some misgivings about what "the one true religion" might be. As titular head of the Lutheran Church in Sweden, Christina delighted in shocking her ministers, spiritual and temporal, by her bawdy stories and unabashed pursuit of pretty women. No one denied her brilliance. She aspired to make Stockholm the foremost cultural center in Europe, and among the learned men invited to court was the French philosopher, Descartes. At three and four in the morning she would summon him to the palace for discussions, and the distinguished man, exhausted by the treks through biting predawns, caught cold and died. In melancholy moments the young Queen mourned her handsome father, Gustavus Adolfus, acknowledged military peer of Caesar, Hannibal, and others in the very select company of strategists. Hero of the Thirty Years War, he was killed in the waning months of that tedious conflict when he was thirty-six, and she a child of six. A superb horsewoman, costumed and raised as a prince, she wistfully remarked how wonderful it would have

(Pa. Hist. & Museum Comm., Harrisburg)

GOVERNOR JOHANN PRINTZ
Unaffectionately dubbed "The Tub"

17

been to serve "an apprenticeship in the art of war to so complete a master." The copy of her portrait presented to the Historical Society of Pennsylvania in 1877 shows a shy, plain face smiling from under a cluster of curls—very feminine in her silk gown. But it is quite misleading as to her spirit, which manifested itself in extraordinary ways. When she approached her eighteenth birthday in 1644, she insisted on being crowned king, rather than queen. Dissuaded from that, she upset the balance of things by conferring knighthoods at random, holding a number of extravagant balls, and spending a fortune to get art treasures to Sweden. When her council urged her to marry, she told the members she would prefer death. In many matters she showed mature wisdom, and in many other matters she was a capricious, headstrong young woman. In 1654, after she had driven able advisers into retirement, she abruptly announced her intention to abdicate, the first major European sovereign to give up a throne voluntarily. While the capitals were still reverberating with the shock of this, she repudiated Lutheranism. At twenty-eight, she had her hair cut short, donned masculine clothes, and rode out of Sweden as Count Dohna, pausing on a leisurely journey to Rome to take a lovely Jewish girl as protégé—the first of a series of women with whom she would have affairs. When she reached the Eternal City she became a Roman Catholic, and her curious career took a humorous twist when a cardinal fell in love with her. This one-sided romance continued through the years when she was verging on the brink of poverty because of her generosity. Twice she went back to Sweden in an attempt to regain her crown, but died in 1689 as a pensioner of the Pope. His Holiness decreed she should be buried in St. Peter's, where she has since reposed—an unconventional figure who lends a unique charm to a corner of the vast church. Four years before she died a German wrote sympathetically, "The Swedes were too stupid to understand her."

Although Christina, child of a loveless marriage, idolized her genial and popular father, she did not share his great ambition to create a Utopia in the New World where all men could dwell together in peace and none would be in bondage. As Queen she paid scant attention to what was happening along the Delaware. "From June 20, in the year 1644 ... to October 1, 1646," Printz complained, "We received no letters." This pattern of indifference made life difficult. Apart from the morale factor, consistently at low ebb, the shortage of goods used for trading with the Indians made the governor's job difficult. And the Dutch, heretofore content with the little post at Fort Nassau (Gloucester, N.J.), began to expand their activities under the prodding of peg-legged Peter Stuyvesant, their superior in New Amsterdam.

Sweden and Holland, on cordial terms, had no intention of going to war over differences on the Delaware, and both Printz and Stuyvesant were aware that confrontations between them, for the time being, would be little more than bluffing matches. With neither side able to muster more than about fifty men, the situation wore the aspect of a comic opera. The Dutch crossed the Delaware and began to construct "strong houses," little more than log cabins, along the Schuylkill and at other points so they could control the fur trade with the Susquehannocks. This tribe, which constantly terrified the easy-going Delawares, lived along the Susquehanna River and hunted mountain lions, elk, and bear. The challenge of big game honed their aggressive instincts to such a degree that among the 15,000 Indians within the area now embraced in the boundaries of Pennsylvania, they were the dominant force. By raids on the Delawares and several small peaceful tribes on the Allegheny and Ohio rivers, they asserted their mastery.

The skins they offered to the Dutch and Swedes were more valuable than the beaver pelts, and "strong houses" along their trails gave the more strategically situated side the opportunity to be the first customer. Printz had his own chain of such houses and, to counter the Dutch intrusion, he would wait until they completed construction of one, then chop down all the trees around the place and build a checkmate station almost on top of his rival's. His moves understandably irritated Stuyvesant, who led a small detachment to the area in a show of force. Happily, all of the encounters were bloodless and eventually the two strong men faced each other across a conference table, and through gritted teeth pledged to be good neighbors.

Such things added to the tedium of Printz's task and he repeatedly asked to be relieved so he could return to Sweden. Each time, in the name of the Queen, he was entreated to remain and, as a reward for his faithful service, he was given the half-devastated Tinicum Island. It was small consolation. He had acquired, undoubtedly through side deals and personal profiteering, a tidy little fortune and preferred to spend it in Europe. The colonists, too, were restive. Except for the freemen, he wrote in 1647,

> all of them wish to be released. And it cannot be otherwise. If the people willingly emigrating should be compelled to stay against their will, no others would desire to come here. The whole number of men, women, boys, girls, and children now living here is 183 souls. . . .

Finally in October 1653, he arranged for his deputy, Lieutenant John Papegaya, to marry his daughter Armegot, appointed him interim governor, took the rest of his family and twenty-five settlers and soldiers, and sailed for home. New Sweden was now reduced to 100 people.

19

From the distance of three centuries Armegot Printz Papegaya is intriguing. About the same age as her queen, she was a strong, independent personality. While she obviously was not as adamant against marriage as Christina, she nevertheless made short shrift of her new husband. He invented some excuse to take the next ship to Sweden, leaving his twenty-seven-year-old wife to preside over the destiny of the settlement until a new governor could be named. "They still tell," Reverend Israel Acrelius marveled ninety years later, "how haughty she was, and she oppressed the poor when in prosperity." From Printzdorp she succeeded so admirably in alienating everyone that she could not even keep a servant.

One of the irritants her father endured under the "good neighbor" policy he and Stuyvesant adopted was the existence of a Dutch fort at present New Castle. As with most such "forts" its complement rarely exceeded fifteen soldiers, and it had been erected as a defiant gesture after a Dutch "fleet" sailed up and down the Delaware "drumming and cannonading." Fort Casimir, from 1651 on became, by its mere presence, a burning issue with Printz. He pleaded without success for the Swedes to dispatch ships to extinguish it, and early in 1653 sent his son home to plead the case personally. On May 28, 1654 the new governor, Johan Classon Risingh, arrived with 350 new settlers, and his instructions expressed the royal desire that the Delaware be secured to the Swedes "yet without hostility." "If the Dutch could not be removed by argument," he was warned not to become belligerent "since a hostile attack is not compatible with the weak power of the Swedes at that place." But the sight of Fort Casimir in a dilapidated condition proved too tempting, and he had little difficulty in forcing its surrender.

His precipitate action spelled doom for New Sweden. In 1655 the irate Stuyvesant led a land-sea operation to the Delaware and Risingh felt it futile to resist. As in all other clashes between Dutch and Swede, it involved no bloodshed. The prize, however, was much greater than the mere recovery of Fort Casimir, for now the Dutch took over all the Swedish holdings, assuring the rank and file they could keep their lands and their local officials on condition they take the oath of allegiance to the Netherlands.

For Armegot Printz Papegaya it was not quite so simple. Her unpopularity made Printzdorp a target for looters, and Swedes joined with some Dutch and Indians in stripping the place of its furnishings. Her high status made the Dutch commandant wary of letting her remain. On August 3, 1656 from Tinicum she appealed to Stuyvesant out of "the great friendship, which he had for my Lord and Father, to let me enjoy" Tinicum and Printzdorp. The former had not been cultivated for nearly 3 years, and is overrun with young under-wood, while the housing standing on it has been still more ruined by the Indians; therefore I have been induced to have the same repaired and the land cultivated by three Fins. . . .

Stuyvesant was probably more impressed by the daughter than any alleged "friendship" for her father and granted permission "to take possession and cultivate the lands of her Lord and Father at Printz-dorp." No mention was made of Tinicum.

In 1657 he confirmed an earlier order permitting Swedes

to concentrate their houses and dwellings . . . in shape of a village or villages either at Upland, Passyonck, Finland, Kinghsessing, on the Verdrietige hoeck, or at such places as by them may be considered suit-able.

By 1660 this mood changed when the Dutch feared the scattered Swedes might be planning an uprising and directed they come closer to the forts. This set off loud protests and William Beekman, Stuyvesant's deputy, reported:

. . . Miss Printz complains, that she cannot move on account of her heavy buildings, also because the church stands there, she offers her land rent free, but nobody as yet shows inclination to live with her. . . . Miss Printz and others also requested to be assisted, if necessity required it, for which purpose I would need here more soldiers.

Scarcely had the Swedes convinced the Dutch to let them stay in their chosen sites, when the whole area came under English rule. The Duke of York's fleet stood off New Amsterdam in 1664 and claimed the terri-tory by virtue of John Cabot's coastal explorations in 1497. Out-manned and outgunned, Stuyvesant did not argue the point, but agreed to the British terms and took a post with the conquerors. The English commander, Colonel Robert Nicolls, sent several ships under Sir Robert Carr to the Delaware to secure Dutch possessions there. Under the pre-text of resistance, Carr's force succeeded in killing and wounding most of the small Dutch garrison at New Castle—the first bloodletting the river had known since the Delawares had massacred a Dutch whaling colony three decades before. As usual the settlers took a new oath of allegiance, this time to Charles II, and were permitted to keep their lands, along with their customs, courts, and laws until a new code was promulgated.

Armegot Printz seems to have charmed the English officials, for we see her, with a servant, manufacturing corn liquor—getting her assistant exempted from militia duty—and, through the English courts in New York, recovering Tinicum after a sale she made of it fell through. In 1669 she was implicated in a bizarre plot the British treated as seditious, although the principal defendant, Marcus Jacobsen who called himself "the Long Finn" and claimed to be the son of the famed Swedish general Konigsmarke, was obviously unbalanced. Together with two others he was charged with going up and down the river trying to enlist the Indians in a rebellion against the English. When Armegot's name came up, Governor Francis Lovelace was more chagrined at her ingratitude than the possibility of her involvement, and no action was taken against her. "The Long Finn" learned how swiftly the English punished sedition, real or imaginary, for he was branded and sold into slavery. His codefendants got off with fines. Armegot stayed in the Chester region until about 1676, renowned for a "temper that often flowed over" but resolute through years of lonely struggle. She died in Sweden in 1695.

While Armegot's reputation for testiness was widespread, it was by no means a characteristic on which she had a monopoly. In spite of the sprawling countryside and their scattered farms, other Swedes got involved in arguments that led to the court at Chester. Between 1676 and 1681 it had a lively criminal docket. Oele Oelson was charged with striking one of the judges and "abusing him with scandalous words." He was fined 210 guilders, but got a discount of 150 when he apologized as ordered. Moens Staecket paid 50 guilders for chasing the wife of Morton Mortense, Jr. "with an axe" and threatening the husband "with a gun" when he came to the rescue. In the same session the same defendant drew a fine of 100 guilders for having "abused and beaten" Andries Boen, and was sued by Morton Mortense, Sr., for slander. Hans Oelsen was charged with striking Roger Peddrick "in the open street with an axe handle", but since there were no witnesses, "the court could not come to any judgment, but order future peace, under severe penalty."

In 1678 Jan Cornelissen "complains to the court that his son Erick is bereft of his natural senses, and is turned quite mad, and he not being able to maintain him, it was ordered that three or four persons be hired to build a little block house, and there to confine him—expenses to be provided for in the next levy or tax." When John Test sued Elizabeth Kinsey for "restitution of five beavers left in her trust," John Ashton represented her as attorney in fact. During the proceedings she came to court, so he asked "to be dismissed . . . that she may manage the suit herself. He says that she is his mistress." When the constable informed the court in 1680 that "Claes Cram, lives in adultery with the wife of Bank Salung" it was ordered "they shall desist, and in case of non-compliance, they shall be apprehended for the next court to act upon." But Claes has a complaint of his own in the next session, suing Hans Peter for slander, "saying he was a thief, &c." Hans was directed to declare himself a liar, acknowledge that Claes was an honest

(Pa. Hist. & Museum Comm., Harrisburg)

MADAME JOHANN PRINTZ
Clothes conscious in a wilderness

23

man and pay him 20 guilders. Andries Inckhooren (Inkhorn) demanded "reason and reparation" from Andries Honman for having "pulled him by the beard and twisted his neck." Honman explained he had gone to Inckhooren's house "in pursuit of a whore and a rogue, and was obstructed by him, when he therefore pushed him aside." The case was dismissed.

This sampling of cases involving the future Philadelphia area gives only a partial picture of the litigation at Upland and Kingsessing, where the court sometimes sat. The more important cases were tried at New Castle and the dockets there were more crowded.

Despite their contentiousness, the early Swedes made a significant contribution to the future of the region in several respects. Rudimentary as they were, the first courts, houses, civil government and farms were introduced by them, and while these had little influence on the eventual development of Philadelphia under the English, they shaped the attitudes of a sizable group of early citizens. The influx of British subjects in the wake of the Duke of York's takeover aroused keen interest in the Swedish technique of home building, but principally because it was fast and economical. Notched logs eliminated the need for nails, but emphasis on functionalism made most Swedes disregard decorative touches and they were usually content with one large room served by ports for windows. They adhered to this frontier look until widespread use of brick in the eighteenth century led them to adopt English and German architectural designs. As farmers they were inexperienced rather than indifferent, and their extensive landholdings were not always as productive as they might have been.

In one field, however, they were matched only by the Delawares. The Swedish bath has not even yet fully attained the freedom of mixed nudity they practiced in their log bathhouses, usually twelve to fourteen feet square. Large fireplaces generated the steam which caused them to perspire, and after stimulating their circulation with birch switches they plunged into a cold creek or rolled in the snow. The similarity between the Swedes and the Indians in this unusual practice is striking. Ordinarily the Swedes made Saturday their bathing day and thus set a precedent which, with some modifications, became an American tradition.

Their relations with the Delawares were exemplary. During the seventeen years they controlled the region they were rigid in refusing to give liquor to the Indians. This strictness earned them the appreciation of tribal chiefs who consistently worried about the enervating effect of "firewater" on the braves. In their casual attitude toward converting the natives to Christianity the Swedes were wiser than they intended. But Benjamin Franklin recounted a story that he may well have invented about a Swedish minister who painstakingly explained about Adam and Eve to the "Susequehannah Indians." When he finished,

an old Indian orator replied, 'what you have told us is very good; we thank you for coming so far to tell us those things you have heard from your mothers; in return, we will tell you what we heard from ours. In the beginning, we had only flesh of animals to eat; and if they failed, we starved; two of our hunters, having killed a deer, and broiled a part of it, saw a young woman descend from the clouds, and seat herself on a hill hard by.' Said one to the other, 'It is a spirit, perhaps, that has smelt our venison, let us offer some of it to her.' They accordingly gave her the tongue; she was pleased with its flavour, and said, 'your kindness shall be rewarded; come here thirteen moons hence, and you will find it.' They did so, and found, where her right hand had touched the ground, maize growing; where her left hand had been, kidney-beans; and where her back-side had been, they found tobacco." The Swedish minister was disgusted. "What I told you," said he, "is sacred truth; yours is fable, fiction and falsehood." The Indian, offended in his turn, replied, "My friend, your education has not been a good one; your mothers have not done you justice; they have not well instructed you in the rules of common civility. You saw that we, who understand and practice these rules, believed all your stories; why then do you refuse to believe ours? We believe, indeed, as you have told us, that it is bad to eat apples; it had been better that they had all been made into cyder; but we would not have told you so, had you not disbelieved the method by which we first obtained maize, kidney-beans and tobacco.

2

"I AM NOT SUCH A MAN":

William Penn Founds a New World "Experiment"

*   *   *   *   *

There is one great God and power that hath made the world and all things therein. . . . This great God hath written His law in our hearts, by which we are taught and commanded to love and help and do good to one another, and not to do harm or mischief one to another. . . . I am very sensible of the unkindness and injustice that hath been too much exercised toward you by the people of these parts of the world, who have sought themselves and to make great advantages by you rather than be examples of Justice and goodness unto you, which I hear hath been a matter of trouble to you and caused great grudgings and animosities, sometimes to the shedding of blood . . . But I am not such a man. . . .

—Penn, writing from England to the Indians, 1682

*   *   *   *   *

"I Am Not Such a Man"

In 1670, twenty-six-year-old William Penn was in London's worst prison, "the stinking hole" at Newgate. He was no stranger to jails, despite his social status and a father who headed the British Navy. Born in 1644, young Penn felt a strong "puritan" spiritual pull from the time he was eleven, comparable to the "inner light" which the Quaker, George Fox, was preaching throughout England. It led him into a distaste for the rich trappings and licentiousness of the Restoration, and his refusal to don the prescribed undergraduate gown and attend compulsory chapel at Christ Church College, Oxford, resulted in his expulsion in 1662. Admiral Sir William Penn, understandably embarrassed, sent the boy to France to study at a Protestant seminary, and when he came back to London in 1664, decked out in "new French pantaloons" with a rapier at his side, it seemed the Continental sojourn had transformed him. On August 30 he visited his father's aide, Samuel Pepys, and thereby found his way into Pepys' immortal diary.

> After dinner comes Mr. Pen, and stayed an hour talking with me. I perceive something of the learning he hath got, but a great deal, if not too much, of the vanity of the French garbe and affected manner of speech and gait—I fear all real profit he hath made of his travel will signify little. . . .

After a brief taste of conflict in the Navy during the Dutch War in 1665, and a hardly less brief sojourn in studies at Lincoln's Inn, he was sent off to Ireland to look after the family properties in 1666. Penn enhanced his new image by posing in armor for a portrait, thus perplexing generations of school children who wondered what a man of peace was doing in the accouterments of war. It was merely a symbol of rank, quickly rendered meaningless in his mind when he traveled to Cork to hear Quaker Thomas Loe preach. The sermon stirred his pietism, and he saw parallels to his own undefined philosophy. The royalist government saw a different parallel. To it Quaker ideas seemed uncomfortably close to the despised Puritanism which had cost Charles I his head and rent England asunder in bloody civil war. From 1661 through 1665 Parliament enacted harsh laws to outlaw religious dissenters and, as one Quaker said, "We were the bulwark that received the shot." During the twenty-five-year reign of Charles II, over 15,000 Quakers would be imprisoned, 450 of them to die in jails. "They go like lambs, without any resistance," Pepys marveled, "I would to God they would either conform, or be more wise, and not be catched."

It did not take long for Penn to be "catched." He was rounded up at a street meeting in Ireland and charged with "riot and tumultuous assembling." His reaction was quite different from the Quakers taken with him. He sent a blistering demand that he be released immediately. Back came word that he would be freed if he promised not to participate in future meetings. It made him more incensed. He insisted on freedom without any conditions, and he got it, being called back to England by his father. Six months later Pepys wrote in his diary: "Mr. Pen, who has lately come over from Ireland is a Quaker again, or some such melancholy thing."

Not only did Penn join the ranks of the Society of Friends—Quakers—in 1667, but also he refused to take off his hat to the King, the Duke of York, or his own father, and published a pamphlet, *The Sandy Foundation Shaken,* which railed against the loose morals of the times. Somehow the officials translated it into blasphemy against the Trinity, and Penn was sent to the Tower of London in 1668. The Bishop of London came to convince him of the error of his ways. "My prison shall be my grave before I will budge a jot, for I owe my conscience to no mortal man," Penn told him, and went back to writing his next pamphlet in the dismal surroundings. *No Cross, No Crown* lashed out at the theater, foppish dress, false pride, and pressed for a return to the unadorned simplicity of the early Christians, along with the observance of the basic precepts of Christianity. Some of it was impossibly priggish, and one aspect was a little troublesome. A childhood illness had left bald patches on Penn's head which he covered with a wig. When he came to a denunciation of women who "curl, powder, patch, paint" he was careful to indict only "false locks of strange colors."

Mrs. Pepys read *The Sandy Foundation* aloud to her husband, who thought it was so well written he wondered how young Penn produced this "serious sort of book . . . not fit for everybody to read." Over a century later Charles Lamb recommended *No Cross, No Crown* to Samuel Coleridge as "a capital book . . . good thoughts in good language."

The Duke of York secured Penn's release from the Tower, and the bristling young author repaid the kindness by writing a scathing attack on religious persecution in England, his famous *The Great Case of Liberty of Conscience.* Significantly one edition is dated "Newgate . . . February 1670." Penn had been arrested yet again, this time for contempt of court and conspiracy. He and others had been arrested for preaching in the street and, when brought before the authorities, he refused to take off his hat. His ensuing trial, at which he conducted his own defense—part of it while locked in a "closet" for being "a saucy fellow" with the judges—became a landmark. Several times the jury acquitted him of the conspiracy charge and each time the judges refused to accept the verdict, sending the jurors back to deliberate, and finally charging them with threats of reprisal if an unsuitable verdict were returned. But the jury refused to be coerced. They were jailed and fined, but on appeal won their freedom with a high ruling that judges had no power to "lead them by the nose." Penn, too, was imprisoned despite the verdict, but only pending payment of a fine for his contempt charge. At first he refused to pay, but finally acquiesced when he found out that his father was dying.

Admiral Penn died on September 17, 1670, leaving his son an annual income of £1,600 and a claim against the Crown for £16,000. But his passing did nothing to soften the attitude of the government toward his heir. In 1671 he was sent to Newgate for six months for refusing to take the oath of allegiance. When he was released, he went on an extended preaching tour through Holland and the Rhine country. 1672 was a much brighter year. Charles II issued a "Declaration of Indulgence" which, to some degree, eased the tensions under which the Quakers operated, and Penn married the beautiful blonde heiress, Gulielma Maria Springett. Their honeymoon was so long his friends wondered if Penn had shifted his energies from religion to romance.

With governmental pressure relaxed the Quakers had time to reassess their position. Should they continue their drive to reform the politicians and the people, or abandon them to the devil and start afresh in America and create a Godly state of their own? There was nothing new in the latter concept. Since 1629 the Puritans had been busy establishing a theocracy in New England, and the Quakers had been their sternest critics, disrupting church services in Massachusetts by breaking empty bottles to show how hollow they thought Puritan theology, and even sending naked Quakeresses up the aisle to suggest the congregation divest itself of the nonsense being preached. In an effort to insulate themselves from such intrusion, authorities ordered Quakers whipped from town to town until they reached the border, and threatened them with death if they dared return. For the belligerent little band of American Quakers the threat was a glorious invitation to martyrdom, and the Puritans responded so enthusiastically that Charles II had to intervene and order executions stopped.

The solution, many English Quakers thought, was a place of their own. Penn later claimed he had an "opening of joy"—a divine revelation—on the subject when he was at Oxford in 1661, and quite coincidentally George Fox, patriarch of the Quakers, sent an emissary to America about that time to look into the possibilities. Later Fox went himself, traveling through the Delaware Valley region, and sending back glowing reports.

Whether or not one subscribes to Penn's belief that he was guided by God's hand, there can be no denial of the symmetry in the pattern that was to evolve into Pennsylvania and produce, among other places, Philadelphia. In 1676 he got a unique opportunity to put some of his political principles into operation. As one of several Friends designated trustees for the newly acquired Quaker province of West New Jersey, he became the principal draftsman for its constitution—"a foundation," he said, "for after ages to understand their liberty as men and Christians." A number of its provisions presaged policies he would prescribe for Pennsylvania: no capital punishment or imprisonment for debt, the right of petition, and the right to trial by jury. One in particular reflects his own experience: "No persons (is) to be called to question or molested for his conscience, or for worshipping according to his conscience."

More and more now he saw the futility of trying to change attitudes at home. "There is no hope in England," he decided in 1680, "the deaf adder cannot be charmed." He asked the King to grant him an extensive tract on the west bank of the Delaware across from the New Jersey River in exchange for the debt owed his late father. On March 5, 1681 he jubilantly told his friend, Robert Turner:

> . . . after many waitings, watchings, solicitings and disputes in council, this day my country was confirmed to me . . . by the name of Pennsilvania, a name the king would give it in honour of my father. I chose New Wales, being as this, a pretty hilly country . . . [but] the secretary—a Welshman—refused to have it . . . *Sylvania* and they added *Penn* to it; and though I much opposed it, and went to the king to have it struck out . . . he said 'twas past . . . ; nor could twenty guineas move the under secretarys to vary the name, for I feared least it should be lookt on as a vanity to me . . . Thou mayst communicate my graunt to friends, and expect shortly my proposals: 'Tis a clear and just thing, and my God that has given it me through many difficultys, will, I believe bless and make it the seed of a nation. . . .

From religion and politics, Penn now turned to land promotion as the theme for his writings. Just a month after he got the charter, the presses turned out *Some Account of the Province of Pennsylvania....* He did not forget his old companions, the Prophets, whose words he so often invoked, but now Moses, Joshua, and Caleb, along with the ancient Greeks and Romans, were put in the garb of colonists, and their pioneering instincts likened to seventeenth-century spiritual adventurers. Nor did he forget his old targets. Those who came to Pennsylvania, he implied, would escape "the great Debauchery in this Kingdom [which] has not only rendered many unfruitful when married, but they live not out half their time, through Excesses. . . ."

(*Hist. & Museum Comm., Harrisburg*)

GULIELMA MARIA SPRINGETT PENN

A beautiful young woman with a beautiful name, Penn's first wife—from all accounts—was obviously as lovely as this modern version suggests. Based on "an engraving of a painting on glass by an unknown artist" it is fairly faithful to the original. The only difficulty is the "original", which appears to be mid-18th century, but could be contemporary, is not fully authenticated. Given these cautions, and the propensity of the artist who did this concept to place Gulielma in a garden, complete with cut flowers and gardening shears (none of which appears in the glass rendition), one can only guess whether Penn would recognize either lady as the one he married.

31

He sketched the outlines of government with a pledge to "settle a free, just and industrious Coloney"; invited "Industrious Husbandmen and Day Labourers . . . Carpenters, Masons, Smiths, Weavers, Taylors, Tanners, Shoemakers, Shipwrights, etc.," whose "Labour is worth more there than here, and . . . provision cheaper"; offered a haven "for those Ingenious Spirits that being low in the World, are much clogg'd and oppress'd about a Livelyhood," assuring them that since "the means of subsisting being easie there, they may have time and opportunity to gratify their inclinations, and thereby improve Science and help Nurseries of people"; and singled out others whose talents might be overlooked in England. Then he got down to the details of cost. As he was to say a few months later, "Though I desire to extend religious freedom, yet I want some recompense for my trouble."

He was concerned for the Indians. From London he sent word to the Delawares that though God

> hath been pleased to make me concerned in your parts of the world, and the King of the country where I live hath given unto me a great province therein, . . . I desire to enjoy it with your love and consent, that we may always live together as neighbors and friends. . . .

But the Delawares did not, as Penn hoped, remain to become an integral part of his "holy experiment." He wanted them, not on reservations, but side by side with his settlers. Neither the settlers nor the Indians were quite that sanguine. As they sold their land, piece by piece, the Delawares gradually moved westward. By 1790, when the first United States census was taken, only 1,300 Indians of all types and tribes were left in Pennsylvania.

They are dimly remembered in Philadelphia today. The scene of the traditional famous treaty "under the elm tree at Shackamaxon" is a patch of green along the banks of the Delaware, flanked by waterfront warehouses and a grim battery of high-voltage transformers. It is hard to imagine as the pastoral Shackamaxon, and a monument deemed "weather-worn" a half-century ago modestly supplants the elm which blew down in 1810. Still, with its prestigious name, Penn Treaty Park, it commemorates sentiments spoken by Penn at one of his many treaty sessions, but not necessarily at this place:

> We meet on the broad pathway of good faith and good will; no advantage shall be taken on either side, but all shall be openness and love . . . We are the same as if one man's body was to be divided into two parts; we are all one flesh and blood.

The Indians could match his eloquence:

"I Am Not Such a Man"

We will live in love with Onas (Penn's Indian name) and his children as long as the creeks and rivers run and while the sun, moon, and stars endure.

Penn picked the name "Philadelphia" from a second-century city in Palestine. It would bring continuity of the Biblical theme of brotherly love, he felt, to the New World. Then he set about looking for a place in his Province to put it. The city, as he said, was named before it was born.

He called it his "great town," his "metropolis," and with only a sketchy idea of the terrain, pictured it as a business district bounded by suburban "liberties" on either side. Those who wished at day's end to shake the dust of commerce could repair to homes beyond the sound of cart and countinghouse. Through the latticed windows of his London land office, the city rose to greatness in his mind. He had heard Upland was a thriving market town, and thought its situation on the Delaware made it an ideal point of beginning. Here his commercial center was already underway, and valuable time would be saved by converting it into his broader scheme. But the surrounding countryside was so dotted with Swedish farms, the site had to be rejected. His cousin and deputy William Markham, sent to the province in 1681, probed farther upriver, and saw beyond the reeds and marshland the picturesque Schuylkill flowing into the Delaware and Philadelphia's destiny was geographically fixed. Some Swedes were there, strung out along the Delaware all the way to Frankford, and occupying farms on both sides of the Schuylkill. They had already endowed sections of the region with names like Kingsessing, Passyunk, Arnomink, Moyamensing—peculiar blends of Swedish, Dutch, and Indian, which survive in the modern city. Their holdings were long, but shallow. Even where the "Neck" widened into a broad expanse, the tracts ran no more than two miles inland. Much as he would honor their titles, Penn was determined they could form no barrier. His agents were instructed to bargain, swapping waterfront acreage for deeper lots or buying up the properties where no alternative remained.

He would bring to his beloved city the latest in urban planning, all the lessons London learned from the devastating fire of 1666 which etched into his mind the dangers of half-timbered houses leaning toward each other across crooked, narrow lanes. Robert Hooke, the mathematician, and Sir Christopher Wren, surveying the charred ruins, had recommended London be redesigned with straight streets intersected at right angles with other straight streets. Penn stressed this in his blueprints. For the commercial center of his "greene, countrie towne" it was essential, and those who would build homes in the "liberties" were urged to set them in the middle of the lot, with space

33

on either side for orchards, gardens, and natural protection against a contagion of flames.

Within the city this meant a gridiron pattern. There were to be, initially, eight east-west streets—three of them north of High (later Market Street) and four south, all projected to run from the Delaware to the Schuylkill. He gave them names representative of "things that Spontaneously grow in the Country, as Vine-Street, Mulberry Street, Chestnut Street, Wallnut Street . . . Pine Street . . . and the like." Penn rejected the proposal they be named for principal lot-holders because it tended too much to "man-worship." North-south streets, except for Broad "in the middle of the City" were to be numbered. High and Broad were each one hundred feet wide, and where they would normally intersect there was to be a ten-acre square for "Houses of publick Affairs. . . ." Today the French chateau-styled City Hall, with its 750 rooms, carries out Penn's purpose. All other streets were to be fifty feet in width, but to give a touch of grandeur to the riverfronts, some latitude was permitted their breadth. Thus the present Twenty-second Street, as close to the Schuylkill as swampy conditions in the seventeenth century allowed, must rest content with the fact that it is wider than neighboring streets, deprived of its intended glory because High Street encountered marsh land 800 feet from the appointed rendezvous. In each quarter of the city Penn wanted an eight-acre park for use "like . . . the Moore-fields in London." These moorfields, just beyond the old London walls, had been drained first in 1527, and laid out in walks in 1606.

Prospective buyers in England could see Thomas Holme's model plan, depicting Penn's dream with geometric precision. The founder expected the city would develop westward, but it would be a century or more before it reached Broad Street. The people preferred to cluster near the Delaware, partially because business concentrated there, and because in the hot summers, a breeze was usually stirring.

In 1682 land sales in the London office were brisk, and the place was oversold by some 13,000 acres. There were other complications. As an inducement to those interested in buying extensive tracts in the province, Penn offered fractional bonuses in the liberties, and lots in the city. As a convenience to absentee owners, the latter were located through a lottery, and quite a few of the choice spots went to people who had no immediate intention of moving to Philadelphia. The prospect of a thriving city seemed to fade under this grim turn of events. What kind of reports would ship captains carry to their home ports when large patches of vacant land, so conspicuously close to the Delaware, were clearly seen from the decks of vessels? To offset this potentially damaging situation,

Penn, by marvelous juxtaposition, shuttled their titles over to the Schuylkill side, believing that by the time they came to take possession, the lots there would equal the market value of those on the Delaware. Thus within sight of ship traffic, Philadelphia would present a panorama of compact energy. So eager were the settlers to get started, many decided not to wait for the official surveys and began clearing land they roughly estimated to belong to them, thus tangling property lines in scores of cases. Penn himself came to his new domain in 1682.

Not all his headaches came from the anxiety of the people to get underway as quickly as possible. Along the high banks of the Delaware there were a series of caves which provided temporary housing. Within a short time some of them would become notorious vice dens, so enjoyable to some of the residents they were in no hurry to find other quarters. Penn ran into an even more monumental problem in the Pennsylvania

(Pa. Hist. & Museum Comm., Harrisburg)

PENNSBURY MANOR

Penn commuted 26 miles up the Delaware from Philadelphia to this picturesque spot near Bristol, Pa. He used his six-man barge for the trips, but he had little time to enjoy the manor house and the nearly seven thousand acres—spending less than two years here. Nonetheless, in anticipation of a long life, he wrote numerous letters and sent from England varieties of plants and shrubs, along with ornamental ironwork and tiles to enhance its beauty. It was still unfinished when he occupied it and there were minor problems such as a leaking roof. In 1938 the Commonwealth of Pennsylvania began extensive archaeological and historical research to reconstruct the house and outbuildings and refurbish the gardens. The digs turned up many original items which were used in the rebuilding, and meticulous work by architects, archivists and archaeologists has reproduced it in the style to which Penn was all too briefly accustomed. Period furnishings, including several of his own things a highboy and his carved chair and highboy, give an air of authenticity.

Assembly, which refused to ratify the liberal charter he had given "The Free Society of Traders," a joint-stock company which had raised £10,000 and bought 20,000 acres in Pennsylvania. Under Penn's formula this entitled them to some 400 free acres in the "liberties" and about eight in the city. Anticipating no obstacles, the Society had already begun brick kilns, a tannery, and glassworks along Tacony Creek in Frankford, along with a grist mill and saw mill.

Along with its domestic sales, the Society intended to run an import-export business, and having a virtual monopoly during the early years, stood in a fair way of reaping a rich harvest. Penn, as proprietor of the Province, had considerable power, but was hemmed in by requirements that he must govern with a freely elected Council and Assembly. As governor he with the Council could propose laws to the Assembly, which had at the time, no power to initiate any of their own. The Assembly could approve or disapprove as they saw fit.

In vetoing the Society's charter as too "feudalistic" the Assembly reflected a curious and perplexing antipathy toward Penn. If the fierce independence they asserted under the banner of an Englishman's rights was heartening, their attitude toward the man who made it all possible was often disheartening. Nor was the strange hostility limited to them; deputy governors and the Council made little effort to collect quitrents and monies due him, while at the same time they unhesitatingly billed Penn for salaries and costs of administration, a burden which eventually helped put him in a debtor's prison in England.

Chagrined at the Assembly's action, Penn gave the Society 100 acres in the city, instead of the considerably smaller land their purchase had warranted. Running from river to river between Pine and Spruce streets, the tier of lots lent added substance to the Society's offices, which were shifted from London to Philadelphia and established at the foot of the hill which has since borne the company's name. While its principal officers were salaried, they devoted more and more of their time to developing their personal holdings, and paid commensurately less attention to the affairs of the corporation.

This, together with a lackadaisical attitude toward collection of long overdue accounts ended the effectiveness of the Society in Philadelphia life. It survived for a while longer as holder of real estate, but the main thrust was gone.

Despite this disappointment, most of Penn's optimistic predictions about the city seemed to materialize. At the heart of it was his theory of religious tolerance, and his personal efforts to bring persecuted sects out of Europe to his holy experiment. With them came their skills which found ways to manufacture linen, paper, furniture, and implements. Penn sought as much diversity of talent as he did diversity of denominations, and because many felt they were doing God's work as well as their own, Philadelphia's fame spread abroad.

Penn's own time in Philadelphia was quite short, but in it he accomplished a good deal of "God's work" himself. His first stay lasted only a year and ten months, from October 1682 to August 1684. Yet in that time he helped set up the government, personally took part in the design and practical layout of Philadelphia, preached, wrote, traveled, played diplomat in the attempted settlement of a boundary dispute with neighboring Maryland, continued his work in land promotion, and finally built for himself the lovely Pennsbury Manor. This pre-Georgian home, now reconstructed north of Bristol, cost over £5,000. It was easily the most imposing and luxurious home in the province, and showed, as one observer put it, that "Penn had inherited some of his father the old Admiral's appreciation of state and dignity," despite his condemnations of pomp and extravagance. In addition, he raised another brick dwelling in the city for his sojourns in town, and named it Letitia Cottage after his daughter.

But church matters and the better promotion of his Pennsylvania demanded his presence in England. Returning, he importuned his friend King James II for the freedom of some 1,300 Friends being held in jail, and then set off on a missionary tour of Holland and the Rhine countries. It was not long, however, before matters took on a somber cast, and from 1688 on his life seemed to run a continual round of grief.

In that year the Catholic James was driven from the throne of England and fled to France, being supplanted by his daughter Mary and her Dutch husband, William of Orange. There were plots to restore him; but if Penn was involved, he seems to have covered his tracks well. Nevertheless, he was suspected of treason, and Pennsylvania was put under a royal protectorate in 1692, while the Council interrogated him for nearly three years before finding him innocent. Although its members were aware of Penn's fierce loyalty to those loyal to him, they could not get adequate proof of his complicity. Pennsylvania was restored to him in 1694, but his beloved Gulielma died, urging him, "Go, my dearest, do not hinder anything that may be good to stay with me; I desire thee to go; I have cast my care upon the Lord." The fifty-year-old Penn was left with three children, two sons—nineteen-year-old Springett and thirteen-year-old William, Jr.—and a daughter, sixteen-year-old Letitia. In March 1696 he married Hannah Callowhill who was about twenty-four, and the next month Springett died. From 1699 to 1701 he was in Philadelphia on his second and what proved to be his last visit. There in 1700 Hannah gave him a son, John, and the schoolboys from the William Penn Charter School, a public grammar school he founded in 1689, composed these verses of congratulation:

> Since children are the Lord's reward
> Who get them may rejoice;
> Nay, neighbours, upon this regard
> May make a gladsome noise.
>
> Therefore, we think we dwell so near
> Dear Governour, to thy gate
> That Thou mayest lend an ear to hear
> What Babes congratulate.
>
> God bless the child (we young ones cry)
> And add from time to time
> To William Penn's Posterity
> The like! Here ends our Rime.
>
> But fervent prayers will not end
>   Of honest men for Thee,
> And for the happy government
>   With whom we all agree.

A few weeks later the family moved to Pennsbury, and for a brief moment Penn could enjoy the luxury of stepping from his imposing barge and walking up the poplar-lined walk to his mansion. Always meticulous about his clothes, the Proprietor ordered items for his wardrobe from England, along with four somewhat more elaborate wigs. Hannah and Letitia caused frowns among the strict Friends by wearing more colorful dresses and gold necklaces with engraved seals. In 1701 he gave his province the Charter of Privileges, to supplement and improve the First Frame of Government. While Penn anticipated Jefferson in asserting fundamental principles of liberty as generalities, he was guarded in the application of those that posed threats to his proprietary interest. Where experience required clarification he was flexible enough to rise to the needs of the occasion. The Assembly was now given full legislative power, and the Council became the Governor's cabinet. The lower counties, which comprise Delaware, were put in position to have a separate legislature, thus removing a persistent source of tension, and this was accomplished in 1704. Penn relinquished many of his personal powers as Proprietor, and the statesmanlike decisions made in that single stroke gave Pennsylvania a constitution that would serve until 1776, and write a basic chapter in American constitutionalism. In 1751, to commemorate the Charter, the Assembly ordered a bell to be hung in the tower of the State House, and chose as a fitting inscription the passage from Leviticus: "Proclaim liberty throughout all the land unto all the inhabitants thereof."

After presenting Philadelphia with a charter, and naming the able Andrew Hamilton as lieutenant governor, he sailed for home to fight off a move in England that would transform charter and proprietary colonies into Crown colonies. To James Logan he wrote from Pennsbury, "I cannot prevail on my wife to stay and still less with Tishe. I know not what to do." Letitia seemed anxious to escape an engagement to a young Philadelphian, William Masters, into which her flirtatious ways ensnared her. Penn was not happy about it, either, but the jilting of Masters troubled the Philadelphia Quaker community.

Just as his own rebellious personality had made his father's life uncomfortable, Penn found the "wild nature" of William Jr., gnawed at his spirit. The boy had married at nineteen and apparently resented his stepmother, but not enough to keep him from leaving his young wife and children with her when he set sail for Philadelphia with John Evans, a young Welshman Penn named to succeed Hamilton as governor. Young William's expensive tastes and disdain for Quaker simplicity had cost his father heavily, and he wrote to James Logan to keep an eye on the youth: "Allow no rambling in New York." It did not take Penn, Jr., long to get into trouble in Philadelphia, as the court records of this city show:

> 1704—1st of 7 mon. (September 1) to wit: The Grand Jury do present some of the young gentry for an assault on James Wood, Constable and James Dough, Watch; making riot at the Inn of Enoch Story by night, in Combes Alley. Namely, William Penn, jun. gent; John Finney, Sheriff; Thomas Gray, Scrivener; and Joseph Ralph, gent. It is charged that Mr. Penn called for pistols to pistol the complainants, but none were seen. The keeper of the Inn, Enoch Story, was of the party but gave no hand and is detained for witness.

Penn's Quaker friends were delighted with the embarrassment partially because they resented the belligerent new governor who was already entangled with the Assembly in a feud over a militia he wanted. Penn, at first, attributed his son's arrest to a plot of his enemies, and sent a blistering note to Philadelphia, demanding justice against the author of "that barbarous affront—I take it as done to myself." But he, in a calmer season, realized that the youngster "is my greatest affliction." The "Waster" apparently did not stay repentant very long, for after being summoned back to England by his saddened parent, he was back in Philadelphia, this time with a dashing, pretty young woman, Lady Jenks, with whom he went off to live in Bucks County, and out of respect for

39

his father, dressed her in man's clothes so they could conduct their escapades with a bit less scandal.

Penn was stunned by the discovery in London that Philip Ford defrauded him of thousands of pounds. Ford, his trusted Quaker agent, had so enjoyed the proprietor's confidence that Penn would sign documents handed him by the agent without even reading them. And when Ford presented to him a huge fictitious debt, Penn mortgaged the whole of his province to the agent and his wife. Ford died without reaping any benefit from his fraud, but his wife fought Penn in the courts, and the last months of 1708 found Penn once more in jail, this time a debtors' prison, where he would spend eight lonely months before friends secured his release. He had been betrayed at home, and he felt deserted by the Philadelphians for whom he had worked so long and hard. Yet he was more sad than bitter when he wrote to them:

> The many combats I have been engaged in, the great pains and incredible expense to your welfare and ease, to the decay of my former estate, of which . . . I too sensibly feel the effects, with the undeserved opposition I have met with from thence, sink me into sorrow, that, if not supported by a superior hand, might have overwhelmed me long ago. And I cannot but think it hard measure, that, while that has proved a land of freedom and flourishing, it should become to me, by whose means it was principally made a country, the cause of grief, trouble and poverty. . . .

He advised his children in 1710:

> Meddle not with government; never speak of it, let others say or do as they please. But read such books of law as relate to the office of a justice, a coroner, sheriff, and constable, also the doctor and student; some book of clerkship, and a treatise of wills, to enable you about your own private business only or a poor neighbor's. For it is a charge I leave with you and yours; meddle not with the public, neither business nor money, but understand how to avoid it and defend yourselves upon occasion against it. . . .

Throughout these years the man's inner strength astounds. In 1693, still under the surveillance of the suspicious William III, he wrote *An Essay Towards the Present and Future Peace of Europe,* projecting a plan for a parliament of nations, and stressing the economic as well as practical value of disarmament which he regarded as the only guaranty of peace and prosperity. In 1696 he offered *A Brief and Plain Scheme How the English Colonies In . . . America, May be Made More Useful to the Crown and One Another*—a plan of union which anticipated Franklin's.

In 1709 he wrote to the Duke of Marlborough, then battling the

"I Am Not Such a Man"

LETITIA STREET HOUSE

Tradition long held this to be the house first occupied by William Penn when he came to town in 1682, but scrupulous historians are hesitant, and all that can safely be said is that it is an interesting illustration of early Philadelphia architecture. It did however stand on the west side of Letitia Street, a small thoroughfare running north from Chestnut between Second and Front, within the half-block Penn deeded to his daughter, Letitia in 1701. In 1883 it was moved to Lansdowne Drive in Fairmount Park where it was more or less reverently regarded by Philadelphians as a repository of Penn's fleeting presence. Standing in semi-splendid isolation it awaits a new breed of historians who will boldly assert its pedigree.

French with his military genius, suggesting peace terms that if they had been accepted might well have averted the French and Indian wars:

> . . . The English Empire on the continent lies upon the south side, and we claim to the North Sea of Hudson's Bay; but I should be goad if our north bounds might be expressed and allowed to the south side of St. Lawrence's River that feeds Canada eastward, and comes from the lakes westward; which will make a glorious country, and from those lakes due west to the River Mississippi, and travers that river to the extreme bounds of the continent westward; whereby we may secure one thousand miles of that river down to the Bay of Mexico, and that the French demolish, or, at least, quit all their settlements within the bounds aforesaid.

Without such a settlement of our American bounds, we shall be in hazard of being dangerously surprised at one time or another, by the French and their Indians; especially if they send but twelve ships of war to attack us by sea, I humbly refer it to the Dukes English, Heart and Head, to secure to his country so great a one, and of that value on many accounts (and no more, I think, than we have a real claim to).

Marlborough's political power was waning, and the scheme came to naught—yet somehow Penn was able to picture the rough outlines of what would eventually become the United States.

Once more the bickering and contention in Philadelphia troubled him, and he finally concluded the only alternative was to negotiate with Queen Anne to change it to royal control:

> My Old Friends—It is a mournful consideration, and the cause of deep afflication to me that I am forced, by the oppressions and disappointments which have fallen to my share in this life, to speak to the people of that province in a language I once hoped I should never have the occasion to use. . . .

A sudden spate of harmony suffused Philadelphia, and on July 24, 1712 he explained:

> . . . Though I have not actually sold my Government to our truly Good Queen, yet her able Lord treasurer and I have agreed it. . . . But I have taken effectual care, that all the Laws and privileges I have granted to you, shall be observed by the Queen's Governors, etc.; and that we who are Friends shall be in a more particular manner regarded and treated by the Queen. So that you will not, I hope and believe, have a less interest in the government, being humble and discreet in your conduct. . . . But be that as it will, I purpose to see you if God give me life this fall, but I grow old and infirm, yet would gladly see you once more before I die, and my young sons and daughter also settled upon good tracts of land for them and theirs after them, to clear and settle upon, as Jacob's sons did. I close when I tell you that I desire fervent prayers to the Lord for continuing my life, that I may see Pennsylvania once more before I die, and that I am
>
> Your faithful loving friend
Wm. Penn

Two months before he wrote, he was paralyzed by a stroke. A little more than two months after, a second stroke virtually put him beyond the grasp of events. Yet with the tenacity so characteristic, he made a partial recovery, only to be stricken again in January 1713. He no longer recognized his grandchildren or his young son, John, but he "played with them lovingly . . . only when he saw his wife at the writing table, hard at work, he looked troubled." Hannah called him "My poor Dearest" and now and then "my second-selfe."

Thomas Story called on him in 1715:

> When I went to his house I thought myself strong enough to see him in that condition; but when I entered the room, and perceived the great defect of his expressions for want of memory, it greatly bowed by spirit under a consideration of the uncertainty of all human qualifications, and

what the finest of men are soon reduced to by a disorder of the organs. . . . Nevertheless, no insanity, or lunacy, at all appeared in his actions; and his mind was in an innocent state. . . .

Penn died at dawn, July 30, 1718. "My poor Dearest's last breath," Hannah wrote, "was fetcht this morning . . ."

From Philadelphia came this tribute:

> It becomes us particularly to say that as he was our Governor, he merited from us love and true honor and we can but have the same regard to his memory when we consider the blessings and ease we have enjoyed under his government, and are rightly sensible of his care, affection and regard always shown with anxious concern for the safety and prosperity of the people, who many of them removed from comfortable livings to be adventurers with him not so much with views of better acquisitions or greater riches but the laudable prospect of retired, quiet habitations for themselves and posterity, and the promotion of truth and virtue in the earth.

Penn like Benjamin Franklin was a prolific writer—publishing over a hundred tracts on a wide range of subjects, all of them reflecting in some way his deep belief that love was the solution to the dilemmas of men and nations. He seems to have been one of the few genuine Christians Christianity has produced. Yet there is nothing ethereal in his approach and none of the uncomfortable fire and brimstone which ministers of his time delighted in hurling at those who ignored the knock. His style is forceful and crackles with the white heat of indignation when he lashes out at the policies of the British government he thought betrayed the liberties of the subject. Almost always, however, it is directed at the actions than at the actors. Since many of his most strident sentences were written in prison they had a background of vivid reality. Like Franklin he compiled maxims, but his were sober, unsmiling epigrams and appeared in print under the title, *The Fruits of Solitude*.

Franklin, by contrast, was always the boy munching rolls as he walked into Philadelphia, an adventurer at life, who grinningly remarked he had great difficulty following the advice he dispensed in *Poor Richard's Almanack*. No pilgrim ever enjoyed his progress as did Franklin, and he was intrigued by the foibles of human nature. An unexpurgated edition of his proverbs would have shocked the staid Americans in the 19th century who cherished such homely little reminders about a penny saved. Both men had a deep respect for the Indians; both were philosophers, Penn in the classic vein, Franklin always pragmatic. Penn summoned an impressive array of ancient sages and saints to support a thesis, and displayed an astounding amount of erudition. The incredible Franklin plucked names from the past only when expedient.

Yet Penn, for all his ostensible fame, is an abstract on the city's landscape. Although he hovers in weathered bronze over his cherished city from atop City Hall, he is as remote to the crowds as if he were a character out of mythology. While, as throughout the entire Commonwealth, Philadelphia has dutifully inscribed his name on some public buildings, his birthday is recalled at half-century intervals. The absence of an authentic adult portrait leaves the populace free to cast him in whatever image they choose. Most associate him with the cheerful double-chinned Quaker who laughs from the label of a cereal box, or Benjamin West's rotund, dour character concluding a treaty with the Indians.
Indians.

At any rate, it is a fair assumption that he bore no resemblance to either. Alexander Calder's statue on City Hall is probably based on the painting made of him in Ireland in 1666 when he was twenty-two and good-looking. Fragments describe him at the celebrated treaty under the elm at Shackamaxon, when he was thirty-eight, as being of a strong, muscular build. A Philadelphia woman whose marriage he attended said he was "rather short of stature, but the handsomest, best-looking, lively gentlyman she had ever seen," which raises an interesting question as to what she thought of her new husband. Franklin, in London, politely questioned the authenticity of a portrait purportedly of Penn which Lord Kames offered him, "because the primitive Quakers us'd to declare against Pictures as a vain Expence." Moreover Franklin said "when old Lord Cobham was adorning his Gardens at Stowe with the Busts of famous Men, he made Enquirey of the Family for a Picture of Wm. Penn, in order to get a Bust form'd from it, but could find none." Calder's work became a conversation piece in the early part of this century when some alert citizens noticed that Penn's extended right arm was pointing to the "red light" district. The gesture of pride, silhouetted against the morning sun unfortunately makes Penn appear to be showering disdain on the unsuspecting city, an item that was quickly discovered by inbound traffic on the Parkway in the 1930's.

These amusing irreverences and the indifference to the founder insulate Philadelphians from one of the most fascinating figures in history. By any standard, William Penn was an extraordinary man, superior in some respects to the cherished Franklin, and matching him, stride for stride, in manifestations of moderninity.

In 1881 a group of Philadelphians endeavored to have Penn's remains removed to the city from his grave in England. Had they been successful, Philadelphians might be more conscious of his presence in the affairs of their remarkable city.

3

THE MODEL CITY:

Penn's Philadelphia Becomes a Living Community

*   *   *   *   *

Philadelphia, the Expectation of those that are concern'd in this Province, is at last laid out to the great Content of those here . . .; the Scituation is a Neck of Land, and lieth between two Navigable Rivers, Delaware and Skulkill, whereby it hath two Fronts upon the Water, each a Mile, and two from River to River. Delaware is a glorious River, but the Skulkill being an hundred Miles Boatable above the Falls, and its Course North-East toward the Fountain of the Susquehannah (that tends to the Heart of the Province, and both sides our own) it is like to be a great part of the Settlement of this Age . . .

—Penn, Letter to The Society of Traders, 1683

*   *   *   *   *

Life and Times in Colonial Philadelphia

More than the Swedes or Dutch, the English paid careful attention to the waterways serving Philadelphia. Shipping was vital to the prosperity of the whole Province. In 1681 a cove near the steep rise of Society Hill caught the imagination of Penn's deputies. Sheltered and pleasant, with an arm of Dock Creek to carry shallow-draft craft to convenient landings, it would provide good harborage for the heavier ocean-going ships. Within a comparatively short time, however, it was so crowded with vessels of all descriptions, nudging each other for space, other outlets for the increasing traffic were needed. Most of this came in the early stages from New Jersey when farmers rowed across the river to sell produce and fowl at the markets. It was augmented by coastal shipping from other colonies and traders from the West Indies. Another natural harbor was found in the vicinity of Arch and Race Streets, north of Dock Creek, and the smaller craft were diverted there—leaving the cove free to serve the larger ships. This, at best, was a temporary expedient. As Philadelphia became an export port, docking facilities would be required, and enterprising Philadelphians with waterfront footage quickly calculated the profits from wharfage fees. By 1685 Penn could say:

> We have had about ninety Sayl of Ships with Passengers since the beginning of '82, and not Vessel . . . miscarried. The Estimate of the People may thus be made—Eighty to each ship, which comes to Seven Thousand Two Hundred Persons. . . . There is . . . a fair Key of about three hundred feet square Built by Samuel Carpenter, to which a ship of five hundred Tuns may lay her broadside, and others intend to follow his example. We have also a Ropewalk made by B. Wilcox and cordage for shipping already spun at it.

Given the requisite manpower docks could be constructed quickly—heavy logs, banded together in huge box-like shapes, could be floated onto the river, filled with sand, stone, gravel and dirt, and sunk into position. Once anchored, flooring was nailed on the top and, by a sectional process, it was possible to take a pier fairly far out, enabling it to handle several ships at a time.

Since vessels from foreign ports often laid over for two months good accommodations were necessary. Merchants found it expedient to build their own docks to facilitate handling cargoes. Small warehouses built on the piers could ordinarily hold enough anticipated exports to load an average vessel with space for thirty tons, thus releasing storage areas in their offices. From 1720 to 1739 the demand for wheat, flour and bread in Europe attracted foreign shipping and during the mid-'30's the annual exports of these commodities alone are estimated to have reached £50,000. While yearly entrances and clearances of shipping fluctuated

46

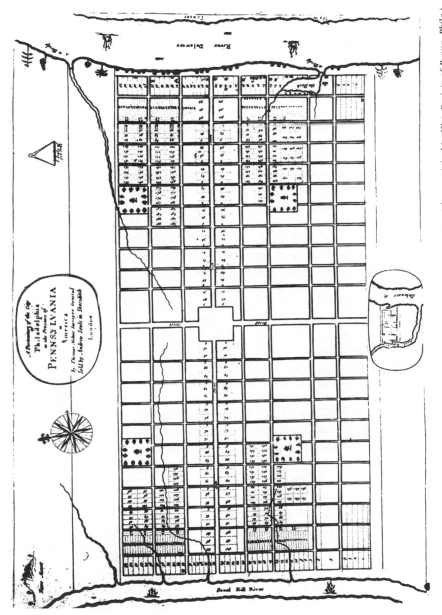

THOMAS HOLME'S "PORTRAITURE OF THE CITY"—1682
Prospective purchasers saw this in the London land office

(Pa. Hist. & Museum Comm., Harrisburg; original in Hist. Society of Penna. Phila.)

during this twenty-year period, only in 1722 and 1723, in the wake of the South Sea Bubble Crisis of 1721, did fewer than a hundred put into port. From 1736 through 1739, over two hundred vessels annually tied up at Philadelphia wharves.

Bitter winter weather frequently closed the port. During 1728 and 1729 fourteen ships, three snows, eight brigantines, nine sloops, two schooners and a number of shallops were frozen in the docks. Reverend Israel Acrelius, who culled many miscellaneous statistics, counted one hundred and seventeen large ships tied up or on the river one October day in 1754. Shipbuilding on the banks of the Delaware added to the expanded maritime scene, and by 1760 Philadelphia had sixty-six wharves —some municipally-owned and quite a few in private hands.

Never content to ship in foreign bottoms, the merchants acquired their own ships as quickly as they could afford them. Like New England they consistently ignored the British Navigation Acts which theoretically limited their commerce to British ports. As early as 1688, Captain John Blackwell, whom Penn brought in from Massachusetts to serve as deputy governor because factional fights in town made it impossible to find an acceptable appointee, was shocked at the total indifference of the Quakers to these restrictive laws. When Samuel Carpenter explained it was common practice to disregard them, the old Puritan, who had commanded the "famous" Maiden Troop in the English Civil War, insisted on referring the matter to Penn in London. He disliked the Quakers, whom he thought were gouging Philadelphians, acidly commenting that they purchased £100 worth of goods abroad and sold it for £400 in the city. He summarized his contempt by asserting the Quaker "prays for his neighbor on First Days and then preys upon him the other six." When he left Philadelphia in 1690 after a turbulent, brief administration, he said, "I have to do with a people whom neither God nor man can prevayle with. . . . Alas! Alas! Poore Governor of Pennsylvania!"

The phenomenal rise of the port, however, was not matched by commensurate foresight in those arteries of land bound commerce, highways. The Quaker-dominated Assembly consistently ignored pleas from the "back country" for an adequate road to link south-central Pennsylvania with Philadelphia. Only a hazardous narrow lane carried produce and products to the city and if a tense farmer successfully negotiated the ruts and rocks, he then faced what he regarded as the perils of the ferry across the Schuylkill. Quaker complacency in the matter was prompted by a belief that the "back country" people could not trade with Maryland to the south, because that colony had enacted a statute in 1704 prohibiting such imports. With cold analysis they concluded farmers could either risk the bad roads or starve. It was incredible logic, and the myopia almost turned into a disaster for Philadelphia. Somewhat surreptitiously, Maryland, aware of the farmer's plight, began in 1739 to survey a road leading into the region, inviting the Pennsylvanians to bring their wares to the port of Baltimore. As far west as Bedford the mountain trails began to turn southerly instead of in the east-west direction the confident Quakers anticipated. Had not the coming French and Indian War forced the Assembly to take a fresh look at the roads out of Philadelphia, it is possible that much of the export trade would have been wholly lost. Philadelphians, in the meantime, were having troubles of their own with streets.

Penn and his aides had been quick to grasp their importance, and what they achieved by 1700 was impressive—the more so when it is remembered the city's population in that year was only about 5,000. The Dutch and Swedes built no roads, preferring waterways and content with trails. In 1675 the English changed this policy, and residents within the jurisdiction of the Upland Court were ordered to "make good and passable wayes from neighbor to neighbor" "... at least ten feet broad, all stumps and shrubs to be close cut by the ground...." Penn's plan for Philadelphia streets was naturally more sophisticated, but his vision went far beyond them. To stimulate growth on the western side of the Schuylkill, highways were projected to Darby and to Haverford. All such rural roads, however, were subject to the whims of abutting landowners, who frequently plowed and planted, and sometimes fenced them. In 1688 Penn told Governor Blackwell to see that "pains be taken of the roads and highways of the [Bucks] county that they be straight and commodious for travellers, for I understand they are turned about by the planters, which is a mischief that must not be endured." Such annoyances did not discourage his dreams of Philadelphia's greatness. To bring New Jersey, as well as the northern reaches of his Province within the magnetic field of Philadelphia's markets, the Council in August 1700 ordered a "King's Highway or Publick Road & the Bridges from the town of Philadelphia to the falls of the Delaware" at Trenton. The "Queen's Path" from Philadelphia to Chester was constructed in 1706; the "Old York Road" in 1711, and eleven years later, branches of it were run to Doylestown and Easton, while in 1721 the "Conestoge Road" was laid out as an extension of High Street with Lancaster as its ultimate objective, but got only as far as Brandywine. The destination was finally reached in 1733.

No one expected the country highways to be paved at the time, but Philadelphians were unhappy about the condition of streets within the city. Samuel Powell, father of a subsequent mayor, said that by 1725 there were still no paved streets, and carts often bogged down in the mires, or churned up such dust on dry days the citizens dubbed the town "Filthy-dirty."

Peter Kalm, visiting from Sweden in 1748, gave a more gentle perspective:

> The streets are regular, pretty, and most of them fifty feet, English measure, broad. . . . Some are paved, others are not, and it seems less necessary since the ground is sandy and therefore soon absorbs the wet. But in most of the streets is a pavement of flags, a fathom (six feet) or more broad, laid before the houses, and four-foot posts put on the outside three or four fathoms apart. Those who walk on foot use the flat stones, but riders and teams use the middle of the street. The above-mentioned posts prevent horses and wagons from injuring the pedestrians inside the posts, and are there secure from careless teamsters and the dirt which is thrown up by horses and carts. . . .

VIEW FROM KENSINGTON

Before settling down to a fairly straight southerly course along the city's numerous docks, the Delaware took a gentle turn here at Shackamaxon near Kensington, giving Thomas Birch several advantages. The spreading elm is the famous Penn Treaty Tree, and it communicates such a sense of serenity that the sound of the boatbuilders axes disturbs neither the fisherman nor the pastoral pair playing with their dog. River traffic is light and the long view of the city and distant church spires is uncluttered. Even the breeze cooperates since it carries the smoke from the pitch pot away from the painter, but the men on the wharf may be having some thoughts about air pollution.

The Model City

Few Philadelphians would have agreed. Grand juries constantly presented this or that street as being dangerous to life and limb due to deep potholes. The myriad of underground creeks eroded the support of roadbeds. Thomas Pownall in 1754 found "stumps or roots of some of the original Pine-Trees" jutting up, and Colonel Henri Bouquet wrote to Richard Peters, "I never Saw anything but dirt and dust in and about your Town." Mayor Thomas Lawrence, while ready to admit that horsemen, chaises and chariots, carts, trucks and the Conestoga wagons drawn by eight horses or oxen kept the thoroughfares dirty, blamed the citizenry for "heaping great Piles of Dirt and Filth near the Gutters, so that the same is raised two or three Feet above them, thereby stopping the Water courses, and in consequence thereof, occasioning an intollerable Stench at this Season, whereby Distempers will in all probability be Occasioned." He issued a proclamation in 1750 ordering every householder to keep the area in front of his place clean.

It was a futile gesture. Forty-three years later Israel Israel asked for some relief from the mounds of trash piled so high that access to his stables was blocked. Since these stables were less than one hundred feet from Bishop White's residence on Walnut Street, one wonders how the popular pastor of Christ Church endured the sight and smell. The populace blamed the mid-18th century mess on the lack of paving, and six months after Mayor Lawrence's decree, the Grand Jury reported to the Court of Quarter Sessions that the city's reputation was at stake. Strangers "who otherwise commend our Regularity, make" the "deep and miry" streets "their first observation." No one offered to contribute higher taxes to relieve the problem, and another grand jury in 1758, obviously inspired by Benjamin Franklin since the report is in his handwriting, demanded Provincial relief. Franklin made clean streets one of his countless crusades, explaining they would mean "greater Ease in keeping our Houses clean, so much Dirt not being brought in by People's Feet; the Benefit to the Shops by more Custom, as Buyers could more easily get at them, and by not having in windy Weather the Dust blown in upon their Goods, &c. &c." He circulated handbills containing these arguments "to each House, and in a Day or two went round to see who would subscribe an Agreement to pay "sixpence a month" for a scavenger, as street-cleaners were ignominiously called. He cheerfully noted that "It was unanimously sign'd, and for a time well executed. "All the Inhabitants of the City were delighted with the Cleanliness of the Pavement that surrounded the Market . . . and this rais'd a general Desire to have all the Streets paved; and made the People more willing to submit to a Tax for that purpose." These recollections, however, were a bit generous, for when the matter was broached to the Assembly in 1758 there was no

51

eagerness to be taxed. Ultimately a lottery was approved and £2,250 was raised, enough to provide paving for the center of the principal streets.

Inasmuch as the General Assembly sat in the State House between Fifth and Sixth on Chestnut Streets, the people turned to it, rather than the weak city government, which was run by committees, a board of aldermen and a mayor. The post of mayor was the least sought honor, and he was selected by his fellow aldermen. If the nominee declined, he had to pay a fine of £30. If he accepted, he was expected at the end of his one-year term, to give a lavish banquet for his friends and associates. This custom ended when Mayor James Hamilton gave £150 to the city treasury in lieu of a feast. In 1747 Alderman Morris went into hiding in Bucks County to avoid being served with notice of his election.

Complaints of every description reached the Mayor's desk, involving not only the streets but the kind of traffic. For a half-century after Penn acquired the province, the Swedish custom of letting hogs run loose was observed. So long as they bore an owner's mark, it was perfectly legal. Cowherds would daily lead cattle they collected from backyards out to grazing grounds, and in the leisurely lope from Society Hill to the nearby green commons, traffic was only slightly inconvenienced. But in other parts of town where the procession had to go a greater distance, commensurate difficulties developed.

With regularity, housewives who led the family cow out at the morning blast from the cowherd's horn, learned at nightfall it had strayed off and was lost. Newspaper advertisements, like a litany of the lost, gave word-pictures of the missing cows, rivaled only by the greater frequency of wandering horses. These, however, generally found their way to inn yards or turned up at stables. In 1752 some Philadelphians asked the Assembly for help in getting rid of surplus dogs, "a great and dangerous Nuisance." "By running out at Travellers and Horses, they have been the Occasion of the Death of one Woman, and breaking the Bones of several other Persons." Kalm's statement that the posts along the sidewalks saved pedestrians from accidents was slightly inaccurate. They were upset when wagons veered onto the footpaths in an effort to avoid collisions—constantly harassed by young men racing their mounts in and out of the congested streets despite city ordinances prohibiting "galloping and trotting" within Philadelphia.

Gouverneur Morris, the handsome, eloquent, urbane member of the Second Continental Congress, lost part of his leg on May 12, 1780 when a runaway horse threw him out of his phaeton and Philadelphia surgeons decided to amputate. His pursuit of women had almost made him a legend in his own time. "Gouverneur is daily employed in making oblations to Venus," John Jay wrote to Robert Livingston from the city

The Model City

LOOKING DOWN MARKET STREET TOWARD THE DELAWARE
Traffic is understandably sparse at 9th and High Streets, for this, in 1799, is a newly-developed section of town, two and a half blocks west of the Presidential mansion occupied by John and Abigail Adams. The horsemen, a segment of the First City Troop, may be practising for ceremonies or catastrophe, for political tensions were running high despite the quiet scene.

in 1779, and after the accident observed to Robert Morris, "Gouverneur's Leg has been a Tax on my heart. I am almost tempted to wish he had lost *something* else." Morris accepted his accident with remarkable aplomb, suggesting that the least known of the surgeons perform the operation so that he might thereby acquire fame. His subsequent career bore out the confident statement that he was still a better man with one leg than most with two.

Philadelphia's street problems were not unique. Franklin on long visits to London worried about their lack of cleanliness, and Americans in Paris during and after the American Revolution pronounced its streets "narrow, nasty and inconvenient" "stinking extremely bad" and without sidewalks. They reported that pedestrians often sank to their calves in mud or worse filth while overhead loomed the constant threat of being splattered with the contents of chamber pots.

Various Philadelphians are credited with having pioneered the lighting of the city's streets. Some say that Quaker John Smith and other public-spirited citizens gathered at Widow Pratt's tavern on

December 21, 1749 to lay plans for putting lamps before their doors, and hiring a lamplighter to tend them. John Clifton was the first to do it in front of his two-story brick house at the southeast corner of Clifton's (Drinker's) Alley and Second Street, below Race. It was a rounded globe, and set an example not only for a number of Philadelphians who followed suit, but started a trend for Newport and other cities. One remarked with pride in 1750 that the city now "only wants the Streets to be Paved to make it appear to advantage, for there is few Towns, if any, in England that are better Illumined with Lamps and those of the best sort." The matter was quickly brought to the attention of the Assembly so that a uniform system of "enlightening the streets, lanes and alleys ... raising money on the inhabitants" could be adopted. In February 1750, the Assembly, ignoring the City corporation, provided for a board of six wardens, meeting each November, to "erect, put up and fix" as many lights as they felt necessary, and to enter into contracts with lamplighters. In September 1751, newly installed whale-oil lamps were lit for the first time. Franklin devised the four-sided ventilated lamp which he said was much easier to clean than the closed globe Clifton used. Londoners may also have been the beneficiaries of Franklin's genius, since he suggested that they change from the globe-type to his concept. A 40-shilling fine failed to protect the new lamps from vandals, and a young man paid that amount for heaving an apple at one. By 1779, a $40 reward was posted by the Clerk of the Wardens for the capture of "some evil disposed persons, who have yet been undiscovered" in a spree where "many of the public lamps ... have been wickedly and wantonly broke and otherwise damaged, and the cups and oils taken out. . . ."

Well lit or not, though, the areas Penn prescribed for use like the "Moore-fields" came along slowly. Ultimately they would become Washington, Franklin, Logan and Rittenhouse Squares, but the belated development of the area west of Broad Street deferred the need for the latter two until the 19th century. Even in the eastern quadrants they seemed hardly necessary, since the bulk of the 30,000 who in 1790 occupied some 6,000 buildings were concentrated in the one square mile between Vine Street to the north, Lombard to the south, and Seventh Street to the west. Thus within a short walking distance open country provided ample pastoral settings for those who needed the relaxation. Unlike the great center square (later named "Penn") where the Proprietor contemplated "Publick buildings," the other four were to remain "open space for ever." All come close to the eight acres decreed by Penn—Logan and Franklin a little more than seven, and Washington and Rittenhouse slightly over six. Throughout the 18th century they were designated as the "northeast" and "southeast," "northwest" and "southwest."

The northeast, later Franklin, wore a forlorn look almost from its inception—inconsistent with its ebullient namesake. Low, wet and marshy, it had gaping holes where clay had been dug out for brick-making. One corner of it accommodated a powder magazine during the Revolution which metamorphosed into a storage place for public lamp oil. A German congregation appropriated part for a cemetery, and this precipitated a law suit.

"Washington" square was conveyed by Penn's commissioners to the city in 1706, in response to a request "for some convenient piece of ground for a comon and publick burying ground for all strangers or others who might not so conveniently be laid in any of the particular enclosures ... [of] certain religious societies." Neither as high nor as level as it now appears, the ground sloped from its western boundary to a deep gulley, through which a creek flowed near Walnut Street. In 1784 a row of red-painted houses at 8th Street marked the end of habitation on Walnut Street.

While waiting for "strangers or others" the city leased the land to Joshua Carpenter for pasture, but when a young woman in his family committed suicide he made a little private burial plot there. Thereafter blacks, some slaves, some impoverished freemen who may have lived in the ramshackle dwellings that lined the south side of Locust Street opposite the square, were there interred. During fairs and holidays as many as a thousand negroes gathered to dance "after the manner of their several nations in Africa ... speaking and singing in their native dialects" and those from Guinea placed rum and food on the graves. "I have spent an hour this morning," wrote John Adams on April 13, 1777 "in the congregation of the dead." He told of his walk

> into the 'Potters Field', (a burying place between the new stone prison and the hospital) and I never in my whole life was so affected with melancholy. The graves of the soldiers who have been buried in this ground from the hospital and bettering-house during the course of last summer, fall and winter, dead of the small pox and camp diseases, are enough to make the heart of stone melt away. The sexton told me that upwards of two thousand soldiers have been buried there, and by the appearance of the graves and trenches, it is most probable to me that he speaks within bounds. To what cause this plague is to be attributed, I don't know—disease has destroyed ten men for us where the sword of the enemy has killed one!

American prisoners of war who died during the British occupation of Philadelphia from October 1777 to June 1778 were buried there. An es-

STATE HOUSE circa 1776

Making allowance for minor errors in perspective this drawing shows how the State House buildings looked to the delegates on July 4, 1776. The wings joined to both the east and west walls by "piazzas" were designed to house State and local record offices, despite the vehement protests in 1736 of the Register General and Recorder of Deeds who did not want to move from their central city locations. The wandering Library Company got permission to use the second floor of the west wing (right of picture) in 1739 and stayed until 1773 when they moved to Carpenters Hall. The first floor of that wing, in 1745, was occupied as living quarters for the Doorkeep of the Assembly and his family. Visiting Indian delegations were temporarily housed wherever space could be found in the wings, but because they were careless about fires their presence gave officials a continuous headache. In 1759 the Assembly voted to build "a small House, suitable for the Purpose" by the brick wall in the Yard. Congress occupied the Assembly room during its sessions in the main building, the four windows on the first floor east (reader's left) of the doorway. Since early legislative sessions were often closed to the public the room had doors. Conversely across the corridor the Supreme Court of the Province was accessible through open arches and people in the passageway must have been disconcerting to the judges and counsel. Within the "piazzas" or breezeways steps led to the second floor of each wing. In 1812 the State empowered local authorities to demolish the wings and the "Piazzas" and replace them with two-story office buildings to serve Federal, state and municipal functions. In the process the historic Assembly room was turned into a court room, the main door of the Chestnut Street entrance was replaced and the cellar for a time became a dog pound. "State House row", as it was called, remained in that condition until the 1876 centennial evoked sentiment to restore the exterior to something approaching its 1776 look. This was not accomplished until 1896-98 through the diligent efforts of the D.A.R. and various committees. Prior to the centennial year the Assembly Room had been converted from a court-room to a museum of items touching the memorable days—Hancock's chair, the Liberty Bell and other artefacts were put on display. It also served as a place for state funerals. In 1848 John Quincy Adams, in 1852, Henry Clay, in 1857, Elisha Kent Kane, the Arctic explorer and in 1865 President Lincoln lay in state. When Independence Hall and the immediate area was transferred to the Federal Government by Philadelphia on January 1, 1951 an intensive reconstruction program was undertaken, with definitive research on a major scale, so that the State House now most nearly approximates its 1776 look except for the 1828 steeple.

timated 900 had been captured during the battles of Brandywine and Germantown. The wounded were carried to the second-floor Long Room in the State House, and the others were herded into the Walnut Street prison. The windows of the prison were shattered on October 23 when the British man-of-war *Augusta*, set afire by a shot from Fort Mifflin, exploded "with a report as loud as a peal from a hundred cannon," according to Thomas Paine. Paine was not exaggerating because the blast was felt as far away as Reading, 56 miles distant, and broke windows within a wide radius of Philadelphia. The British provost, so notorious for his brutality that Sir Henry Clinton gave him a captaincy as a safety precaution in the event the Americans took him, did not replace the panes. Without blankets and almost starved, approximately 100 died, and "were . . . dragged by the legs along the floor to the dead carts." More mass burials occurred during the Yellow Fever epidemic of 1793, and in 1795 the city closed it to further interments.

As Philadelphia began to move westward in the early years of the 19th century the creek was covered and a formal design of walks and trees adopted between 1815 and 1817. The Society of the Cincinnati, having started in 1811 to collect funds for a monument to Washington, got permission to raise one in the center of the square. With much pomp and ceremony the cornerstone was laid in 1833, and the area named for the general, amid the "50 varieties of trees, 7 of which are European and 43 native, 2 of which . . . were introduced by Lewis & Clark from the Rocky Mountains." The Society was still collecting monies in 1877, hoping to finish the monument in time to mark the centennial of Yorktown in 1881, but Washington has to be content with the cornerstone.

The area came into its own in the 1800's, however, as a literary and cultural center. Just off the Square in 1823 at the Prune Street Theatre, "Home, Sweet Home" was first sung in 1823; at 725 Walnut Street was the office of Lewis E. Redner who wrote the music for "O, Little Town of Bethlehem." Sep Winner, composer of "Little Brown Jug" was inspired by the bird imitations of a neighborhood black known as "Whistling Dick" and transformed one of his tunes into "Listen to the Mocking Bird" which, in addition to being a favorite of Abraham Lincoln's, sold twenty million copies. The Athanaeum, a subscription library founded in 1813 to provide more cosmopolitan reading, moved into the splendid Italian Renaissance building on South Sixth Street in 1847, while a few doors farther down, at No. 245, lived Marshal de Grouchy, forced from France by Napoleon's charge that it was he who lost the battle of Waterloo.

In 1869 a Philadelphia ordinance decreed that new city-county office buildings should replace all structures in Independence Square, including the historic State House. Once more, outraged Philadelphians appealed to the Pennsylvania General Assembly, which directed such construction either in Washington or Penn Squares, the site to be chosen by voters in a referendum. It added, however, that upon completion of the new building, "All the present buildings on Independence Square, except Independence Hall, shall be removed." The electorate selected Penn Square for the new city hall, and the Centennial celebration in 1876 may have saved the other 18th-century buildings from the demolition. In any case, it was happily not carried out and twenty-five years later in 1895, the State legislature repealed the offending clause. Uncluttered by "Publick buildings", Washington Square was able to retain its soft serenity.

4

"KEEP THY SHOP and thy shop will keep thee":—*Franklin's Almanac*
Business and Community Grow Together

* * * * *

"... it is not enough to bring money,
but one must also bring an inclination to work ..."

Pastorius' Pennsylvania (1684)

* * * * *

"Wealth is not his that has it,
but his that enjoys it."

Poor Richard's Almanack (1736)

* * * * *

Life and Times in Colonial Philadelphia

A lthough the lessons of the London fire of 1666 shaped much of Penn's planning for Philadelphia, the Assembly and Council were slow in taking steps to prevent fires. Arson was outlawed in the criminal code of 1692, but it was not until 1696 that definitive measures were enacted requiring householders to keep a twelve to fourteen foot swab and a bucket on hand, and prohibiting the use of fire to cleanse a foul chimney. Smoking in the streets was banned. Fines, from 10 shillings to 40 shillings, were earmarked for the purchase of leather water buckets. In 1700 two buckets were required, and no more than six pounds of powder could be kept in any house or shop within forty perches (a stone-masons measure) from any residence. Sensitivity to this peril is reflected in the stiff penalty of £10 attached to a breach.

The city acquired its first fire engine in 1718, a crude pumper Abraham Bickley imported from England. Resembling an early farm wagon with a side-handled pump, it failed miserably in "the great fire of 1730" which burned out a store on Fishbourne's wharf and damaged Jonathan Dickinson's "fine house." Officials quickly ordered three more engines, 400 leather buckets, 20 ladders and 25 hooks. A special tax was levied to provide the funds. Two of the engines, along with 250 buckets, arrived from England in 1731, but the third was built by a Philadelphian, Anthony Nicholls, in 1733. He demonstrated that it "played water higher than the highest" of the London machines, but his pumping mechanism, and wood fittings instead of brass, made the engine cumbersome, and the City Council decided not to let him manufacture others of the type for Philadelphia.

Franklin, under the guise of an elderly man, wrote a letter to his newspaper in 1735: "Being old and lame of my Hands, and thereby uncapable of assisting my Fellow Citizens, when their Houses are on Fire, I must beg them to take in good Part the following Hints . . . ." Those careless in carrying "living . . . Coals in a full Shovel . . . out of one Room into another, or up or down Stairs, unless in a Warmingpan shut . . . may be forced, (as once I was) to leap out of your Windows, and hazard your Necks to avoid being overroasted." He favored laws against "too shallow Hearths, "and the detestable practice

of putting wooden Mouldings on each side of the Fire Place, which being commonly of Heart-of-Pine and full of Turpentine stand ready to flame as soon as a Coal or a small Brand shall roul against them. . . . Those who undertake Sweeping . . . and employ Servants for that Purpose, ought to be licensed by the Mayor; and if any Chimney fires and flames out 15 Days after Sweeping, the Fine should be paid by the Sweeper,; for it is his fault. We have at present got Engines enough in the Town, but I question, whether in many Parts . . . Water enough can be had to keep them going for half an Hour together. It seems to me some Publick Pumps are wanting; but that I submit to better Judgments.

After an extensive fire in "Budd's Long Row," Front Street near the Drawbridge, in 1736, Franklin and several others decided to form a fire brigade, and thirty volunteers responded:

we agreed to meet once a month and spend a social evening together in discoursing and communicating such ideas as occurred to us . . . to keep always in good order and fit for use a certain number of leather buckets, with strong bags and baskets (for packing and transporting of goods) which were to be brought to every fire.

They called it the Union Fire Company and Franklin was chosen to lead it. In 1738 the Fellowship Fire Company, with thirty-five men, was established and kept its engine in a house on a lot in Second Street near Market, and hung the ladder under the eaves of the butchers' shambles near the meal-market. The Hand-in-Hand Company was formed March 1, 1742, The Heart-in-Hand, February 22, 1743 (Washington's eleventh birthday) and The Friendship, July 30, 1747—all three had a membership of forty.

Franklin, familiar at first-hand with the procedures in London and Boston, was the guiding hand. Each unit had a "Fireward" or fire chief to "direct the opening and stripping of Roofs by the Ax-men, the pulling down burning Timbers by the Hookmen, and the playing of the Engines. . . ." Roofs on the older frame houses presented a particular peril, and Franklin wished "that either Tiles would come in . . . or else . . . Roofs (be made) more safe to walk upon, by carrying the Wall above the Eves" as the newer homes in the city featured. Everyone within a reasonable radius of a fire was expected to help, bringing their leather buckets to the scene, where under the supervision of the chief a line of men passed the filled buckets while the empties were returned through a line of women.

Three types of hose were available, the English with woven cylindrical sections of hemp or linen; the Dutch of thick sewn leather; and the German of hemp without seams, and later of linen, called "watersnakes" by the *Pennsylvania Gazette* of March 24, 1772. Of the three countries, the Netherlands was the most advanced, being the first to design an air-chamber fire engine, and making a sailcloth suction hose water-tight by cement. Almost a half-century after their founding, the Union in 1791 had eighty, and the Friendship one hundred twenty feet of hose, while both had at least two working engines—more than any of the expanded number of companies. Luckily the city was spared throughout the 18th century any heavy damage from fire—the worst consuming several stores filled with produce near the Drawbridge over Dock Creek.

Richard Newsham of "Cloth-Fair, London, Engineer" produced many of the engines used in the colonies, advertising his wares through handbills. Some Philadelphia companies were among his customers, but in 1768 Richard Mason "living at the upper end of Second Street" designed one with the levers at the ends instead of the sides, and the Northern Liberty Company bought the first one he produced. Thereafter Mason was in demand, and before he quit the business in 1801, he established quite a production record. Others like Samuel Briggs tried to get in on the market, but the two he offered between 1791 and 1796 were failures. Patrick Lyon, the best blacksmith in town, invented an engine with greater pressure in 1794, but its merit was not fully recognized until 1803.

Lyon achieved minor fame in a less palatable manner, when he was falsely accused of complicity in the "great bank robbery of 1798." The United States Bank, awaiting the completion of its new home temporarily stowed its money in Carpenter's Hall and Lyon was given the order to make the requisite locks and other security devices. Despite these and other elaborate precautions, even to watchmen patrolling the area with dogs, thieves managed to break through. In the wave of hysteria that followed bank officials suspected Lyon, and he was held in Walnut Street Prison for three months with barely enough food to sustain him, when the culprits were finally apprehended. Joseph Hopkinson represented Lyon in a suit against the bank officers for false arrest, and won a verdict of $12,000, which was later compromised at $9,000.

The prospect of the honest, poor blacksmith fighting the rich bankers made it a cause celebre, and Lyon became a popular figure. Joseph Neale painted him by his forge, and the canvas is among the more absorbing art memorabilia of early Philadelphia housed at the Pennsylvania Academy of Fine Arts.

Meanwhile the Assembly continued to tighten restrictions so that fire hazards might be eliminated. In 1731 coopers and bakers were required to ply their trades in shops built of brick or stone and possessed of large chimneys. Haystacks were not allowed within 100 feet of any building, and no more than 200 faggots could be stacked in firewood piles. In 1795 the city was authorized to prohibit wooden buildings east of Tenth Street and could specify that each dwelling have six buckets exclusively for fire-fighting. The firing of guns, squibs and rockets was brought within its regulatory powers.

Notwithstanding their high civic purpose fire companies had to contend with mischief-makers. Some "evil minded, dissolute Persons" made off with "the nossels of most of the Pumps in Market Street" in 1744 and

HIGH STREET MARKET

High Street from Front to Second was the original site of the public markets in the early 1700's. As wind and weather eroded the wooden stalls they were replaced in 1759 with brick-pillared types shown here. Separated by alleys, the structures came to within forty feet east of Second, on the west side of which stood the city hall and court house. For revenue and convenience the sheds were extended to Third Street, but when the city council voted in 1773 to build another group between Third and Fourth irate citizens protested. After having their petition denied in council, then in a law suit, the said citizens, arguing the project would be an encumbrance on the street, quietly dismantled at night all workmen did during the day. For good measure they carried off the lime and destroyed the limehouse. The unsentimental British occupying the city from October 1777 to June 1778 used the markets to stable some of their horses. When the city tried again in 1786 to build out to Fourth, there was no organized opposition. The first half of the 19th century saw the sheds reach 17th Street. In 1859 dismantling began to clear Market Street for increased traffic. Head House Market in Society Hill gives a present picture of what the past was like. The view of the First Presbyterian Church on High Street shows how the markets narrowed the width of the "cartways."

1745, and the Sun Company in 1779 lost some of its baskets and buckets to thieves after battling a fire on Chestnut Street. Through the long, hot summer, it appealed to the rascals to return the equipment, apparently with little success.

The volunteer firemen usually held their meetings at taverns and after dues and fines were collected, and items pertinent to firefighting were ticked off the agenda, they settled down to the more convivial business of drinking and debating. Quaker John Smith, thrifty of time, thought some of these discussions were not "profitable," but nothing was unprofitable to Franklin. In addition to the fellowship he so thoroughly enjoyed, he was able to keep his finger on the pulse of public opinion, and often to prod it in the direction he wanted it to go.

He had long thought of the idea of fire insurance—the success it enjoyed in London and the disaster that befell a Charleston, South Carolina group in 1735, when an extensive fire wiped the venture out. Philadelphia's good fire record and the advantage of trained fire brigades combined to minimize the risk, particularly when policies would be sold only to those least likely to have fires. Coopers and bakers, working with forges and ovens, would be among those excluded if they operated their business out of their homes. Those otherwise eligible would be required to have trap doors leading to the roof, with iron-handled access ladders. The majority of fires were caused by faulty chimneys, and roofs were therefore highly vulnerable. Policyholders would have to agree to use only company-approved chimney-sweeps.

Still the Union Company, in and of itself, was not large enough to warrant the establishment of a fire insurance company. It would require the cooperation of the eight brigades throughout the city, and eventually the others that were forming in various sections. His own unit, however, provided a point of beginning. By 1750 all but one of its members had signed articles of agreement "to make up the Damage that may Arise by Fire among this Company." A year later he asked each company to designate two members to meet at the "Sign of the Royal Standard" in Market Street "to Consider such Matters as they may think will Tend Most to the Utility of The Inhabitants in General." With his exquisite, unhurried sense of timing Franklin thus laid the groundwork for his major move. On February 18, 1752 his *Gazette* announced that articles of insurance would be available at the courthouse every Saturday afternoon until April 13, where they could be signed by those wishing to subscribe. Governor James Hamilton was the first, and Franklin the second. The articles were carefully copied from those of the Amicable Contributionship in London, and its "hand-in-hand" emblem was also adopted, under the title "Philadelphia Contributionship for the Insurance of House from Loss by Fire" with the "Contributors . . . equal Sharers in the Losses as well as the Gains." Policies would be written for seven-year terms and limited to an area within ten miles of Philadelphia in Pennsylvania. Franklin was elected to chair the board of twelve directors. Philip Syng, a silversmith and one of the directors, designed the seal, "four Hands united," with this motto: "Philadelphia Contributionship."

Policyholders were requested to affix the company's "firemark" to their houses so the firefighters would be careful not to aggravate the damage by indiscriminate wielding of axes. Edward Shippen neglected to do this, and the Board surveying the aftermath of a blaze in his home found "much of the damage was done thro' Indiscretion." In 1758 a man was hired to attach the "marks" to insured properties.

Peter Bard on Water Street filed the first claim in December 1753, and the Board, conscious of the public relations value in quick settlements, met and ordered "the water and dirt to be cleared from the floor & to glaze all sashes that are not broke. . . ." In an account of the fire, Franklin's *Gazette* announced "the House being insur'd, the Damage will be immediately repaired, without Cost to the Owner."

With a virtual monopoly, the Contributionship became increasingly selective in its risks. By 1769 it banned issuance of policies on all frame structures, and in 1774 announced that it planned to refuse coverage to residences whose shade trees were too close, since these added to the hazard and impeded fire-fighters. Before the matter was resolved the Revolution took the center-stage, and the Company faced new problems. Since some policyholders temporarily abandoned their homes in 1776, the Company had to see that their chimneys were swept as American, and later British soldiers billeted in them, were not likely to concern themselves with such details. The situation was further complicated by the shortage of chimney-sweeps and, during the British occupation, by the wrong kind of currency with which to pay them. When the war moved south in 1781 the tree question recurred. While the policyholders intensely debated the quarrelsome problem, legislation was slipped through which required all trees along city streets, alleys or lanes to be cut down to eliminate danger of fire. An irate citizenry quickly caused this measure to be repealed. The Contributionship, nonetheless, was adamant in its position so far as its members were concerned, and rejected a proposal that those who wanted to keep their trees and their policies could do so by paying an extra-risk premium. The tree-lovers, among whom was Dr. Benjamin Rush, formed their own group, the Mutual Assurance Company, in 1784, with which a homeowner willing to pay a little more and keep his trees trimmed so they grew no higher than the eaves, could get a policy. Symbolically, the Mutual's emblem was "The Green Tree."

Ten years later two more companies entered the field. The Insurance Company of North America had begun operations in 1792 as Philadelphia's answer to Lloyds of London, concentrating on marine risks. Seeing ships put out to sea with vessel and cargo covered by Englishmen disturbed a number of Philadelphians, who felt they were watching money flow into foreign pockets. John Copson, back in 1721, had tried to make such protection a local matter, and opened "An Office of Publick Insurance on Vessels and Merchandizes . . . at his house in the High Street." But Copson, like the London "gentlemen at the Coffee House" had to find "Persons of undoubted Worth and Reputation" to pledge reimbursement to the owners in case of loss, in return for a fee based on a number of factors—the condition of the ship, its destination, the experience of its master and so forth. It was a betting game, with the owner betting on the integrity of the underwriter, and the latter on wind, weather, ship-handling, pirates, privateers and hostilities. William Penn was skeptical of its worth. "I am tender as to insurance and did nothing in it for the *Hopewell*," he wrote in 1702, and then in 1705 acidly commented, "J. Askew insured for £100, but the insurer broke and the twenty guineas (premium) lost. Ensurers fail much."

In 1731 Francis Rawle had a chapter on marine insurance in a book Franklin published for him, *Ways and Means For the Inhabitants of Delaware to Become Rich*. It sufficiently inspired a number of individuals who clustered around the London Coffee House in Philadelphia to subscribe for the coverage of voyages in the manner and tradition of Lloyds. Although by 1760 they had banded together as underwriters, the personal equation made the task of insuring onerous, finding out from each individual how much of the risk he wanted to assume. Lloyds had long since overcome this obstacle, and in a single stroke of the quill-pen could handle any venture.

The North American group approached the matter somewhat differently. They raised $600,000 through subscriptions, hired a weather-beaten old sea captain to inspect ships seeking insurance, and when all the necessary data was before the board of directors, the risk was weighed and if accepted, the premium and term were fixed. If their investors got a smaller return in the form of dividends, they correspondingly had little to fear from any single catastrophe. The stockholders had met in an auspicious place to choose their board. On December 10, 1792 they gathered in the Declaration chamber at the State House— and the next day the new directors met at the City Tavern. By December 12 they leased a brick building at 223 South Front Street at an annual rental of £100.

But 1793 was hardly the best year to begin. News reached the city

COLBY COMMUNITY COLLEGE LIBRARY

26137

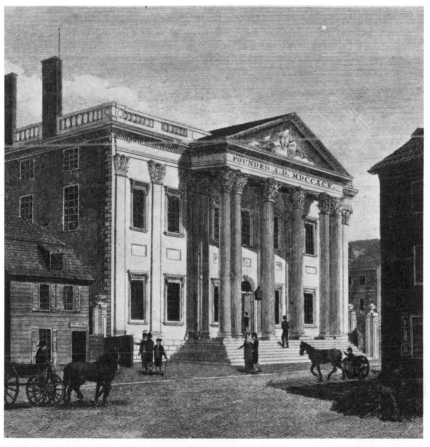

BANK OF THE UNITED STATES

On Saturday, Dec. 23, 1797, the *Gazette of the United States* exulted: "Wednesday morning the workmen of the new Bank of the United States struck their scaffolding and unfolded the novel and enchanting scene of a truly Grecian Edifice, composed of American white marble . . . " Birch pictures it as it looked two years later, and it still stands at 120 South Third Street a durable tribute to Alexander Hamilton, the workmen and the architect, Samuel Blodget, Jr. Blodget apparently felt the entire structure should have been marble, but mounting costs must have negated that idea, and in 1806 he was still concerned that "the brick sides are an injurious deviation." Although the Bank was chartered in 1791, it was nearly seven years before it could occupy these premises. In the interim Carpenters' Hall served as its headquarters. Claudius LeGrand stone cutter, prepared the marble work in his yard at 10th and High Streets, and 1500 sheets of copper, 48" x 24", each weighing 8 pounds, were ordered from England for the roof. When Congress refused to renew the 20-year charter in 1811, Stephen Girard bought the building for his private banking operations. In 1816 President James Madison, who had fought Hamilton's plan to establish the Bank, as an American "Bank of England", realized the worth of the idea. A charter was granted to the Second Bank of the United States, and the directors sought to buy back this structure from Girard. His refusal led to the handsome Graecian temple-type around the corner on Chestnut Street. Girard and his successors continued banking operations here until 1926, when the Girard National Bank vacated it. After remaining unused for three years it was leased to the American Legion until June 1944. In August 1945 it became the principal office of the Board of Directors of the City Trust, and thereafter was used as a temporary Information Center for visitors to Independence Hall area. It is the oldest bank building in the nation.

that a new French Republic had been set up, and Louis XVI overthrown. Washington at the Presidential mansion on High Street did not share the enthusiasm of many Philadelphians for reasons that were to become abundantly clear. The Revolutionary government in Paris was demanding American assistance under the mutual aid pact of 1778—ships to safeguard their possessions in the West Indies and money and supplies to fight off a threatened invasion by England. The impact of events on ocean traffic posed an immediate dilemma for the North American Insurance association. Washington proclaimed neutrality, but it gave little comfort to American shipowners who feared the United States lacked sufficient naval strength to enforce it. Since the carriage of goods to the port of either belligerent made a vessel subject to seizure by the other, the new company quickly wrote exclusion clauses disclaiming liability for losses "occasioned by War." Just as it was bracing itself for a decline in policies because of the international crisis, yellow fever brought all commerce into the port of Philadelphia to a standstill. In 1794 the directors decided to expand their operations to the fire insurance field, as a hedge against the vagaries of the maritime business. Then it encountered the frenetic force of Pennsylvania politics.

Shortly after it organized the group had applied to the state legislature for a corporate charter. It cited all the benefits that would accrue to the people of the Commonwealth from a financially stable organization. Most immediately Philadelphians would profit from the stimulus it would give to shipping and to local merchants. The application was referred to a committee, and kept there because the private underwriters attacked it in the press and in the Assembly, stressing the theme that such a giant would wield too much influence in governmental circles. One irate correspondent sent off a letter to a newspaper, citing an example of how two incorporated insurance companies in England had been involved in the widespread corruption of British officials and hoped "the legislature of this state will not establish a precedent of so dangerous a nature . . . which may eventually destroy the constitution of the country." Others earnestly defended the application. The yellow fever epidemic silenced critics and champions alike, and the possibility of war with either France or Great Britain preoccupied those not sufficiently disturbed by the other problems.

North America weathered the crises, and when the prominent financier Thomas Willing made application to incorporate The Insurance Company of the State of Pennsylvania, much of the steam was drained from the arguments advanced against the earlier applicants. Governor Thomas Mifflin signed the charter for the Insurance Company of North America on April 14, 1794 and for its rival on April 18.

"Keep Thy Shop . . ."

Both the Hand-in-Hand and Green Tree firemarks had been cast in lead by John Stow, of Pass and Stow, the Philadelphia firm which in 1753 was called upon to recast the Liberty Bell which cracked on testing after its arrival from London. North America chose as its design a six-pointed wavy star, done in lead and mounted on wood. It commissioned a plumber, Robert Haydock, 38 South Second Street, to make the devices. It issued its first fire policy on December 10, 1794 to William Beynroth "on German Dry Goods" in "House No. 211 High Street for three years," for which he paid a $72 premium for $8,000 coverage, and received an $8 discount for paying in full. However his "Badge (the star) & Policy" cost $2. In 1796 the company decided on a more sophisticated emblem, an eagle on a rock, and boldly offered fire insurance anywhere in the United States if "premiums adequate to the risk . . . be paid."

Firemarks served purposes other than reminding firemen to be careful. In the 18th century a favorite tactic of mobs was to threaten to "pull down" houses of their opponents. The fragile shields might serve to cool the passions of volunteer firemen involved in such protest marches, but they definitely reminded the ringleaders that if the place was put to the torch, the owner would suffer no economic loss. On the other hand, John Dickinson found this theory was circumscribed with provisos. When the British burned "Fair Hill," his country seat, in 1777, he filed a claim with the Philadelphia Contributionship. This was rejected on the peculiar ground that the mansion was destroyed in full view of a crowd which did nothing to interfere with the vandalism. Dickinson, one of the leading colonial lawyers and author of the "Letters from a Farmer in Pennsylvania," which figured prominently in the early stages of the arguments with Britain over the rights of the colonies, was unable to convince the company he should be compensated.

The heavy concentration of population and houses within less than the square mile between Delaware and Seventh, Vine to Lombard, in 1777—35,000 in some 7,000 buildings—gives a graphic picture of the potential fire problem Philadelphia faced. Since 1690 brick had been the dominant material for exterior construction, although frame structures—some dating from Penn's time—were still to be seen. Peter Cooper's colorful eight-foot canvas of the city in 1720, with a multiplicity of spires and some five-story structures, was more imaginative than real in some respects, for the city's first four-story edifice, still standing in time-disguised form at the northwest corner of Third and Market, only dates from 1795. Architecture as a formal profession was in its formative stages, and its antecedents are to be found in the diligent work of the master carpenters, who founded their association in 1724 "for the purpose of obtaining instruction in the science of architecture. . . ." How well these almost obscure carpenters succeeded is evident in the clean-lined State House (Independence Hall), Christ Church (where the first successful American reproduction of English Palladian ordinance is to be seen), and the magnificent "country seats" such as Mount Pleasant and Woodford, along with others in the so-called "Colonial Chain" in Fairmount Park, as well as the superb home of James Logan, "Stenton," "Wyck" and others in Germantown and through Bucks, Montgomery and Chester Counties. Unlike lovely Williamsburg which is largely reconstructed, Philadelphia's unique charm lies in its scores of original buildings which echoed to the sights and sounds of history. It is believed that hundreds, many masked with later "improvements" and alterations, still stand.

The most pretentious place of the era was built by William Bingham about 1788, on the west side of Third Street above Spruce and occupied the block back to Willing's Alley. Charles Bullfinch, the Boston architect, who saw it in 1789 said it equalled those

> in the most luxurious part of Europe. Elegance of construction, white marble staircase, valuable paintings, the richest furniture and the utmost magnificence of decoration makes it a palace in my opinion far too rich for any man in this country.

Bingham, who made a vast fortune while in the West Indies during the Revolution, returned to the city at war's end with the requisite money and taste to accomplish his ambitions. Inspired by the Duke of Manchester's London house, his home was, as might be expected, far larger. Three stories high and "very wide" it stood forty feet back from Third Street and was approached through two ornamental gates by a semicircular drive. Off the marbled mosaic-floored center hall, whose marble staircase was wide enough to accommodate floral decorations on either side, were Bingham's public rooms where guests found to the right the study, the library and banqueting room, and to the left the ballroom, several parlors and a beautiful conservatory. On the second floor was a drawing room, dining room, card room and bedchambers. Anne Willing Bingham's bedroom was of "state" proportions and contained a seven-foot four-postered canopied and curtained bed. Paintings and statuary, collected during the couple's European visits, adorned the mansion which looked out onto three acres of gardens, replete with rare plants and, during the summer, tubbed orange, lemon and citron trees taken from the shelter of the large greenhouse.

Bingham imported Lombardy poplars to border the grounds, and these became the progenitors of many that were planted in and about the city.

To afford privacy he had a large wooden fence constructed around his place—a source of annoyance to curious Philadelphians who had to push for possession of a few knotholes to glimpse the grandeur of the setting.

In 1797 he acquired another mansion—the spacious Italian-styled home of former Governor John Penn, which once stood on the site of the now-demolished Horticultural Hall in Fairmount Park. "Landsdowne," as it was called, occupied some two hundred acres, and gave Bingham an alternate place in which to entertain. But the Binghams were not destined to enjoy the luxury of either establishment very long. On a sleigh-ride Anne Bingham contracted a cold that turned into "galloping consumption" and died in Bermuda, where she was taken in hope that the more favorable climate would help. She was 37 at the time of her death in 1801. Bingham shortly afterward went to Europe, and apparently died of a stroke in Bath, England in 1804, aged 52. A trust created under his will was not terminated until 1964, when there were 315 beneficiaries.

The city residence was sold at auction on November 22, 1805 to a group who planned to convert it into an exclusive club for Philadelphia businessmen. When there were not enough subscribers it was converted into a fashionable hotel. Fire gutted the mansion in 1847 and it was torn down. Three years later, Jacqueline Kennedy Onassis' great-great grandfather Bouvier, a cabinet-maker and mahogany dealer in Philadelphia, built a row of brownstone homes on the lot, some still standing. Lansdowne passed into the hands of Maria Bingham Baring, Anne's beautiful daughter, then in the second of her three unsuccessful marriages. Napoleon's brother, Joseph Bonaparte, after a brief turn as king of Naples and Spain, occupied it for several years after the fall of the French dictator.

Bonaparte, known in the city as Count de Survilliers, also had a home at the southeast corner of Twelfth and Markets. His daughter, Princess Zenaide Charlotte Julie married her cousin, Charles Bonaparte, and the couple came to live in Philadelphia in 1824. Both were scientific-minded, the husband gaining some measure of fame for his four-volume work on *American Ornithology* and the wife for her skill in another area, painting. Lansdowne was set on fire July 4, 1854 by some youngsters playing with fireworks, and suffered some damage. In 1866 a philanthropic group of citizens purchased it and presented it to the city in the belief that the comparatively small amount needed to restore it would render it an attractive addition to Fairmount Park. The Park Commissioners razed it, instead, and in the Centennial year, 1876, Horticultural Hall, designed by the greenhouse expert, Herman J. Schwartzman, rose in its place. An impressive iron and glass structure, reflecting the Moorish-Arabic mood that was then fashionable in Philadelphia, it was admired as the American counterpart of the Crystal Palace in England and the Alhambra in Granada. It was allowed to decay during the depression years of the 20th century and finally was torn down.

From the beginning Philadelphians were keenly interested in horticulture. Penn and his friends were highly enthusiastic about the productivity of the soil, and while their primary concern was with crops, flowers were not overlooked. Up at Pennsbury, the founder had formal gardens, typical of the landed English gentry, and his Scot gardener was regarded as one of the best so long as his attention was not distracted by the bottle.

Johann Kelpius, the mystic monk of the Wissahickon in 1694 was probably the earliest botanist in America, including in his quest for the "elixir of life" cultivation of medicinal herbs. Dr. Christopher Witt, a former member of the cult, and erstwhile artist and physician "removed his flower beds close to" the fence between his Germantown home and that of Francis Pastorius in 1711, and five years later Pastorius responded by throwing a poem on Witt's "Fig Tree" over the same fence. James Logan, who came to Philadelphia in 1699 as Penn's secretary and was destined for greatness in Pennsylvania history, planted shrubs and trees around his Germantown home, Stenton, that offered in after-years pleasure and solitude to Secretary of State Thomas Jefferson when he visited the place. Jefferson's deep and definitive interest in obtaining exotic examples of flora and fauna for Monticello, absorbed some of his leisure time while he was in Philadelphia, and Secretary of the Treasury Alexander Hamilton was also quite knowledgeable on the subject.

The most famous botanist in the thirteen colonies was John Bartram, whose hand-hewn stone house in West Philadelphia is something of a shrine for all horticulturists. Testimonials to the beauty of his gardens abound in the writings of many distinguished visitors from home and abroad. A Quaker with limited education, he tells how, at age 29, he was inspired to make the subject his lifework:

> One day I was busy holding my plow (for thee seest that I am but a simple plowman, and being weary I ran under the shade of a tree to repose myself. I cast my eyes on a daisy. I plucked it mechanically and viewed it with more curiosity than common country farmers are wont to do. . . ."

Thus it began. He made the three-mile trek into Philadelphia to a bookshop and purchased some books on botany, and hired a schoolmaster to give him a three-month course in Latin. A year later, in 1729, he sufficiently impressed James Logan with his dedication that Logan presented him with Parkinson's *Paridisi in Sole Paradistus Terrestris,* whose title alone would have been enough to discourage an ordi-

"Keep Thy Shop . . ."

MOUNT PLEASANT

Peggy Shippen persuaded Benedict Arnold to buy this house for her wedding gift in 1779, but since the Spanish minister, Don Juan de Mirailles had a lease until the fall of 1780, Arnold's treason denied them residence. Visiting Captain John Macpherson who started building it in 1761, John Adams in 1775 pronounced it "the most elegant seat in Pennsylvania." A more recent authority says it "remains the finest colonial house north of Mason and Dixon's line." Macpherson, said Adams, "has been nine times wounded in battle . . . made a fortune by privateering; an arm twice shot off, shot through the leg, &c." Here he raised "two pretty daughters" and two sons and lost their mother in 1770. Adams met the second spouse, a "clever Scotch wife" whom Macpherson married in 1772 on a trip to Scotland. John, Jr., whose portrait attributed to Trumball, hangs in the dining room, was killed in December 1775 in the siege of Quebec, an expedition in which Arnold played a heroic role. William, the other son, could not get rid of the British commission his father purchased for him when he was 14, and was wounded in the Battle of Monmouth as an English officer before he finally joined up with the Americans in 1779. Baron von Steuben rented the house in 1780 but no one knows whether he lived here, and in 1781 it was sold to Colonel Richard Hampton; in 1783 to Blair McClenachan and in 1784 to Edward Shippen, Peggy's father. In 1792 Shippen sold it to Jonathan Williams, a great-nephew of Benjamin Franklin, and poetically enough, first superintendent at West Point where Arnold turned traitor. In 1868 the house became an integral part of Fairmount Park. Macpherson remains, however, little known, the most colorful of the inhabitants—a testy character who dabbled in astronomy, compiled a cryptic city directory and boasted he invented a vermin-free bed.

nary person with such a perfunctory background in Latin. Bartram's determination was not to be denied by this, any more than a lifelong fear of Indians and rattlesnakes kept him from long journeys into woodlands far distant from home. Availing himself of the delightful practice of the "age of enlightenment" to correspond with total strangers known to have similar interests, Bartram won both applause and patronage from Englishmen. When he besought the help of Franklin in getting funds to permit him to make his botany a full-time vocation, he was overwhelmed with the enthusiastic response. In the *Pennsylvania Gazette,* March 10, 1742, Franklin wrote:

> ... as John Bartram has had a Propensity to Botanicks from his Infancy
> ... and is an accurate Observer ... acquainted with Vegetables and
> Fossils, and Books treating of them ... and had by many Ships sent over
> to some of the Members of the Royal Society in London ... Plants,
> Seeds and Specimens as were new and unknown to them ... we the
> Subscribers to induce and enable him wholly to spend his time ... in
> these Employments, have proposed an annual Contribution for his En-
> couragement. . . . . ."

Bartram's extraordinary progress had not only made his advice and
help sought by eminent Europeans, but enriched his cultural abilities as
well. The word pictures he painted of "the vernal and autumnal
flowers—these so nobly bold—those so delicately languid!" illustrate
the distance he traveled in his swift rise from a poorly educated farmer
to a man of letters.

That Bartram helped inspire Franklin's American Philosophical Society in 1743 is shown in the priority given botanical research and related
minerological matters in the organization's announced purposes:

> all new-discovered plants, herbs, trees, roots, their virtues, uses, etc.;
> methods of propagating them, and marking such as are useful, but partic-
> ular to some plantations, more general; improvements of vegetable
> juices, as ciders, wines, etc.; new methods of curing or preventing
> diseases; all new-discovered fossils in different countries, as mines, min-
> erals and quarries; new and useful improvements in any branch of math-
> ematics; new discoveries in chemistry; such as improvement in distilla-
> tion, brewing, and assying of ores, new mechanical inventions for saving
> labour, as mills and carriages, and for raising and conveying of water,
> draining of meadows, etc.; all new arts in trades and manufactures ...
> and all philosophical experiments that let light into the nature of things,
> tend to increase the power of man over matter and multiply the con-
> veniences or pleasures of life.

Impressive as Philadelphia's scientific community was, it contributed nothing to the fundamental problem of identifying the location of
its citizens.

The first city directories were published in 1785. Francis White, a
broker on Chestnut near Third undertook the initial project. Since
houses were not numbered, residents were listed "between" streets,
as "Alibone, Wm., captain, Front, Callowhill and Vine streets." One
living on a corner could be located with slightly more precision, as
"Fulton, Robt., miniature painter, corner Second and Walnut
streets." Captain John Macpherson, who sold Mount Pleasant to
Benedict Arnold, issued a directory later in the year but restricted oc-
cupational listings to subscribers, and those who gave flippant answers

such as "none of your business" or refused to disclose their names were recorded precisely in that way.

Part of the difficulty was resolved in the fact that, until the yellow fever epidemic of 1793 at least, virtually all merchants—as has been noted—lived and worked at the same address. When they began to build homes as far west as Seventh Street, there was much speculation whether they would not find the "walks to and from their counting-houses and businesses" fatiguing. This was due more to the condition of the sidewalks than the distances involved, although many Philadelphians of the era were not overly enthusiastic about walking. Coaches, however, were still a symbol of status as late as 1772, when only eighty-four of the 20,000 citizens owned carriages. Quakers who could well afford them shied off from this "conspicuous consumption" for a time, as an unnecessary mark of vanity. The Anglicans, untroubled by such thoughts, outnumbered other denominations by far in pride and possession. Du Simitiere who collected all sorts of odd items and data, felt impelled in 1772 to draw up a list of owners, and classified carriages by three types. The most expensive was the "coach," which only ten of the wealthier owned. The "post-chaise" or "chariot," differentiated only by the latter's coach box for the driver, were closed three-seaters. Since forty-five chose this type of vehicle, it was the most popular and seemed to satisfy the various creeds as well as cost factors. Twenty-nine, mostly Quakers, selected what Du Simitiere described as "coach-wagons," although a less grandiose term would be "buggies." Franklin disdained any of these trappings while in Philadelphia, but enjoyed being carried in a sedan chair to the meetings of the Constitutional Convention in the State House, in the summer of 1787. Four husky prisoners from Walnut Street Prison were enlisted to convey the aged Doctor.

Ownership was not all vanity. Quite a few, like David Franks, who had a store near Christ Church, a town house near City Tavern and the fine "country seat" at Woodford, some four miles out of the city, needed such transportation. But merchants like Abel James, a leading businessman of the city, had a "coach-wagon" although he lived on Water Street by Elfreth's Alley, and had stores on the nearby wharf.

It was not until about 1795 that stores began to appear west of Fourth on Market Street. The merchandise mart held fast to its traditional boundaries between Front and Second, and from Arch to Chestnut for the best part of the 18th century. Shutters often gave a clue as to whether a house was strictly residential or partly a shop, if perchance no sign was exhibited. Drop-leaf shutters could be used for dual purposes—the lower half when extended provided open-air display, while the upper-half cut the glare from the sun. Neither type of shutter, drop-leaf or folding—or the canvas awnings, dissuaded the pigeons who were so numerous in the city that it became a popular sport to sit on the roof and pelt them in flight with sticks, stones, or the riskier method of shooting.

Race Street, from Second to Third was the dry-goods section, and the several retail stores there were kept by women for the most part. Millinery stores and ladies' shoe stores dotted Second Street, all the way from Dock to Spruce, but eventually all shoe stores moved to Market Street. Henry Manly was the first to operate a shoe store in Philadelphia, and before that itinerant salesmen fitted customers. John Wallace, just before the Revolution, opened a shoe shop exclusively for women, featuring worsted, satin and brocade types, most or all of them imported. Before 1800 it was rare to find any stores in Third Street and none at all in Fourth or Fifth. When expansion extended that far, other merchants doubted whether they would succeed. When President Washington and Robert Morris lived in the houses on Market Street, just east of Sixth, only Sheaff's wine shop was in the neighborhood. The block was so quiet that not even the "western wagons" intruded, regarding Fifth Street as their outer limit.

Auctions attracted large crowds. The public vendues around the year 1740 and later were held under the northwest corner of the court house on Second Street. When the office of public auctioneer was vacated in 1742 Reese Meredith outbid John Clifton, £110 to £100 to secure the post from the city corporation. During the 1760's a spate of private auctions held on the immediate outskirts of Philadelphia in Southwark and Northern Liberties cut so sharply into the city shopkeepers' trade they demanded the State impose a 5% levy. At the same time large Philadelphia importers were angered when their British suppliers undercut them by acting as double agents—using as many as one hundred fifty salesmen, or "correspondents," to sell goods directly to small shopowners or auctioneers. After the Revolution the legislature cut down on the latter, permitting only three within two miles of the State House. Those not able to get licensed moved their activities to the west bank of the Schuylkill, safely out of range of the State duties. Jonas Phillips used the "large brick house" over the Middle Ferry, and John Chaloner held his sales in a stone stable at the Upper Ferry. These two were the "pioneers" in the area, but were quickly followed by so many other auctioneers that by 1783 all sorts of inducements were offered to draw prospective customers, such as "free carriage rides," "free ferry fares" and the like. Sales were always in the afternoon, beginning at 1 p.m. sharp and the mornings were set aside for bringing in and setting up the goods.

Only grocery stores and drug stores remained opened at night. Merchandising, as an art, did not develop until about 1790 when James Stokes opened a "fancy retail hardware store" with bulk windows in the former Old Coffee House at the southwest corner of Market and Front.

Buck-handled "Barlow" penknives, scissors, gilt and plated buttons "curiously arranged" on circular cards fascinated youngsters and country people in town for the market. On Tuesday and Friday evenings they could be seen "lounging with their arms folded" in front of the lighted window, transfixed by the items. But when Mr. Whitesides from London opened a "fancy dry-goods store" with bulk windows in his residence at 134 Market Street, Philadelphians were not quite ready for some aspects of his "true Bond Street style." They admired the "fine mull-mull and jaconet muslines chinses and linens suspended in whole pieces . . . and entwined together in puffs and festoons," but were somewhat embarrassed by the "powdered, bowing and smiling" clerk.

Much of the beautiful furniture produced in the city between 1750 and 1790 was influenced by Thomas Chippendale, the London craftsman whose book, *The Gentleman and Cabinet-Makers Director* was published in England in 1754. Chippendale enthusiastically revived the motifs of the Louis XIV period, but many of his designs were traditional and already in use by the more knowledgeable artisans. Still his authority was such that both in England and America most woodworkers followed his lines without deviation. Philadelphians, on the other hand, showed a marked degree of independence. With carvers equal, if not superior to, any in the British Empire, they exhibited bold creativity. If their adaptation of suitable architectural forms to furniture was not wholly unique, they translated them with such consummate confidence that Philadelphia Chippendale achieved a singular quality. In selecting themes for elaborate carvings they unhesitatingly discarded more ponderous classical subjects to delicately portray Aesop's Fables like "The Fox and the Grapes." They put pediments on their highboys and fluted slender columns.

The wealth of Philadelphia was sufficient to encourage this kind of ingenuity, but cabinetmakers did not ignore the much wider market that either could not afford or, for matters of creed or taste, wanted less ornate pieces. Highboys, chests-on-chests and other handiwork of well-known craftsman—in whatever price range—were matters of quiet pride to their owners, and occupied places of honor in many Philadelphia parlors. It was not unusual for the family to ruffle through drawers for apparel in the presence of company.

Life and Times in Colonial Philadelphia

To politically-sensitive Philadelphians one aspect of Chippendale's designs had particular appeal. His depiction of three carved busts atop "a desk and bookcase" reintroduced a 16th century Italian technique which had found favor with the influential French designer, Jean Lepautre, who about 1665 surmounted a roccoco cabinet with a Roman military head. Benjamin Randolph, "Cabinet Maker at the Golden Eagle in Chestnut Street", incorporated Chippendale's bearded man in his ornate business card. Soon on Philadelphia bookcases and desks appeared busts of John Locke, the English political philosopher who believed individuals had rights to "life, liberty and property" and occasionally some of John Milton, whose *Aerogapatica* enunciated belief in freedom of thought. More significant was the popularity of two contemporaries, Franklin and Washington, who must have observed with some satisfaction their mahogany busts in the furnishings of the more affluent Philadelphia homes.

At least one of the magnificent chairs made in the city touched the hem of history. Used by the Speaker of the Pennsylvania General Assembly at its sessions in the State House, it was occupied by John Hancock during the Continental Congress which adopted the Declaration of Independence, and by Washington when he presided eleven years later at the Constitutional Convention. Franklin in the closing moments of that Convention said throughout the debates he had looked at the sunburst on the back of the chair, and wondered whether it was a rising or setting sun. Now happily, he concluded, it was the sun ascendant. Few other than specialists in the field know that Thomas Folwell constructed that chair, but the general anonymity in which he has been enveloped is characteristic of almost the entire remarkable group of Philadelphia cabinet-makers.

The grandeur of Philadelphia Chippendale was not typical of the furniture in middle income homes, where red walnut served as a substitute for mahogany and rush-bottom chairs with maple posts and slats were frequently seen. The "plain people" used settees made of unpainted white pine, which were whitened by "unsparing scrubbing." "Settles," were settees that had a concealed bed. Before the Revolution carpets were something of a rarity, and in 1760 a Scotch carpet twelve feet square was a novelty to people accustomed to having white floors sprinkled with clean white sand. The sand provided artistically inclined housewives with the opportunity of making it "into a variety of fanciful figures and twirls with the sweeping brush." Wits invited to a home affecting the use of carpets thought it quite humorous to tip-toe around them or to ask their hostess whether it was safe to walk on them. Large china punch bowls were indispensable, but seemed to be accident-prone if estimates are correct that over half of them had been mended with cement, or where the break was more complicated, threaded with wires. It was rare to see china on dinner tables, and glass tumblers were equally rare. Plate, silver or pewter, depending on the home, was predominant. Delftware imported from England, pewter platters and porringers, "made to shine along 'a dresser' " were commonplace, but china tea pots and coffee pots "with silver nozles" were "a mark of superior finery." Sideboards made their appearance after the Revolution, and

BINGHAM MANSION

William Bingham may have been a dull, pompous fellow to some of his contemporaries, but he had a talent for making and keeping a fortune—part of which he translated into magnificent homes. Standing on the corner of Spruce Street, William Birch sketched the Third Street "prospect" of the showplace mansion, but its splendor pales against the poignancy of the young woman and child sitting on a doorstep, whom the lad in the group across the street finds more fascinating than the architectural splendor of Bingham's brick wall. Even the guard posts are decorative, contrasting sharply to the more functional kind opposite. The pedestrians appear to be in their Sunday best. Presumably they are not Binghams, judging—imperfectly—by the decorous and modest dress of the ladies. In much colder weather the dashing young Harrison Gray Otis told his lovely wife back in Boston he spotted Maria Bingham walking with her beautiful 35-year old mother, Anne. Maria was waiting for the first of several divorces, and Otis observed her "in a dress . . . you will hardly believe it possible for a lady to wear at least at this season. A muslin robe and her chemise, and no other article of cloathing upon her body. I have been regaled with the sight of her whole legs for five minutes together, and do not know 'to what height' the fashion will be carried." He was not complaining, but Abigail Adams did—snorting that the Bingham women wore such low-cut dresses they looked like "nursing mothers." Within five years William and Anne Bingham were dead, and this house was the scene of a "public vendue" of his personal property in November 1805. The unimaginative auctioneer's advertisement identifies the items cryptically, and lists only such familiar faces as Voltaire, Rosseau, Franklin and "a full length portrait of Mrs. Siddons in the Grecian Daughter," among the objects d' art.

china and plate were displayed in "corner closets with glass doors." Windsor chairs were invariably painted green, "like garden furniture in France," de Saint-Mery observed on a visit—which is not strange since they were widely used in England, where they originated, for outdoor purposes.

In October 1768 Philadelphians were advised by Plunket Fleeson that he had for sale "American Paper Hangings, Manufactured in Philadelphia, of all kinds and colors, not inferior to those generally imported; and as low in price." Fleeson may have been more successful with his offerings of "paper mache," for while English and some Chinese papers were used sporadically, it was not until 1790 that wall-papering became more widespread.

The city had several good silversmiths. Philip Syng, Jr., did the inkstand which graces the desk in the Declaration chamber of Independence Hall. At Wintherthur extensive experiments are being undertaken to compare the silver content used by British and American silversmiths during the 18th century, and early findings have disclosed that the English craftsmen met the full 92.5% sterling requirement, while a sampling of the American specimens indicate a variation of as much as 16% and a tendency to be generous with copper. Whether Philadelphians were suspicious of some of their own artisans in this, or whether they preferred the English workmanship, Joseph and Nathaniel Richardson, sons of a Quaker silversmith, formed a partnership in 1777 to import from London. Their first order, placed on December 17, 1777 to John Masterson in London, was poorly timed. The British were in Philadelphia, the Americans at Valley Forge and the presence of the war made futures too indefinite for the purchase of luxury items. Three months later the brothers interrupted their correspondence with Masterson, citing the conflict as the reason. In 1783 they renewed relations, but called them off in 1785 because "Our late Assembly have laid a duty of two shillings currency per Oz upon all Wrought Silver Plate . . . imported into this state . . . ". Six years later the partnership was dissolved. Although some one hundred and forty silversmiths worked in Philadelphia between 1680 and 1800, only sixteen were listed in the census of 1790.

Fire engines, art, carpenters and craftsmen, Philadelphia's artisans and "mechanics," all converged on the snow-blanketed evening of January 22, 1784 on Market Street between Sixth and Seventh. Congress had formally ratified the Treaty of Peace with Great Britain a week earlier, and in anticipation of the great event the State of Pennsylvania had commissioned "the ingenious Captain Peale" to construct a triumphal arch "exactly in the stile of . . . the Romans," but with "illuminated Paintings with suitable inscriptions." Throughout December

Philadelphians watched the forty-foot high wooden structure, with its triple arches stretching fifty-six and a half feet across Market Street, being hammered into place, while Peale worked feverishly in a room in the State House to complete the paintings. Only one facade was to be so decorated, the back of the superstructure covered with plain canvas. Within, an array of ladders and landings reached the shelves where most of the 1500 lamps were to be placed. The central arch was twenty feet high, and the two flanking arches fifteen. Across the entabulature panels showing the lilies of France; the State's coat of arms; the closed doors of the Temple of Janus; the sun of France amid a galaxy of thirteen stars; and clasped hands holding olive branches—all with suitable inscriptions. The four ionic columns which supported the whole were garlanded with painted flowers native to America. Over the flanking arches were transparencies depicting the country leaning upon a soldier surrounded by military trophies, and Indians busily building churches in the wilderness. The central arch, reminiscent of ancient Rome, bore the initials S P Q P, (*Senatus Populusque Pennsylvanianum*) which supposedly translated into "The Senate and People of Pennsylvania." At the base of each of the four pedestals other illuminated scenes showed a library with emblems of the arts and sciences—a tree bearing thirteen fruitful branches—a laurel-crowned Washington as Cincinnatus returning to his plow—and militia at drill. Surmounting all of this, across the top balustrade, were statues of Justice, Prudence, Temperance and Fortitude, with a bust of Louis XVI between the first two, and a pyramid cenotaph honoring the war dead between the others. The place of honor where Romans fixed their victorious Caesars in chariots, was left vacant and purposely enshrouded in secrecy. This was to be Peale's supreme touch—a dominant figure of Peace, holding a flaming torch, gloriously lit up by lamps concealed in a fluff of clouds, slanted into place along a night-obscured taut rope from a nearby rooftop. Her arrival was to signal an artillery sergeant to set off the fireworks, all neatly hidden along with him, behind the statuary. But as Peace began her memorable trip, one of the rockets prematurely exploded and the canvas caught fire. In a trice the arch was a blazing inferno, the crowd plunged into panic, the sergeant burned to death and Peale, a rib broken by a plank, was seared and shaken as he tried to make his way home, rescued by a sleigh at Third and Market when he almost fainted. Scores were injured and robbed, and at dawn only the charred frame, in skeletal sobriety, remained. Gouverneur Morris, who had no time for the liberal politics of Peale, wrote to Alexander Hamilton on January 27, 1784:

> I would entertain you with a *splendid* account of the Illumination and fire Works which, if we may believe the Philadelphia news Papers, were

to have been the most splendid imaginable but I arrived too late. . . . The Exhibition would have been perfectly ridiculous, but for the Death of one spectator & the wounds of others. . . . I have been however to see the Place . . . and truly if the Projectors had intended to fire their City, it was an ingenious Invention. Only think of a large wooden Stage, raised in the middle of a street, to hang canvass on, with a number of lamps o' the inside, & no Precautions against the Flames. You will perhaps be curious, as I was, to know what put it into their Heads. The account I received is to this Effect. The Quakers, who have more than one reason for not illuminating their Houses, and some others who have on this occasion at least one reason for the same Thing, wished to save both their Glass and their Principles . . . & then out popp'd Captain Peale. This is a Politician by Birth, & a Painter by Trade. . . . He it seems is one of those who have supported the Revolution by the Powers of Eloquence, notably displayed at the Corners of Streets to such audiences as can usually be collected in such Places. . . . (He) was employed to prepare Decorations & Devices for the triumphal Arch, & to superintend the Expenditure of . . . six hundred Pounds, appropriated by Government to the splendid Exhibition. At the same Time all Illuminations were forbidden, & by a wise Foresight, Squibbs were also prohibited. This you see is the age of Coalitions, and so, blessed be the Peacemakers.

5

"DEATH'S PALE ARMY":

Medicine and Progress Didn't Always March Hand in Hand

* * * * *

Of Lawyers and Physicians I shall say nothing, because this Countrey is very Peuceable and Healthy; long may it so continue and never have occasion for the Tongue of the one nor the Pen of the other, both equally destructive to Men's Estates and Lives; besides forsooth, they, Hang-man like, have a License to Murder and make Mischief.

—Gabriel Thomas, Philadelphia, 1698

* * * * *

Life and Times in Colonial Philadelphia

During the American Revolution a soldier's chances of surviving battle were 1 in 98, but if he was hospitalized the odds sharply dropped to 1 in 45. Ignorance and indifference explained much of the dismal ratio, but it is also a commentary on the physicians, whom Washington thought generally were "scoundrels." Admittedly the profession suffered from the many who enlisted as "surgeons" or surgeon's mates" fraudulently so they could get better rations, better pay and better quarters. Forged credentials were not uncommon, but the Medical Department of the Continental Army needed no assistance from inexperienced fakes. It achieved disaster proportions with men whose qualifications were, by 18th century standards, impeccable. There were, to be sure, contributing factors, such as a woeful lack of supplies and a tense fight at the top level between Dr. Benjamin Rush and Dr. William Shippen, both of Philadelphia. But one of the basic difficulties was that even the best of doctors thought the human body contained twice as much blood as it did—and just as one sucked poison from a snakebite, so it was thought infections could be cured by venting the blood. Washington, stricken in 1799 by what modern medical men believe was a streptococcic throat, was so weakened by bleeding he had no strength to combat the infection.

The conceit of academic training posed perils in another direction. Introduced to the manifold mysteries of anatomy in Edinburgh and London, some colonial physicians like Rush too often ignored the obvious to search for the obscure. At Valley Forge he stood on the banks of Valley Creek pondering the causes of the "putrid" (typhoid) fever which was taking hundreds of lives, while watching soldiers upstream washing their dirty "Linnen" and those downstream drinking the water. Rush worked out an elaborate theory of a miasma—the favorite idea of the profession that poisonous vapors rising from decomposing animal or vegetable matter and marshy lands infected the air. Washington was much closer to the truth when he constantly warned the troops to drink only from approved springs. To give Rush and his contemporaries their due, however, it should be remembered that he had written an excellent handbook for the Army on sanitary precautions, and there were some positive advances in medicine emerging from the age.

Philadelphia furnished a favorable climate for such development. It was spared the superstitions that paralyzed New England in the 17th and early 18th centuries. There ministers and "demons" dominated, and physicians were apt to follow theology in diagnoses. Quaker practicality rejected such aberrations. The earlier Dutch and Swedes were also untroubled by the supernatural, although fascinated by the Finns and their belief in black magic and occult healing. The Delawares, like many tribes, had "medicine men" who not only did strange dances, but who were highly skilled in setting fractures, and competent to a degree in the use of herbs and plants, although admittedly they assumed the resemblance of a plant to an ailment was the Great Spirit's way of prescribing a cure, thus snakeroot for snakebite. Gabriel Thomas in his propaganda promoting Philadelphia was not the only one who thought there was little need for doctors. Across the Delaware in New Jersey, Charles Gordon wrote to his physician-brother in England,

> you may come as a planter, or a merchant, or as a doctor of medicine. I cannot advise you, as I can hear of no diseases here to cure, but some aguos and some cutted fingers and legs, but there are no want of empiricks for these already. I confess that you could do more than any yet in America, being versed in Chirugery and Pharmacie, for here are abundance of herbs, shrubs and trees, and no doubt medical ones for making drugs, but there is little or no Imployment this way.

Thomas Spry, who served the area from Upland to New Castle between 1670 and 1680 as a lawyer-surgeon may have demonstrated the need to practice two professions to make a living.

But the Philadelphia area, despite Thomas and Gordon, was not free from disease. Smallpox was "very mortal and very general" in the city in 1701. Often it was imported, and on Penn's maiden voyage on the *Welcome* in 1682 he miraculously escaped contamination while ministering to scores of stricken passengers, thirty of whom died. In 1726 a ship from Bristol was ordered to put in near Old Swede's Church, rather than docking within city limits, so that victims aboard could be led off through the woods to the "Blue-house tavern" out South Street, where, happily, all recovered. In 1730 "great mortality" followed an epidemic, and the next year Dr. John Kearsley and some of his medical students submitted to innoculation to set a public example. Kearsley later claimed credit for being "the first that us'd ... (it) ... in this Place," although not the first in colonial America, that honor belonging to Zabdiel Boylston, who braved clerical wrath in Boston to have himself, his son and two slaves, innoculated in 1721, and was almost lynched. Philadelphia, being more enlightened, watched with interest when doctors in 1736-37 did a test pattern of immunization. Of 130 persons (33 white adults, 64 whites under 12, 4 "mulattoes" and 29 "negroes young and old") only a child died when the disease struck during those years. Franklin lost his four-year old son, "Franky," but through his tears, dispelled "a current Report" that it was caused by "inoculation":

> I do hereby sincerely declare, that he was not inoculated, but receiv'd the Distemper in the common way of Infection. ... I intended to have my Child inoculated, as soon as he should have recovered sufficient Strength from a Flux with which he had been long afflicted.

Life and Times in Colonial Philadelphia

He had championed inoculation as a "safe and beneficial Practice" since 1730, and in 1759, while in London, was asked to write a preface to a book on the subject by Dr. William Heberden. In it Franklin said he had made a survey "Some years since" in Philadelphia "of the several Surgeons and Physicians who had practis'd Inoculation" and found "upwards of 800 (I forget the exact number) had been inoculated at different times, and that only four . . . had died." His statistical recollection was right, for he had asked for the data in 1751-52 when he was reading a French pamphlet dealing with the topic. Thomas Jefferson, then twenty-three and bearing a letter to Dr. John Morgan, came to Philadelphia for immunization in 1766, and "was placed in a cottage house, back from the city, near to the Schuylkill." Isolation was part of the elaborate procedure which, together with strict dietary precaution, made inoculation a traumatic experience for many understandably scared patients. Jefferson was so unruffled he barely mentioned it. To deliberately induce a mild case of a disease as a safeguard against it puzzled quite a few, but gradually it came to be accepted. From Valley Forge in 1778, Washington whose face bore the scars of his own bout, warned governors and recruiting officers to send no soldiers who either had not been immunized or previously stricken. His requests were blithely ignored, and scores had to be inoculated in the encampment under the least favorable conditions.

Franklin's insatiable mind naturally encompassed medicine. He published books, ranging from the scientific to the home remedy types like *Every Man his own Doctor,* and in 1752, assisted a Dr. Evans in using electricity on a young woman who had been suffering from convulsions for ten years. There were plenty of areas for him to probe. Philadelphians were annually bothered by malaria, as well as "hooping Cough" or "Chincough," measles and the usual run of childhood diseases, as well as the broken bones and the more complicated and less understood afflictions. He played a prominent role in the founding of the Pennsylvania Hospital for the "relief of the Sick and Miserable" and its cornerstone bears the inscription he wrote.

Built in a clearing between 8th and 9th, Spruce and Pine Streets, the hospital admitted its first patients in December 1756, transferring most from the late Judge John Kinsey's home on High Street. It was the fulfillment of the hopes of Dr. Thomas Bond, whose three trips to Europe had convinced him of the need for such an edifice. It also marked the culmination of five years intensive work by laymen like Franklin, who had acted as secretary of the board of managers and ultimately, in 1755, as president. In that capacity he instituted two traditions which still prevail in the Hospital—a fifty-cent fine for late or absent board members and the requirement that each provide his own chair. Franklin's chair, mingled anonymously with others, is still used. Franklin's friend, Dr. John Fothergill of London, sent medical books in 1762, and a set of crayon anatomical drawings by Jan Van Riemsdyk "half as big as the Life." John Adams on August 30, 1774 saw them in a visit to the hospital:

> Dr. Shippen . . . shewed Us . . . (the) exquisite Art. Here was a great Variety of Views of the human Body, whole, and in Parts. The Dr. entertained us with a very clear, concise and comprehensive Lecture upon all the Parts of the human Frame. The Entertainment charmed me. He first shewed us a Set of Paintings of Bodies entire and alive—then of others with the Skin taken off, then with the first Coat of Muscles taken off, then with the second, then with all—the bare bones. Then he shewed Us paintings of the Insides of a Man, seen before, all the Muscles of the Belly being taken off. The Heart, Lungs, Stomach, Gutts.

Still in their glass cases, the drawings, in natural colors, afforded medical students of the day their first intensive look at the human organs, since cadavers were rarely used, and then in secret. Public fear of grave-robbers made Shippen's lecture room on North Fourth Street, above High, a place of trepidation, accentuated by its approach down an alley that led to a long back-yard. The atmosphere was conducive to such songs as:

> The body-snatchers! they have come
> And made a snatch at me;
> It's very hard them kind of men
> Won't let a body be!
> Don't go to weep upon my grave
> And think that there I be;
> They haven't left an atom there
> Of my anatomy!

In 1774 Dr. Abraham Chovet who, with his family, fled to Philadelphia from an insurrection in Jamaica, advertised he would begin a series of "Anatomical and Physiological lectures" on December 7 at 6 p.m., "At the Anatomical Museum in Videl's Alley, Second Street." He said he would use "his curious collection of anatomical wax-works and other natural preparations," and "As this course cannot be attended with the disagreeable sight or smell of recently diseased and putrid carcasses, which often disgust even the students of Physic," he hoped his "undertaking will meet with suitable encouragement."

When young Drs. Morgan and Shippen began teaching medicine at the College of Philadelphia, Dr. Bond suggested clinical work could be done at the hospital. The college soon added to its faculty young Benjamin Rush, fresh from London and Edinburgh. Dedicated though they were, physicians like Rush were enchanted with lengthy Latin terms, which more often confused than clarified. Most medical theory at the time proceeded on the basis that, at the root of all disease, was a fever. All too often the treatments prescribed were no more effective than those devised by the large number of quacks in the city. The dread "yellow fever" calamity of 1793 underscored this.

Endemic in the Caribbean and along the South American and African coasts, the disease swept up the Eastern Seaboard at irregular intervals. It struck Boston, New Haven, New York, Norfolk and Charleston, but invariably Philadelphia was the hardest hit. Heavy rains on its many creeks and ponds added to the marshy land sites, and this, coupled with tropically hot summers, made it an ideal breeding ground for mosquitoes. As America's leading seaport, the city was constantly exposed to the possibility that a passenger or crewman who had contracted the illness would arrive undetected. A small quarantine station had been set up in the Delaware to inspect incoming vessels, chiefly on the lookout for smallpox. When inbound traffic was well spaced, diseased persons could be intercepted, depending on the diligence of the inspectors. When it was heavy one could slip through, and with yellow fever one was enough. The mosquitoes could convert the victim into an epidemic.

In 1699 the scourge struck in autumn. "Great was the fear that fell upon all flesh," Quaker Thomas Story recorded in his journal: "I saw no lofty air or countenances, nor heard any vain jesting; but every face gathered paleness, and many hearts were humbled. . . ." Isaac Norris, Sr., concurred: "This is quite the Barbadoes distemper . . . not a day nor night has passed for several weeks, but we have the account of the death or sickness of some friend or neighbour. It hath been sometimes very sickly, but I never before knew it so mortal as now; nine persons lay dead in one day at the same time; very few recover. All business and trade down. . . ." Five of his own family were among the 220 dead.

In 1717 it returned, and again in 1741 when it was described as the "Palatine distemper" and blamed on the German immigrants who had been cramped aboard ships bringing them to Philadelphia. From June to October 1741, 250 died, and Dr. Bond called it "yellow fever" and thought it was introduced by sick passengers from Dublin. 1743 saw a milder attack, but it was clear to physicians that Joel Neaves died of "a true, genuine yellow fever. . . . He also gave it to others about him, and they to others; yet but few of them died." In 1747 Noah Webster surmised it was the "bilious plague," preceded by influenza. Philadelphia had "the epidemic pleurisy" in February 1748 which took its toll, and in 1754 and 1755, another, attributed to the "Dutch distemper," ascribed to servants imported from Germany and Holland.

During the summer of 1793 there was an outbreak of influenza. July,

LIBRARY BUILDING

The Library building was just 10 years old when Birch made this engraving. Its design was taken from Swan's *Collection of Designs in Architecture*, two sets of which were among the books Franklin and his friends gathered for the Company since founding it in 1731. First located at the Pewter Platter Inn, the library was removed to various sites before it settled in this handsome structure. During the Revolution subscribers found it at Carpenter's Hall which made Franklin uneasy because of the "combustible material" stored in the cellar. While occupying Philadelphia in 1777-78 the British used the collection with more respect than they showed other city institutions. When it was decided to build across Fifth Street from the State House William Bingham commissioned a statue of Franklin to be sculpted in Italy. The aging statesman, when consulted about costume, asked that he be shown in "A Gown for his dress and a Roman head." He was dead when it was hoisted to the niche over the door in 1792, but vivid rumors circulated that every night the statue hopped down and headed for the nearest pub. So upset was his newspaper-publisher grandson, Benjamin Bache, ("Lightning Rod, Junior"), that he kept cold vigils to insure his idolized grandfather stayed put. The Library in the nineteenth century gradually got so large it once more was moved into two buildings around 1878, and currently can be found at 1314 Locust Street. Franklin's statue is there, safely indoors. The building here shown was torn down in 1887 to make way for the Drexel Building, which in turn was torn down in the 1950's to make way for a facsimile of the Library Company edifice for the expansion of the American Philosophical Society.

however, seemed normal enough, with some severe cases of scarlet fever, but cholera and malaria rates were average. With eighty physicians, the city felt it was competent to cope with any outbreaks. The tight clique of twenty-six Edinburgh-London alumni had formed themselves into the "College of Physicians"—and thirteen of the older members decreed themselves "fellows," with Dr. Rush regarding himself as the dean.

The 47-year-old Rush was living at 83 Walnut Street, the first house adjoining the northwest corner of Third. Daily he made his rounds with horse and buggy, but seldom was he called to Water Street. On August 5, however, Dr. Hodge, who lived there, sent him a message asking that he take a look at his fever-wracked little daughter. Rush, always meticulous in his note-taking, observed that her skin had turned yellow, and two days later, the child was dead. Shortly afterward, a clerk named McNair, living in the same neighborhood, was seized with pains symptomatic of "bilious fever," and despite being bled and purged, died within a week. Others were felled. Those who recovered had a yellowish cast to their skin. Although Rush had previous experience with yellow fever, he was inclined to regard these attacks as variations of the familiar "malignant and bilious" fever-types. Then he was called to the bedside of Mrs. Peter LeMaigre on Water Street for consultation with Drs. Foulke and Hodge. As the three puzzled over the dying woman they began to compare her condition with other recent cases they individually attended, and discovered that they each had been treating an unusual number involving the same condition. When they discussed the possible cause the rotting coffee on nearby Ball's Wharf was mentioned. Instantly Rush declared that was the villian, and in his professional opinion, it produced "a putrid miasmata." "As yet," he wrote on the 21st to his wife, who was summering in Princeton, "it has not spread thro' any parts of the city which are beyond the reach of the putrid exhalation which first produced it." But from the three to five burials that took place on a normal August day, the toll began to mount. On Saturday the 24th, seventeen were interred. The following afternoon Rush again wrote to his wife: "The fever has assumed an alarming appearance. It not only mocks in most instances the power of medicine, but it has spread thro' several parts of the city remote from the spot where it originated." Philadelphia's ears became constantly attuned to its church bells, and one of the city's four daily newspapers, the *Advertiser,* responded to the growing hysteria by inanely urging that everyone "contribute all in his power to prevent the spreading of disorders." It suggested "the Fire Companies would render essential service upon this occasion if they would cause their engines to be exercised daily, until rain should fall, in wetting the streets. Which at the same time would prevent their getting out of order for want of use."

"Death's Pale Army"

Governor Mifflin ordered Falstaffian Dr. Hutchinson to advise him whether a contagious disease was abroad. Hutchinson asked Rush who replied, "The fever was confined for a while to Water-street, between Race and Arch-streets; but I have lately met with it in Second-street, and in Kensington; but whether propagated by contagion, or by the original exhalation, I cannot tell. . . ." Hutchinson reported to the Governor: "It does not appear to be an imported disease; for I have heard of no foreigners or sailors that have hitherto been infected."

In 60-year-old Matthew Clarkson, Philadelphia had an outstanding mayor. Chosen for the post by his fellow aldermen in 1792, he had virtually no power since the city government was still run on the committee system. A former judge, Clarkson was a trustee of the Mutual Insurance Company (Green Tree) and the largest underwriter in town. His immediate contribution to the crisis was a display of remarkable calm.

Rush urged him to have all the city streets, beginning with Water, cleaned. Someone wrote to the *Federal Gazette* that instead of putting garbage in the yards or down the cellar where it "putrifies," it would be well to toss it into the street, so "the dogs would devour the meat, and the cows the vegetables." The correspondent also recommended "we . . . pay an additional tax, to have the Scavengers call at our houses three times a week" rather than "be sowing the seeds of death in our own borders." The mayor invoked an old ordinance requiring householders to sweep their walks and gutters and put their rubbish in piles every Monday and Thursday, so the scavengers could collect it the next day. Other suggestions poured into the editors—sprinkling vinegar throughout the house; diffusing tobacco smoke; keeping tarred ropes in rooms and on the person; and hanging camphor bags around the neck. To purify the air some began lighting bonfires, but one letter warned that in the dry August weather this was more of a peril than a purifier. The latter added, however, that morale would be improved if the tolling church bells were silenced.

Clarkson asked the College of Physicians to recommend steps. They immediately fell to bickering over whether the fever was domestic or imported; the methods of treatment, and, after savoring their beloved Latin terms, offered the same advice given by letter-writers. The most delicate point they made was the marking of infected houses. It conjured scenes from Daniel Defoe's *Journal of the Plague Year* which those bookstores still open found in sudden demand. Readers searched the fictional account of London's experience in 1665 for ideas to combat their menace. It just added to the gloom, for Defoe's black-cloaked men who called through London streets, "Bring out your dead!" came shiveringly alive in the silent blacks who were pushing corpse carts through the deserted Philadelphia streets, seldom followed by any mourners.

91

While the conclave of doctors were meditating miasma, the individual who recommended bells be muted, wrote another letter to the *Advertiser:*

> As the late rains will produce a great increase of mosquitoes . . . it will be agreeable to the citizens to know that the increase of those poisonous insects may be diminished by a very simple and cheap mode . . . Whoever will take the trouble to examine their rainwater tubs, will find millions of the mosquitoes fishing about the water with great agility, in a state not quite prepared to emerge and fly off; take up a wine glass full of water, and it will exhibit them very distinctly. Into this glass pour half a teaspoonful or less, of any common oil, which will quickly diffuse over the surface, and by excluding the air, will destroy the whole brood . . . A gill of oil poured into a common rain-water cask, will be sufficient; large cisterns may require more. . . .

This was too elementary for the College of Physicians, and they ignored it. By September 1 Rush put the number of deaths at 325 and the mayor estimated 140. People avoided each other, sniffing their camphor or saturating themselves with vinegar. Naval heroes like Barry and Truxtun headed south. President Washington went to Mount Vernon and Secretary of War Knox hurried to New York. As lesser Philadelphians tried to flee to other states, their way was blocked, and some were hurled from a coach as it passed through New Jersey. Thousands gathered in a tent city on the west bank of the Schuylkill or went farther inland. But back in the depleted Philadelphia, a new breed of heroes arose. Mayor Clarkson, finding himself virtually alone as the fever sent aides and aldermen into exile or sick beds, advertised for willing citizens to lend a hand. One of those who responded was Stephen Girard, the French immigrant who was amassing a sizable fortune from foreign trade. Lonely and despised as a Shylock by those who borrowed money from him, he picked the disagreeable duty of administering the improvised hospital which had been set up on the protesting William Hamilton's estate, Bush Hill, at 18th and Buttonwood Streets.

Elizabeth Drinker wrote in her diary:

> This provided a large house, barn and stable, all of which were at once filled with yellow-fever patients . . . Almost at once the hospital partook of the general panic and demoralization. On the sixteenth of September the managers . . . after inspection of the hospital reported it exhibited as wretched a picture of human misery as ever existed. A profligate, abandoned set of nurses and attendants (hardly any of good character could be procured at that time) . . . rioted on the provisions and comforts, prepared for the sick, who were left almost entirely destitute . . . The dying and dead were indiscriminately mingled together. The ordure and other evacuation of the sick were allowed to remain in the most offensive state imaginable . . . it was in fact a great slaughter house, where victims were immolated on the altar of riot and intemperance . . . No wonder, then, that a general

dread of the place prevailed throughout the city, and that a removal to it was considered as the seal of death. . . .

Trenches were dug on the grounds where patients awaiting admission were laid, adding to the funereal atmosphere. The smell was so noxious that the gallant Mayor, going out to swear in an official, retreated for two blocks to perform the ceremony. Girard ignored the unpleasant odors, pitched in and purged the place of the rascally nurses. He set up administrative procedures, had the place thoroughly scrubbed, procured beds and blankets and managed to obtain experienced French doctors to head the medical staff. Unlike Rush and those who insisted on massive blood-letting and emetics, the French handled their patients more gently and used techniques learned in the West Indies. Some of the Philadelphia physicians began to doubt Rush's procedure, and these he denounced as enemies. The feud became so bitter, as charges and countercharges by the physicians appeared in the press, journalist Philip Freneau protested

> Doctors raving and disputing
>   Death's pale army still recruiting
>   What a pother,
>   One with 'tother
>   Some a-writing, some a-shooting.
>
> Nature's poisons here collected
> Water, earth and air infected
>   O! what pity
>   Such a city
> Was in such a place erected.

Negroes were thought to be immune, and they became the unsung heroes of the tragedy as they undertook the mighty task of searching out the stricken, carrying them to Bush Hill, burying the dead, and caring for youngsters who strayed into the streets from houses where their parents were dead or dying. Even when the disease dispelled Rush's belief in their immunity, these valiant men and women carried on. Absalem Jones and Richard Allen, who had founded the first organization for blacks in the United States—the African Society—in 1787, were self-educated and highly respected citizens. Their nonsectarian society was designed to give mutual aid to members on sickness and to care for widows and fatherless children. Now they had taken the whole city of Philadelphia under their wing.

As late as September 17, when a thousand deaths were acknowledged, Dr. William Currie cheerfully continued his daily announcements that there was no yellow fever in the city. As October arrived frost was anticipated—but the same mildness that typified the whole year continued, and with it, the fever. Doctors took note of marks on corpses, jotting down every detail and commenting that some of the red spots looked like mosquito bites. Rush, stubbornly clinging to his theory of bleeding, worked heroically around the clock. His sister and several medical students who refused to leave him were all dead. Letters and newspapers were soaked in vinegar—bedclothes were drenched with vinegar and dried—children and adults alike smoked cigars—and the smell of tar and camphor hung heavy in the air. At City Hall, 5th and Chestnut Streets, undertakers displayed coffins and, while competing for prospective customers, let their horses eat oats from the crudely constructed wooden boxes. Few people ventured onto the streets. Shops were shuttered, houses closed. Those who did appear were gaunt with fear and fatigue. Funerals were lonely processions of a single carrier and an "inviter," both strangers to the deceased. A young Quaker lawyer, John Todd, Jr., had moved his family to the comparative safety of Grays Ferry, but felt it his duty to come into the city daily to care for the property and estates of his clients. He had a vivacious wife and two young children. He was suddenly stricken, and barely managed to reach his home. His wife, still weak from the birth of their second child, watched him helplessly die in her arms. She caught the fever, and almost died, and her newborn infant contracted it and had his little life snuffed out. When the epidemic ended, she and her surviving son went to live with her mother, Mrs. Payne, at 4th and Walnut Streets. Mrs. Payne kept a boarding house and there the handsome young widow was introduced to James Madison by Senator Aaron Burr. Eleven months later she became Dolly Madison.

Blacks attending those ill at home encountered strange things. Sometimes the sick would get out of bed and lie on the floor, asking to be measured for coffins. Amid all the charity there was avarice. Landlords evicted without worrying about the condition of tenants. A wealthy widow got money from the relief Committee for several destitute tenants, then seized their clothing and turned them out. One man, whose wife died, recovered from the fever blind and penniless, with two small children to look after. His landlord confiscated his furniture and clothing, and threw him from his sickbed into the street. "Not a ray of alleviation of the present calamity breaks in our city," Rush wrote his wife; "All is thick and melancholy gloom." In September, 1,443 died. October's toll would be higher.

Throughout the seige the Pennsylvania Hospital tried to protect its patients from infection by banning yellow fever victims. It felt Bush Hill was adequate, and feared the disease would sweep through the "Hospital Family" as the ward patients were called. Dr. Foulke managed to get two admitted; it caused consternation, and the hospital asked him to take steps to insure the safety of the others. But Foulke had gone to the country, and the hospital found only two physicians still in town—one of them Rush. He came down with a severe attack in mid-October, but struggled back to his practice within a short time, heartened on October 21st that the death rate of 60 a day was half of the peak period. The following day 82 died, and thereafter it steadily declined. Matthew Carey later fixed the number of burials between August 1 and November 9 at 4,044. Not all interred were victims of the fever, but these were more than counterbalanced by the uncounted who died on the outskirts of Philadelphia as they attempted to flee. In St. Mary's churchyard, Fourth above Spruce, burials during 1793 and two later epidemics in 1797 and 1798, were so frequent gravediggers did not have time to dig sufficiently deep. To cover the shallow graves, for reasons of sanitation, 1500 tons of dirt were dumped over the grounds, thus accounting for the raised level now seen in the cemetery.

Rush persisted doggedly in his "bleed and purge" technique and denouncing "putrefactions" on ships, docks and in gutters as the cause of yellow fever. He speculated about the possible influence of the moon's phases, and faithfully recorded the daily Farenheit readings along with comments on the weather. In the severe recurrence of the fever in 1797 he even commented on the large number of mosquitoes without realizing the role they played in the epidemics.

The Philadelphia newspapers in October 1793 savagely attacked his treatments—the *Gazette*'s Fenno denouncing it as a "lunatic system" and attributing to the French Revolution Rush's enthusiasm for bleeding. William Cobbett's *Porcupine Gazette* prefaced a stinging article with

> The times are ominous indeed
> When quack to quack cries purge and bleed.

Rush's faith in mercury, which he called "the Samson of Medicine," led Cobbett to comment:

> I verily believe they have slain more Americans with it, than ever Samson slew of the Philistines. The Israelite slew his thousands, but the Rushites have slain their tens of thousands.

He depicted Rush as a "poisonous trans-Atlantic quack," and public indignation against the doctor and his supporters mounted to a point where they were in danger of physical assault. Dr. Philip Syng, Physick, soon to be "the father of American surgery," from his home at 4th and

95

Delancey, credited Rush with saving his life, but his testimony did nothing to abate the storm. Rush brought suit against Fenno, but dropped it—but he instituted a libel action against Cobbett and relentlessly pursued it until the latter fled to avoid paying the judgment Rush ultimately won.

Others, as well as Dr. Physick, survived the drastic methods Rush employed, but Secretary of the Treasury Alexander Hamilton wisely went to a French physician when he fell victim.

While woefully ignorant of the blood content of the body, Philadelphia doctors were sophisticated in much of their medical thinking. Morgan, when he graduated from Edinburgh in 1763, revolutionized the theory of the origins of pus in an extraordinary thesis that demonstrated it did not proceed from solid tissue as theretofore believed, but was secreted from blood vessels during infection. Before he returned to Philadelphia to start a medical school he won almost every honor Europe could offer. His insistence that doctors should have liberal arts training as a requisite for professional schooling laid the foundation for modern medical education. His classmate, William Shippen, Jr., advocated that obstetrics be handled by physicians—a blow to the time-honored establishment of midwifery. Philadelphia had deep respect for women like Mary Broadway, who died at 100, and Mrs. Lydia Darrach, at Second and Dock Street, who delivered more babies than any of her associates. But Shippen's credentials in the field were imposing, and his Edinburgh thesis, *DePlacentae cum Utero,* in 1761, was highly regarded in Europe. Shippen set up a series of lectures in 1765 for "those Women who have Virtue enough to own their Ignorance, and apply for Instruction," thus proferring a helping hand to midwives even if his invitation had barbs.

Through the Revolution, Morgan, Shippen and Rush got into heated controversies over the conduct of the Medical Department of the Army. The impetuous Rush, using his authority as a member of Congress, drove Shippen to a court-martial. His vindictiveness led to friction with Washington, as well, and made him an enviable target for writers like Fenno and Cobbett.

Self-righteous, puritanical and often obnoxious, Rush still had some good qualities, and one of these was his persistent interest in the treatment and care of the mentally disturbed.

To the credit of the founders of the Pennsylvania Hospital, their petition for a charter in 1752 indicated their own concern for "the Numbers of People, the number of Lunaticks or Persons distempered in Mind and deprived of their rational Faculties . . . some of them going at large are a Terrour to their Neighbors . . . [and] few or none of them are so sensible to their Condition, as to submit voluntarily to the Treatment. . . ." With good reason, it might be noted, for the hospital paid a blacksmith for

"Death's Pale Army"

"1 pair of handcuffs, 2 legg locks, 2 large rings and 2 large staples, 5 lincks and 2 large rings and 2 swifells for legg chains." On John Adams' visit in 1774 he saw

in the lower Rooms under the Ground, the Cells of the Lunaticks, a Number of them, some furious, some merry, some Melacholly. . . .

It was all too easy to get a person committed since any one of the managers or the physicians attached to the hospital could simply write out an order. In many cases, legal proceedings led to commitment, but many

WALNUT STREET GAOL

The artist seems to have become more interested in the housemoving than the Walnut Street Prison he was sent to sketch. Light and location suggest this is the Debtor's division which faced Prune Street. While it hardly held sentimental attachment for citizens who spent some time there, some distinguished Philadelphians were in residence when this view was made, including Robert Morris, financial genius of the American Revolution. His overspeculations in land triggered ruin for himself and hundreds who followed his lead. Washington visited him during the early part of his three-year stay. The "felons" were housed in the building facing Walnut Street. The mobile home, destination unknown, has attracted fascinated spectators, including the little girl with her father in the foreground. The dog standing by the tall top-hatted man in the far right of the picture is absorbed in action of the dog who apparently attached himself to the procession. The lamppost portends a brighter future when imprisonment for debt would be banished and Penn Mutual Life Insurance Company would rise on the ground which, particularly on the Walnut Street side, meant misery and death for American prisoners of war under the brutal administration of the British provost marshal, "Bloody Bill" Cunningham, who later was hanged in England—but not for war crimes.

97

were accomplished by the simple stroke of a pen. There was no fence around the building until 1760 and the morbidly curious used to go to the windows in the basement and tease or stare at the patients. Even a wooden palisade did not prevent this, and in 1762 the managers ordered a "hatch door" cut, with a notice that "persons who come out of curiosity to visit the house should pay a sum of money, a Groat at least, for admittance." In 1767 the Board ordered that "the Hatch door be kept carefully shut . . . and no Person be admitted . . . without paying the gratuity of Four Pence . . . and that care be taken to prevent the Throng of people who are led by Curiosity to frequent the House on the first day of the week to the great disturbance of the Patients."

Stephen Girard's wife, Mary, was admitted as a lunatic "paying patient" on August 25, 1790 after wandering through Philadelphia streets and moving through a succession of boarding houses. Girard had recoiled against committing her, but became convinced her irrationality might bring her harm. Five months later she was pregnant, and stories began to circulate that a black sailor got into the loosely-guarded cells. Regardless of how it happened, the hospital asked Girard to remove her, afraid he might insist on including her maternity and child care in the original fees. Girard had no such intention, and she was permitted to remain and was delivered on March 3, 1791. The infant "was put out to Nurse with John Hatcher's Wife, at 10s Per Week" but lived only until August. The managers tightened security around the mental ward by denying admission to anyone "unless introduced or allowed by one of the Managers, Physicians or by the Steward, to which resolution the Cell-Keeper was strictly to Attend, and to keep the Gates and Wards locked in future. . . ."

Patients "eloped" from the hospital with regularity. Thomas Perrine "a remarkably neat and tidy sailor" escaped from the cells and got up into the cupola atop the East Wing in 1765 and stayed there until his death in 1774. After attempts to dislodge him failed, the managers decided to put bedding there and send food up to him. "He never left these cramped quarters for any purpose; he was also noted for his long nails, matted beard and hair and for his insensibility to cold, since he never, in the coldest weather of nine winters, came near to a fire."

Rush's interest in mental instability extended over a long period, and in an age that produced so many "fathers" it is not surprising to find him being hailed as "the father of psychiatry." Among his prolific writings is a brief attempt at a psychological study of the impact of the war upon the minds of the citizens. To the task of treatment he brought his abiding faith in blood-letting, sometimes extracting 20 to 40 ounces at a time, still blissfully unaware the body had half as much blood as he thought. He devised a "gyrator," or revolving machine, to be used in "torpid Madness" and a "tranquilizing chair" which, with a box over the patient's head and stocks for the feet and straps for the wrists and arms, looks anything but pacifying. To his credit, however, was his deep conviction that mental disorders were a disease, and should not be treated with cells and shackles. Repeatedly he urged managers to abandon forcible restraint, chains and straightjackets whenever possible, and suggested

> Certain Employments . . . be devised for such of the deranged people as are Capable of Working, spinning, sewing, churning, &c. might be contrived for the Women; Turning a Wheel, particularly grinding Indian Corn in a Hand Mill, for food for the Horses or Cows of the Hospital, cutting Straw, weaving, digging in the Garden, sawing or plaining board, &c. &c. would be Useful for the Men.

One who may have driven many to lunacy was Philadelphia's first dentist, a Dr. Baker. In the absence of toothbrushes, which were as yet undiscovered, people rubbed their teeth with a chalked rag or with snuff, although some men deemed it effeminate to be seen cleaning their teeth at all.

These primitive conditions notwithstanding, the next dentist in sight was a Doctor LeMayeur who, in 1784, advertised tooth transplants, stating that he had successfully transplanted 123 teeth in the preceding six months. In the same advertisement he offered two guineas for every tooth which might be offered by "persons disposed to sell their front teeth or any of them!" He achieved a financial success, and pleased at least one patient who admitted, however, that it was two months before she could eat with them. Since dentists were rare even in London or Paris at the time, LeMayeur, with such advanced concepts must have been close to what was best in the western world. Bad teeth were commonplace among 18th century Philadelphians, although Philadelphia belles thought New York girls had worse.

Like all colonial cities Philadelphia had its share of quacks, and all assumed the title of doctor. Thomas Anderson, apparently dissatisfied with being a glazier, opened an office in his home in 1772 as a specialist in the treatment of venereal diseases. As an incentive he offered free advice and "chirugical assistance" daily, 10 a.m. to 2 p.m. and from 4 to 9 p.m. The "Saxnay medicine" he used

> will effectually and radically cure every sympton of the venereal disease, without pain or sickness, or any confinement, whatever. . . . They are taken by the most delicate of both sexes, at all seasons of the year, and by fishermen in water.

He promised cures "on moderate terms" for "Gleets and seminal weaknesses, in both sexes, impotency, fistulas and obstructions in the urinary passage." Piles he offered to cure without charge, but he carried medicines for a host of other ailments, including Baron Van Swieten's worm plumbs, Daffy's elizir, and Dr. Stork's tincture for toothache. In 1773 a Dr. Day came to town, offering cures for gall-stones, assuring the public "The medicines he administers are very good to take, and gives no uneasiness, but works off gently by urine." Like Anderson, he did not limit himself to this area. For "a dollar each" he sold a "bottle and a box . . . that infalliabily cures the worst of fevers and agues, or the worst rheumatisms: He greatly assists the eyes in both young and old. . . ." The advertisement continues

> Any gentlemen that hath occasion for a private lodging in any difficult disorder, may be accomodated at the Doctor's in Vine-street, near Fourth-street. He hath his name over the door in brass letters.

Presumably this service was designed for those who did not avail themselves of Dr. Anderson's talents. Dr. Anthony Yeldall was available for "any case of Physic or Surgery" but

> omits saying anything of his abilities in practice, his well-known travels for these five years past through different parts of this continent, and the many surprizing cures that, under God, have been performed by him . . . speak more powerfully than anything that can be here inserted. . . .

He hinted that the demand for his services had been so great that heretofore he could not leave his office but

> in order to render himself as useful to his fellow-creatures as possible, he will, for the future attend at the houses of such patients as are not able to attend on him either in town or country; those that live in the country may, by sending an account of their disorder, have advice and medicines as the nature of their case may require.

Some who knew their problems could buy Dr. Ryan's "worm destroying sugar plumbs" for 7s 6d per dozen

> one of the best purges in the world for gross-bellied children that are apt to breed worms, and have large bellies; their operation is mild, safe and pleasant; they wonderfully cleanse the bowels of all stiff and clammy humours, which stop up the parts, and prevent the juice of food being conveyed to the liver and make blood, which is often the case with children, and is attended with a hard belly, stinking breath, frequent fevers. . . .

100

"Death's Pale Army"

There were attempts to banish these quacks and bring the practice of medicine into some form of regulated system. A bill designed to accomplish this was introduced in the General Assembly in 1794 but failed to pass. So Philadelphia doctors headed for the 19th century, trained and untrained alike. The stethoscope would not be invented until 1819; percussion of the chest by tapping would not be popular until 1808 when Napoleon's physician took up the discovery made in 1751; the clinical thermometer would not be used until after the Civil War; urine and blood analysis was unknown throughout the 18th century, and Philadelphia physicians would gird themselves for a new debate about childbed fever and the value of washing their hands.

6

"A SYREN'S PART":

Philadelphia Loved the Theater, But Not All Philadelphians

*   *   *   *   *

Too oft, we own, the stage with dangerous art
In wanton scenes, has play'd a Syren's part,
Yet if the Muse, unfaithful to her trust
Has sometimes stray'd from what was pure and just
Has she not oft, with awful virtue's rage
Struck home at vice, and nobly trod the stage?
Then as you'd treat a favourite fair's mistake,
Pray spare her foibles for her virtue's sake;
And whilst her chastest scene are made appear
(For none but such will find admittance here)
The muse's friends, we hope, will join the cause,
And crown our best endeavours with applause.

—Prologue, Opening Night, April 15, 1754

*   *   *   *   *

"A Syren's Part"

"How many plays did Jesus Christ and his apostles recreate themselves at?" asked young William Penn in *No Cross, No Crown,* "What poets, romances, comedies, and the like did the apostles and saints make or use to pass away their time . . . ?" Not receiving a satisfactory answer by 1682, it was inevitable that among the things he would proscribe in his province would be "such rude and riotous sports and practices as prizes, stage-plays, masques. . . ." Pennsylvanians who transgressed were liable to a twenty shilling fine or a short term at hard labor in the tiny jail. The British Crown, however, which reviewed all legislation condemned this as an intolerable limitation on "healthy and innocent diversions," which, measured against the bawdiness of the Restoration theatre, anything produced on a stage in Philadelphia was likely to be. Pragmatism more than priggishness was at the base of the Quaker theory. Plays were a waste of time and unproductive, but there was an element of self-righteousness. "Plays, parks, balls, treats, romances, musics, love-sonnets, and the like, will be a very invalid plea . . . at the revelation of the . . . judgment of God," Penn had dogmatized, impliedly consigning lives like Shakespeare's to a wasteland.

Having battled monarchs in more direct confrontations the Quakers were not about to relinquish their principles, and since Philadelphia was their stronghold, magistrates determined that no wandering minstrels would profane it. It took non-Quakers more than a half-century to venture timidly onto a stage, and then it was an amateur affair put on at the College under the guise of an elocution exercise.

In 1723 an itinerant showman set up a stage south of the city line. The General Assembly designated the Speaker to ask Governor Sir William Keith to prohibit the performance. But Keith was no Quaker and, amid all the provincialism of Pennsylvania, he missed the flair of London. He built an austere-looking mansion, still standing in Graeme Park in Bucks County, hoping the twenty miles from town would discourage city officials as well as province officers from bothering him. Within the residence, the fine woodwork, pedimented doorways and marble-trimmed fireplaces attest his appreciation of the material world—a taste his inner circle of non-Quaker friends sampled in the lavish parties. Keith not only rejected the suggestion to stop the show, but announced he intended to go see it. James Logan, simultaneously Mayor and Secretary of the Province, told irate Philadelphians he was powerless to interfere. Despite the stage it was hardly theatre. The producer, who introduced himself to the audience as "your old friend Pickle Herring," apparently put together a program of jokes and tricks, for when he returned in 1724 he advertised as "newly arrived" some "Roap-Dancing." One of the performers was a seven-year old girl "who danced and capered upon a strait roap, to the wonder of

103

all spectators." Another had a woman whirling for a quarter of an hour with swords pointed at her eyes, mouth and breast. The Quakers were distressed at this double intrusion. Even Franklin found it politic at the moment to join the chorus of condemnation. Mayor William Plumsted, however, was made of sterner stuff. When a visiting company headed by Thomas Kean and Walter Murray sought his sanction in 1748, he offered them the use of his warehouse on Water Street below Pine, and from January 1749 to February 1750 they offered their repertory of twenty-four plays, including Addison's *Cato, Richard III,* Dryden's *Spanish Friar,* Congreve's *Love for Love, The Fair Penitent, The Beaux Stratagem,* and *George Barnwell.* Presbyterians allied with the Quakers in cries of indignation, and the City Council was warned such plays would encourage "Idleness" and draw "great Sums of Money from weak and inconsiderate People."

After this breakthrough, Plumsted's remained dark until April 15, 1754 when Lewis Hallam, invited by bolder spirits in Philadelphia, brought his troupe to town, fresh from successes in Williamsburg and New York. The Quakers renewed their fight, but Governor James Hamilton, on assurances there would be nothing "indecent or immoral" and that the tour would be limited to thirty plays, gave it his benediction. With a broader selection than their predecessor the Hallam company opened with *The Fair Penitent,* after reciting as a prologue the apologetic verse at the head of this chapter. *Miss in Her Teens* was the second offering on opening night, and Franklin's *Gazette* reported the two plays were greeted by "a Numerous and Polite Audience, with Universal Applause."

Still, it was 1758 before Philadelphians got another glimpse of the company, and its new manager David Douglass. Douglass was authorized to build his own theatre just over the city line, on the south side of Cedar (later South) at Vernon (later Hancock) Streets. The theatre on "Society Hill," as it was known, was sold a year later and converted into three houses. In 1952 the owner of the corner house noted that the wall dividing the rooms was thicker than the outside walls, possibly indicating it was the original proscenium wall of the theatre.

Both the Quakers and Presbyterians were aroused and took steps to eliminate the plays. The Friends first went to Judge William Allen. "His reply," the annalist Watson wrote, "was repulsive, saying he got more moral virtue from plays than from sermons. As a sequel, it was long remembered that the night the theatre was opened, and to which he intended to be a gratified spectator, he was called to mourn the death of his wife." The General Assembly was more receptive and limited the season from June 25 to December 28, 1759. One of the performers,

(*Hist. & Museum Comm., Harrisburg; original in Hist. Society of Penna., Phila.*)

JAMES LOGAN
Stature among the elms

Watson reported with satisfaction, was Francis Mentges, a dancer who "had talents above his original profession and was, in the time of the Revolution, esteemed a good officer, and was continued in the United States' service long after the peace."

In 1760 a new theatre was erected, larger than its predecessor, at Fourth and South,

> an ugly ill-contrived affair outside and inside. The stage lighted by plain oil lamps without glasses. The view from the boxes was intercepted by large square wooden pillars supporting the upper tier and roof . . . the front bench in the gallery was the best seat in the house for a fair view of the whole stage.

A rough-cast red brick and timber structure, the Southwark Theatre had the lines of a church with the belfry straddling the steep sloped roof. The skittish proprietors, wary of the law, used to advertise "a Concert of music" after which there would be a free lecture or dialogue on the vice of scandal. Racier plays were toned down and sophisticates in the audience complained that actors did not always follow the script.

Douglass was an entrepreneur. With "The Southwark" as the first permanent theatre in America, he set out to establish others in the principal cities and, sensitive to the growing nationalism, labeled his troupe, "The American Company." As a token of his interest in native playwrights he scheduled, in 1767, a comic opera by a twenty-year old Philadelphian, Thomas Forrest, *The Disappointment: or, the Force of Credulity*. It lampooned so many of the city's leading characters that Douglass acceded to demands that it be cancelled before it was presented. The bemused Forrest had set the scene on Petty's Island in the Delaware, where the easily-recognizable public figures made fools of themselves looking for pirate's gold. The most permanent value of the aborted play was his direction that one song be sung to the "tune of Yankee Doodle," thus fixing an earlier date for its popularity than had been supposed. Forrest's cancellation led to vehement protests by young Anthony Wayne and others who found the hastily inserted substitute, *Prince of Parthia* tedious and boring. Douglass was on much safer ground, for the *Prince* was the product of a gentle Philadelphia poet, Thomas Godfrey, Jr., who in addition to acceptable credentials as a graduate of the Philadelphia College, used the early Christian era for his setting. Son of a glazier and self-taught mathematician, young Godfrey is believed to have been born at the present 135 Market Street, where his father acquired a dual measure of fame by renting rooms from Benjamin Franklin in 1736 and inventing the quadrant. The elder Godfrey died when his son was thirteen, and never knew the recognition he was to get posthumously for his contribution to safety at sea. The son, too, was denied seeing his romantic tragedy produced, for he died four years before in North Carolina from yellow fever. This might have been a blessing since its next, and most recent staging was in 1915 when the Zelosophic Society of the University of Pennsylvania resurrected it under strict orders that all parts had to be performed by men. The 1767 audience was more fortunate since the American Company had two beautiful actresses, a Miss Wainwright, and Miss Margaret Cheer. Miss Cheer was as astute as she was attractive. In 1768 she married an admirer, Lord Rosehill, and, appearing in the next

ST. PETER'S CHURCH

Built to keep Anglicans living a few blocks south of High Street from deciding "to stay at home and neglect divine Service, or go into dissenting Meetings", St. Peter's took five years (1758-1763) to complete. Raised on ground at 3rd and Pine given by Thomas and Richard Penn, proprietaries who forsook Quakerism for the Established Church, this exquisite structure retains its high-pewed charm and the unusual feature of the pulpit at the opposite end from the chancel. This affords worshippers a chance to shift in their box pews. While it came into being because muddy conditions of neighboring streets to the north discouraged residents from making the trek to Christ Church, it found itself in the same quandry—a committee reporting in 1768 stating: "The Streets leading to St. Peter's Church not being paved are often so bad that people cannot come to Church." The graceful spire and tall tower in 1842 supplanted the small cupola shown here on the west end—about the only major alteration to the church in the more than two centuries it has stood. In 1778 some cold Hessians removed a section of wooden fence surrounding the churchyard for firewood. Major Edward Williams, Royal Artillery, wrote that the British commander would pay a "reasonable allowance" for damages. In 1961 the pastor presented a bill to the British Treasury for $760,000—based on 183 years of compound interest at 6% for the initial debt of $18. The Chancellor of the Exchequer pointed out that since the event occurred before the Treaty of Versailles in 1783, claims by citizens of the colonies which had not been settled, were under the treaty terms to lie against the successor governments, and gave the minister the choice of Pennsylvania or the United States. However he sent his personal check for $18 which the clergyman accepted in full settlement. The church yard is crowded with celebrities including Charles Willson Peale, Benjamin Chew, Nicholas Biddle the banker, Lewis Hallam, Jr., "father of the American theatre" and naval hero Stephen Decatur, killed in a duel.

107

season as Lady Rosehill, commanded a weekly salary which would now approximate $270 a week.

Forrest continued his puckish ways. To the consternation of his targets, he took his play to New York and had it published as a book. It got wide and amused circulation in Philadelphia. His propensity to practical jokes got him a court-martial and reprimand after the Battle of Germantown, but the scene of his rebuke apparently had other pleasant memories for, after maintaining a note brokerage house at 425 Market Street in Philadelphia, he moved his residence to Germantown from whence he was twice elected to Congress. In 1796 he revised and enlarged *The Disappointment* and published it as a novel.

In 1769 the Southwark offered *The Padlock,* which had been a rousing success in London the year before. A newspaper critic said in addition to "the most crowded and brilliant Audience" it attracted "Some Ruffians in the Gallery, who so frequently interrupted the Performance, and in the most interesting Scenes" that the management should admonish three-shilling customers they had no right to clamor for songs not listed on the program, and have constables handy to evict noise-makers. These patrons, however, became progressively worse, and in 1772 Douglass was offering a £10 reward for capture of the culprits who carried "away the iron spikes which divide the galleries from the upper boxes." The "gallery gods," as they called themselves, imported the English custom of pelting performers and pit alike with oranges and pears. When Philadelphia was caught up in the excitement of the French Revolution, they would single out an "aristocrat" in the audience and demand he stand and bow to them. If he refused, the whole lower level came under a barrage of spit, beer and rotten fruit. During one performance the orchestra had to flee.

The long struggle of the Quakers to ban the theatre got an unexpected assist from the Continental Congress in 1774. In the Articles of Association through which they hoped to get the cooperation of the thirteen Colonies to improve such things as agriculture and manufacture, they called for frugality, and subscribers promised to "discountenance and discourage every species of extravagance and dissipation, especially all horse-racing, and all kinds of gaming, cock-fighting, exhibitions of shews, plays, and other expensive diversions and entertainments." Although this was resolved in Carpenter's Hall, Philadelphians had mixed reactions.

Working through uncontrolled vigilante committees, Congress soon learned its pious proposals were paving the way for unbridled mob terror. A woman was advised to "decline" giving a proposed ball; some horse-racers were made to express repentance and promise "proper atonement" for their "enormity," and one victim growled:

> If I must be enslaved, let it be by a KING at least, and not by a parcel of upstart lawless Committee-men. If I must be devoured, let me be devoured by the jaws of a lion, and not gnawed to deth by rats and vermin.

Douglass took his American Company off to the West Indies, leaving the Southwark deserted until the British came to the city three years later. Then a group of officers interested in amateur theatre, dubbed "Howe's Thespians" reactivated its stage, giving thirteen plays between January and June 1778. One of the most active was 27-year old Captain John André, who was quartered in Franklin's house during the occupation and appropriated a portrait of the philosopher-politician as a souvenir. The painting, by Benjamin Wilson, was returned to the United States by the British in 1906 and has since been in the White House. The multi-talented André, although said by some to be a "poor actor" (a fact grimly underscored in 1780 when he was captured on his "spy" mission), was a skilled writer and was useful in editing and preparing prologues to the presentations. With Captain Oliver deLancey he painted most of the scenery, one of their major efforts being a backdrop described as

> a landscape presenting a distant champagne country, and a winding rivulet, extending from the front of the picture to the extreme distance. In the foreground and center, a gentle cascade—the water exquisitely executed—was overshadowed by a group of majestic forest trees. The perspective was excellently preserved; the foliage, verdure and general coloring artistically toned and glazed.

The "curtain" remained for the rest of the theatre's comparatively long existence, and provided a background for a skit in 1780 dramatizing his seizure by three country yokels.

The "Thespians" had no problem getting women for the feminine roles, most of whom in the estimation of the janitor were of "no character." Such an estimate may have been jaundiced, but there is some indication that enlisted men often shared their wives with officers. Professional actresses, when available, were used. On one program Miss Hyde "sang 'Tally Ho' between the play and the farce."

While the British were enjoying themselves, Americans celebrated the return of good weather and the French Alliance at Valley Forge on May 11, 1778 with an amateur performance of their own, converting a hillside into an open-air amphitheatre. An officer wrote to his sister:

109

... the theater is opened. Last Monday *Cato* was performed before a very numerous and splendid audience. . . . The scenery was in taste and the performance admirable. . . .

If the enemy does not retire from Philadelphia soon our theatrical amusements will continue. *The Fair Penitent* with *The Padlock* will soon be acted. . . .

Cato was a natural choice for a premiere. Addison's works were popular throughout the colonies, and the play was Washington's classical favorite. It was a virtual anthology of statements patriots found useful: "What a pity is it that we can die but once to serve our country" was condensed and vastly improved by Nathan Hale under unhappy circumstances. "It is not now a time to talk of aught but chains or conquest; liberty or death" was more stirring in Patrick Henry's version. When Washington attended Southwark as President in 1791, he preferred *The Poor Soldier*, and is said to have requested that it be repeated several times—a point which may have some psychological implications.

When the British withdrew from Philadelphia in June 1778, Major General Benedict Arnold, his leg shattered in heroic action at Saratoga the' previous October, led an occupation force into the city, while the main army under Washington pursued the English through New Jersey. Arnold and his men took up the pursuit of pleasure where the British had left off, with elaborate banquets, balls and plays. Congress, bereft of the outstanding men of 1776 except for a few, shared the annoyance Pennsylvania officials felt about his extravagance and policy of coexistence with the suspected Tory element in town. Congress, on October 12, recommended once more that the states suppress "theatrical entertainments, horse racing, gaming, and such other diversions as are productive of idleness, dissipation, and a general depravity of principles and manners." Arnold ignored the sentiments which were aimed, in large part, at his activities. Samuel Adams sourly observed that some officers "have condescended to act on the stage; while others, and one of superior rank, were pleased to countenance them with their presence." Angry at Arnold's contempt, it adopted a rule on October 16 that

any person holding an office under the United States who shall act, promote, encourage, or attend such plays shall be deemed unworthy to hold such office and shall be accordingly dismissed.

"What a lot of damned scoundrels we had in that Second Congress," Gouveneur Morris reflected in a letter to John Jay. "Yes, we had," Jay agreed.

"A Syren's Part"

STATE HOUSE

The light indicates this sketch was made in late afternoon, probably on a Sunday in 1798. Mother and child are walking toward Sixth Street, across which is the theatre district—New Theatre, Rickett's Circus and the fashionable Oeller's Hotel. The lonely-looking horse tethered in front of the tavern, and the lack of activity around the State House, suggests the rider had no trouble finding a table. The watch box, hard by the steps to the main entrance of the State House is strategically located. The United States Supreme Court occupies the second floor of the building with the cupola, while the first floor serves as the new City Hall. Just beyond the proud mother, the three vertical windows is part of a building in which Gilbert Stuart had his center-city studio.

After the war Pennsylvania kept tight restrictions on the professional theatre. Lewis Hallam, Jr., now managing The American Company, told Anthony Wayne in 1784 he intended to buy the "acrostique machine" which had carried its French inventor 80 feet in the air, attach it to the Southwark and lift it 1300 miles above the State House where "The height will subtilize and enlighten the ideas of the play and make them more sublime, more rarified, and inoffensive to the most immaculate Puritans."

The fight to reopen the theatre dragged on interminably. Heartened by what he felt was the diminishing influence of the Quakers, Hallam brought his petition to every session. Wayne, elected in 1785 was unable to help, although eloquent speeches attributed to him seem to indicate his willingness to compromise his personal opposition to censorship, by suggesting Hallam be given a monopoly for a $2,000 annual license fee,

111

that ticket prices be regulated, and the Supreme Executive Council authorized to approve plays in advance of their showing. In 1785 a committee recommended lifting the ban, but the liberal-controlled legislature finally rejected it by four votes—sensitive to the powerful coalition of Presbyterians, Quakers and Baptists. "The Saints and saint-like folk have too much influence," Cadwalader Morris said in 1784 and it was equally true until 1789, when the back-country liberals were finally outvoted by the combination of eastern conservatives and liberals. One of the factors tipping the scale was the anxiety of some legislators to have Philadelphia selected as the site for the national capital.

The New Theatre on the north side of Chestnut Street above Sixth was begun in 1791, and enthusiasts claimed it was "a perfect copy of the Bath Theatre." Its opening for dramatic presentations had been scheduled for 1793, but the yellow fever scourge that year delayed it until February 17, 1794. The most impressive theatre yet built in America, it was 90 feet wide and 134 feet deep, seating 765 in three galleries and another 400 in a parquet of thirteen rows. Saint-Mery, the French traveler, observed its oil lamps were raised or lowered to control the light on particular scenes, a technique used in Europe. He thought the intermissions were "more indecent" than in France, so much so that women turned their backs to the stage. The exuberance of opening night, however, was pictured by the *New York Magazine* for April 1794:

> The managers have used their utmost endeavors to form a theatre of elegance and convenience. That part of the theatre, before the curtain, forms a semicircle, having two rows of boxes extending from side to side, with another row above these on a line with the gallery in front. The boxes are lined with a pink coloured paper, with small dark spots, and supported by pillars, festoons of crimson curtains, with tassels intervening, and a profusion of glass chandeliers, form an assemblage that captivates the eye, and renders the whole a most pleasing spectacle. The paintings and scenery are equal to the generality of the European, and do the greatest credit to the pencil and genius of Mr. Milbourne. The dresses correspond with the elegance of the whole. The emblematical device over the stage is very applicable, and well executed—it represents an eagle hovering in the air; beneath it a boy holding a blue ribbon on which is inscribed, 'The eagle suffers little birds to sing.' Shakespeare.

The "gallery gods" needed no invitation. They continued to interrupt plays and concerts when it struck their fancy, which, for the more genteel, was far too frequent.

Drama in Philadelphia would take on greater dimensions in the next century. The Walnut Street Theatre, built in 1809, is the oldest surviving playhouse in the English-speaking world. The New Theatre in Chestnut Street had its proudest season in 1797-98 when it offered thirteen new pieces and twenty revivals and afterpieces. Fire destroyed it on April 2, 1820. It was rebuilt and opened again in 1822, one of its most memorable moments occurring on October 16, 1850 when Jenny Lind, the "Swedish nightingale" gave her first Philadelphia concert under the management of P.T. Barnum. In May 1855 it was torn down, and its marble facade, along with other materials, was sold. The four marble columns brought $25 each.

Eclipsed by its more pretentious successor, the Southwark stayed in business until 1813, was partially burned on May 9, 1821, but its ancient walls found new significance when the structure was converted into a distillery which survived until 1912.

Hallam, who labored so long in behalf of drama for Philadelphia, lived his last years at 410 Fifth Street, just below Pine. The New Theatre billed him as "The Father of the American Theatre" when he gave his final performance in 1808. Somewhat poetically he died the same year, aged 68 according to reliable sources, although the Philadelphia *Daily Advertiser* in the obituary said he was 75. He is buried in the churchyard of St. Peter's, Third and Pine, but no marker tells precisely where.

7

THE CHARMS THAT SOOTHED:

Music Calmed Many a Savage Philadelphian

*   *   *   *   *

Written out of temper on a Pannel in one of the Pues in Salem Church:

"Could poor king David but for once
  To Salem Church repair
And hear his Psalms thus warbled out,
  Good Lord, how he would swear!"

*   *   *   *   *

The Charms That Soothed

Congregations in Philadelphia's 18th century churches probably sang no better than that which inspired the above verse, but for sixty years they were the closest one could come to anything approximating a musical concert. Not even the Puritans took the stiff position assumed by the Quakers about music, and by 1750 the city lagged far behind Boston, New York and Charleston in this sphere of the arts. Still Philadelphians were spared homespun hymns like those of William Billings which drove a New England clergyman to take his text from Amos: "The songs of the temple shall be howlings." Visiting Christ Church, the Moravian Meeting and the "Romish Chapel," John Adams in 1774 pronounced the renditions "very sweet and soft indeed." All three had organs—vanguard of the growing number which Francis Hopkinson surveyed in 1790 with the conclusion that too many organists forgot "the congregation have not assembled to be entertained" by a display of their "powers of execution." "It is as offensive to hear lilts and jigs from a church organ," he told Bishop White of Christ Church, "as it would be to see a venerable matron frisking through the public streets with all the fantastic airs of a columbine."

Christ Church was also having difficulties with singing. In 1785 the vestry ordered "that clerks be required to sing such tunes only as are plain and familiar to the congregation; and ... the singing of other tunes, and the frequent changing of tunes, are deemed disagreeable and inconvenient." Hopkinson probably did not share that sentiment, unless the "other tunes" were imported from Massachusetts. A lawyer, signer of the Declaration of Independence, designer of the American flag and lastly, a Federal judge, his whole life was set to music, a theme reflected in his composition, "My Days Have Been So Wondrous Fair." This pastoral piece, reminiscent of the neoromanticism of the age, is believed to be the first non-religious composition in America. Dedicating eight songs to Washington, Hopkinson described himself as a "Lover, not a Master, of the Arts," but he was an intense devotee who traveled to London to hear Handel's *Messiah* rendered "by the best hands" and carried reams of music by the masters back to Philadelphia to share with his close friend, Robert Bremmer.

Bremmer, a Scot, was one of some forty music teachers in Philadelphia in 1763, and brought with him a reputation as a composer and virtuoso. Hopkinson, already an accomplished organist and harpsichordist, came to further his studies at Bremmer's school near the London Coffee House, and despite Quaker frowns helped arrange a subscription concert series for Bremmer in 1765. It proved so successful it was repeated in 1766, and set in motion other series. Signor Giovanni Gualdo had come to the city in 1767 to open a wine cellar, and when this failed, established a music store in Front Street in 1769, providing a wide range of services, from repairs to lessons along with a good stock of string instruments and flutes. He quickly established his genius in the widening circle of afficianados, and gave concerts in which he interspersed his own compositions with those of the more famous. Highly successful as these were, Gualdo's financial problems seemed insoluble, and in 1771 Hopkinson gloomily reported to John Penn, "Music is at present in a very deplorable condition here. Sgr. Gualdo lies in Chains in one of the Cells of the Pennsylvania Hospital." Bremmer was back in England and prospects did not seem bright. "Except Forage and myself I don't know a single Votary the Goddess hath in this large city." But the next year was more encouraging. At Christ Church the "Hallelujah Chorus," in which he took part, drew enthusiastic crowds, and Michael Hillegas, who was to be the first Treasurer of the United States, expanded his music shop into possibly the most complete in the colonies. John Adams regarded Hillegas as a "great musician" who talked "perpetually of the forte and piano, of Handel, etc., and songs and tunes."

In attempting to break the barrier, Hopkinson got considerable help from the American Company at the Southwark Theatre. A few hired musicians were generally on hand to support the cast and soothe the audience, and in 1769 Douglass announced that "on Opera Nights" they "will be assisted by some musical Persons, who as they have no view but to contribute to the Entertainment of the Public, certainly claim a Protection from any Manner of Insult." Thus he enticed timid amateurs from the little music clubs that met weekly in various taverns. Whether his advertisement made the audience more tolerant is not recorded.

The College of Philadelphia, whose Anglican provost, Dr. William Smith, delighted in assailing Quaker stolidity, altered its commencement program in 1773 from the traditional pattern of hymns to have the Royal Irish Regiment Band play lively martial airs.

Quakers could do little about the British troops stationed in the city to be on hand in case Indians went on another rampage in the interior of the Province. In 1769 Alexander Macraby gave an account of some of the informal concerts they presented:

> Seven sleighs with two Ladies and two men in each, preceded by fiddlers on horseback, set out together ... to a public house a few miles from town, where we danced, sung, and romped and eat and drank, and kicked away care from morning till night, and finished our frolic in two or three side-boxes at the play.

116

This the sober citizens could live with, but his "serenade" was something else:

> We, with four or five young officers ... drink as hard as we can, to keep out the cold, and about midnight sally forth, attended by the band, march thro' the streets, and play under the window of any lady you choose to distinguish; which they esteem a high compliment. In about an hour all the blackguards who sleep upon bulks, with gentlemen of a certain profession, are collected round, drawn by that charm which soothes a savage beast, and altogether make it extremely agreeable in a fine frosty morning

The Revolution brought its own brand of music, as militiamen drilled to the fife and drum. Since the musicians were novices they clung to "Jack, the Brisk Young Drummer" until some Philadelphians thought it their most effective weapon to drive the enemy insane. With Washington's victory at Trenton, the best prize of battle was the little Hessian band which was paraded through town in January 1777, and created such a sensation, it was kept in Philadelphia to give concerts while other prisoners of war were sent off to Lancaster and Carlisle. When the British captured the city in October, Loyalists were assured of fine music. "Assemblies, concerts, comedies, clubs, and the like make us forget there is any war ...," Hessian Captain Johann Heinrichs wrote on January 18, 1778.

War's end brought new opposition to music, this time from the Presbyterian Whigs, but it was short lived. In 1783 John Bentley, who led the orchestra at the Southwark estabilshed a fortnightly "City Concert" which continued through 1784. The press notices, seldom explicit about the programs, mention Signora Mazzanti as a featured soloist, and leave unidentified "some favourite catches and glees," "several favourite airs," and "a glee and chorus from the opera of Castle of Andalusia." Bentley got into an argument in 1785 with some of the leading musicians and went off to New York, so for two years there were no concerts of his dimension. Alexander Reinagle, son of an Austrian musician, but raised in Edinburgh, came to Philadelphia in 1786 and "by virtue of his superior talent and individuality" took "control of the musical affairs of the city." He offered twelve fortnightly concerts at the City Tavern, including works of Handel, Bach, Toeschi, Stamitz, Fiorillo, Lachnith, Breval and Corelli, whose compositions captivated Philadelphians. A program lists a "Sonata Piano Forte" by Reinagle, but managers often inserted the performer's name in the space where the composer's normally appeared, leaving later generations in considerable doubt whether the artist was playing his own work.

Chamber music, predominantly private, has left little traces of its odyssey through Philadephia's history. Apart from knowing its soft intimacy was ideal for the back parlors or drawing rooms, nothing remains to suggest the selections most frequently requested or played. Some of it was interwoven in the larger, formal concerts and is identified, but in the main, letters and diaries of the period furnish no clue as to the most popular pieces. Some "French gentlemen, Musicians" announced their availability in 1793 for "such Ladies and Gentlemen of this City, as might be pleased to have Music performed at their own Houses." Their specialty, whatever it might have been, vanished with "Mr. Oeller's Hotel" or "Mr. Merkel's, No. 224, at the sign of the Drover, Northeast corner of Calowhill and third streets" where they could be contacted. Chamber music, for the most part, was probably non-professional except when a host or hostess wanted to impress guests. Some prominent personages had music rooms in their homes, Franklin and Mayor Samuel Powell among them. Powell's, removed from his home on South Third Street, has been reassembled in the Philadelphia Museum of Art. Strawberry Mansion in Fairmount Park has an opulent room designated as such, but its size suggests that it was a synonym for ballroom. In any event it was added in 1825.

The New Theatre in Chestnut Street was completed sufficiently in February 1793 so that concerts could be held, even though the dramatic presentations had to wait for a better equipped stage. The *Federal Gazette* in recounting the premiere was more carried away by the audience than the performance:

> ... the boxes exhibited a blaze of beauty—the pit was a display of respectable judges and the gallery was filled with orderly, well disposed citizens whose decency of behavior deserves the greatest applause ... that part of the entertainment, wherein Mrs. Morris' abilities in *Kiss me now or never* and Master Duport's dancing came in, seemed to afford the most attractingly delightful sensations. ...

Franklin's grandson, Benjamin Bache, a Francophile, used his newspaper reviews to blast Washington's neutrality policy which denied revolutionary France economic aid. The slanted stories were so patently obvious in their sympathies that a reader would have had no way of knowing, short of having attended, which selections at the premier provoked the most audience reaction.

"The band is well chosen and full; the audience could have dispensed with the noise of the kettledrums. The favorite *Ca Ira* was the first air played. The orchestra by attending to the call for it, and by a voluntary repetition ... shewed that they did not forget their audience was American. . . ." On February 25 he praised the orchestra but suggested it might be well "now and then, to give the gallery some simple tunes more agreeable to the taste of the generality of the audience." On the 28th: "Last Wednesday the house was again crowded. The orchestra opened with the President's march, and then, after repeated calls from the *mountain,* favoured the audience with *Ca Ira.* The Minister of the French Republic was present and was greeted by three huzzas."

Four years later it was a different story. The United States, under President John Adams, was on the brink of a war with France. The Philadelphians, while never quite as rabid about the French as Bache would like to have believed, except for a loud minority, were swept on the emotional tides of patriotism. Hopkinson's *President's March*

(Kean Archives, Phila.)

ZION LUTHERAN

Although this building was only three years old when the Birches etched it, Zion Lutheran's congregation dated to 1769. In that year the prototype was raised here at the s.c. corner of 4th and Cherry Streets. Considered the largest and finest in America by many, the church encountered a series of disasters. In 1777 the British converted it into a hospital—in 1793, 625 members died in the yellow fever epidemic—and on Christmas Eve in 1794 it was totally destroyed by a fire started by a box of hot ashes left unattended in the vestry room. Undaunted, the parishoners built the church here pictured in less than a year and a half, and it was made memorable by the official ceremonies commemorating Washington's death in 1799. The "Dead March Monody" performed as a part of the doleful music selected for the occasion is still preserved at St. Michael-Zion Lutheran Church, Franklin above Race Streets, which was built in 1870 when the congregations merged, and this church was sold, torn down and replaced with a row of stores. Fire still haunted the site, for in 1878 these stores were consumned in a blaze.

took on new significance. *Ca Ira* was anathema. The times called for a spirited song, but Hopkinson had been dead for seven years. His son, Joseph, also a lawyer, recalled how he came to write *Hail, Columbia!*—

> A young man belonging to it (the theatre), whose talent was high as a singer, was about to have a benefit . . . he called on me one Saturday afternoon (at 338 Spruce Street) . . . (and) said that if he could get a patriotic song, adapted to 'The President's March' he did not doubt of a full house; that the poets of the theatrical corps had been trying . . . but had not succeeded. I told him I would try. . . . He came the next afternoon, and the song, such as it is, was ready for him. . . .

Thousands tried to get into the Chestnut Street Theatre to hear Gilbert Fox sing it on Wednesday, April 25, 1798, drawn by an advertisement the day before which simply said that after a play and epilogue "an Entire *New Song* (written by a citizen of Philadelphia), to the tune of *The President's March,* will be sung by Mr. Fox, accompanied by *full band* and the following *Grand Chorus. . . .*" William Cobbett, the eccentric Englishman who published *Porcupine's Gazette* across the street from Christ Church put an editorial beside the advertisement:

> It is not often that I interest myself in the success of *Theatrical Representations,* but I cannot help bestowing a word or two in approbation of what is advertised for tomorrow night. Mr. Fox has, with singular propriety, admitted a Song, . . . adapted to *The President's March,* which has long been the national, and is now the popular tune. Long, much too long, have the lovers of the drama been shocked and insulted with the sacrilegious hymns of atheism and murder, and the actor, let his theatrical merits be what they may, who, by his voluntary choice, first breaks through the disgraceful practice, and appeals to the virtues in place of the vices of his audience, deserves every mark of applause, which it is in the power of the public to bestow.

He was equally enthusiastic in his review on April 28:

> Never was anything received with applause so hearty and so general. The *Song* was sung at the end of the comedy . . . it was called for again at the end of the pantomine, and again after all the performance was over, and encored every time. At every repetition it was received with additional enthusiasm, 'till, towards the last, a great part of the audience, pit, box and gallery, actually joined in the chorus. It was very pleasing to observe, that the *last* stanza received peculiar marks of approbation. Every one was closed with long and loud clappings and huzzas, but no sooner than the words—
> 'Behold *the Chief who now commands*'
> were pronounced, than the house shook to its very center, the song and the whole were drowned in the enthusiastic peals of applause, and were obliged to stop and begin again and again, in order to get a hearing.

120

Bache's *Aurora*, Jefferson's backer, was predictably disgusted at an audience who were "admirers of British tyranny" and had cheered the "ridiculous bombast, the vilest adulation of the Anglo-monarchial party, and the *two Presidents*." Their ecstasy "knew no bounds, they encored, they shouted, they became Mad as the Priestess of the Delphic God!" The intense newspaper war between the *Gazette* and *Aurora* spurred added interest, and the New Theatre had a packed house for many nights running. When President and Mrs. Adams and the Cabinet appeared on April 30 and May 1 the management distributed free copies of the song, while publishers like Benjamin Carr at 122 Market Street were busy with orders from many parts of the country. In New York, where it drew large crowds, it was given the title, "Hail Columbia— Death or Liberty," and Philadelphia adopted the more abbreviated version by which it is now known. Its broad appeal stimulated a variety of song writers, but the work never caught the public fancy. *Hail Columbia!* had the advantage of a familiar score and the propitious moment, and climaxed a long struggle of one man to raise the city to a ranking position in American music. If Hallam could be hailed as the first man of the American theatre, Francis Hopkinson's crusade for good music deserves comparable recognition.

Philadelphians boasted they had become the outstanding city in America at the end of the 18th century in musical achievement. If so, it was hardly the genius of its people that merited it. There was a quiet appreciation among the more cultured and cosmopolitan, which produced the chamber music and sent young ladies off to tutors. The wealthier citizens, like the Bingham's in their lavish mansion, and the Powells in their "music rooms," did little to further the careers of struggling artists. This was to be reserved for a later period. The French presence, with scores of well educated aristocrats, gave support to the "concerts" and helped impose more exacting standards for talent. As much as anything the fact that Philadelphia was the national capital from 1790 to 1800 must be recognized as a contributing force. Foreign musicians, accustomed to the practice of royal patronage, expected the national government to fill that role, and aspirants flocked to the "metropolis."

Hail Columbia! and songs of that genre commanded the same widespread response as comparable pieces have done in every age, for they are direct, uncomplicated mirrors of a national mood. Yet there was a surprising depth of interest, as the concerts and programs at the New Theatre evidence, in the more involved compositions of Italian writers, most of whom have since faded into obscurity. Even the economic indicators point to that, as craftsmen in Pennsylvania began to build organs and harpsichords and make violins.

Franklin's own critical understanding of music is often overlooked in the amusement his invention of the "armonica" engenders today. Taking the old casual process of tapping table glasses with a knife, he designed special glasses, hemisphere-shaped with specific sized holes and varied diameters, and using thirty-seven, found them "sufficient for three octaves with all the semi-tones." By delicate grinding he tested them against "a well-tuned harpsichord." The instrument captivated Europeans, one artist giving a concert in England in 1762 and then taking it to Austria and Italy. In Vienna it was introduced in the Imperial Court and Maria Antoinette became a pupil. In Italy Metastasio composed an ode for a royal wedding in which Franklin's invention provided the accompaniment, the "nuovoa istrumento di musica . . . inventata dal celebre Dottore Franklin". In Germany it brought him as much fame as his experiments in electricity, and Mozart and Beethoven were among the many European composers who wrote compositions specifically suited to it.

The fad never quite caught on in America although, with characteristic pride, Franklin brought the idea he had conceived abroad to the city for its first American performance in December 1764 in Lodge Alley at the Assembly Room. It seemed to evaporate entirely by about 1800, attributed to the "nerves" performers got from the reverberations. It might have had greater success for a far longer period had Franklin attributed the idea to some ethereal inspiration, rather than beer glasses—but that is the enduring charm of the man.

8

"THE LINE OF BEAUTY":
The Painter's Brush Found Fertile Ground in Penn's Model City

*   *   *   *   *

Painting done in the best manner by Gustavus Hesselius from Stockholm and John Winters from London. Viz. Coat of Arms drawn on Coach, Chaise &c or any kinds of ornaments, Landskips, Signs, Show Boards, Ship and House Painting, Guilding of all sort, Writing in Gold or Color, old Pictures cleaned and mended.

—The Pennsylvania Gazette, December 11, 1740

*   *   *   *   *

Life and Times in Colonial Philadelphia

The plight of the Philadelphia painter is mirrored in this advertisement. Thomas Pratt, toward the end of the 18th century said sadly the fine arts were "very poorly encouraged." Benjamin Rush agreed that "portrait painters . . . have been obliged to travel occasionally from one state to another to support themselves. . . ." Gustavus Hesselius could vouch for that. He had long worked in Maryland and Delaware before settling in Philadelphia at age 53, in 1735. Much as he might have liked to concentrate on portraiture, the alternate services listed were the stuff of the artist's life. Few escaped the sight of seeing their hard-learned talent reflected in the design of a sign for some prosaic pub, battered by winter winds and blistered by summer sun. Yet for most such signs were an accurate measure of their abilities. Rare indeed were those competent to portray a face invested with life and warmth.

In 1740 Philadelphians were not inclined to order "Landskips" unless they were "perspectives" of their own country estate. Such work usually went to journeymen who peddled from one to another and, like their mediocre renditions, drifted aimlessly into anoynmity. Eventually the Peales would sketch the Schuylkill, and Birch and Sully catch its beauty in the soft light of 19th century summers. In Regency London and bookstalls along the Seine engravings of these vistas, particularly those showing the Grecian splendor of the pink-columned waterworks, would find an eager market. Philadelphians themselves would melt into languid appreciation of the river's loveliness, but not yet. In the 17th and 18th centuries, they were too immersed in the act of creation.

By 1762 they began to buy "Glazed Pictures" at the Kennedy's Print Shop, 2nd and Chestnut, which featured "scriptural, historical, humorous and miscellaneous" subjects. The technique of putting glass over a picture and tracing it in color could be executed swiftly by deft hands, but European experience was so superior the Kennedy brothers imported their initial stock. Framed in a black molding with goldleafed corners the pictures, usually small, relieved the white-washed starkness of rooms that were not apt to know wallpaper until 1790. Only the affluent like Dr. Franklin could afford such innovations in his new home, "A plain brick building, three stories high, about forty feet front, thirty feet deep, with an entry through the centre." Deborah Franklin had misgivings about hanging any until Franklin returned from London, partly because of the wallpaper. With the exception of "The Pickter of the Erel of Bute," she wrote, she had deposited in his room "all your close and the pickters as I donte drive nailes leste it shold not be write."

The Kennedys prospered and in 1770 adopted "The Sign of West's Head" as their trademark, basking in the reflected glory of their fellow Pennsylvanian. They offered an extensive array of "elegant Gardens"

124

and pastoral scenes, foreign and domestic. Some others took advantage of the increased interest. Nicholas Brooks invited the public "to regale themselves" with his acquisitions, each "exhibited in a convenient Room." John Winters in Arch Street still clung to portraits, specializing in Holbein's "heads." All this, however, was peripheral art, and the city's cultural progress had to be measured by the "heads" of its citizens, rather than those of Henry VIII, Anne Boleyn or the Queen of Scots. The Quaker distaste for vanity and concern over "graven images" eliminated most of them as customers. A few would reconcile the temptation with the text and pose, but with the scrupulous supervision members of the sect exercised over their brethren's activities, they were rare exceptions to a well observed rule. Penn is a case in point.

In 1740 Hesselius, in this field, was rivaled only by Robert Feke, who came from his Newport, Rhode Island home annually to make "likenesses" of Philadelphians, until 1750 when he drops out of sight. Hesselius (1682-1755) was a sort of spiritual wanderer, constantly searching for self-discovery through religion. When he came to America he was a Swedish Lutheran, then in Maryland joined the Church of England and between 1743 and 1750 was a member of the Moravian Church in Philadelphia. Sensitive art experts read into his paintings signs of inner tensions, although the struggle to free himself of the European tendency to flatter his subjects goes more in the direction of integrity in art form than a purification process of the soul. He was at his best with two Indian chiefs, whom Thomas Penn commissioned him to paint in 1735 at Pennsbury. Their abject look of resignation has been hailed as a mark of Hesselius' realism, and given rise to effusions about foreknowledge the two Lenni-Lenapes supposedly had of the doom of their noble race. Historically, they were undoubtedly glum about the possibility of fraud in the celebrated "Walking Purchase," by which certain boundaries were to be fixed. The walk had been discussed and deferred since 1686, but was imminent at the time of the paintings. It finally took place in 1737 and any suspicions the Indians had at the moment of sitting for Hesselius were confirmed at that time, for Thomas Penn's highly trained walkers, following a devious route, walked twice as far as was anticipated and acquired twice as much land.

Like Gilbert Stuart a half-century later, Hesselius emphasized face rather than costume. Feke preferred more distance from his subject. A comparison of the two artists can be seen in Hesselius' loose, competent but somewhat bland "head" of Charles Willing, and Feke's depiction of his wife. Mrs. Willing seems self-conscious of her amply proportioned body, but the artist's precision in the designs on her figured dress gives

(Pa. Hist. & Museum Comm., Harrisburg; original in Hist. Soc. of Penna., Phila.)

LAPOWINSO
Hesselius caught the Delaware chief's apprehensions about the "Walking Purchase."

credibility to the definition of her face, and she emerges, overweight and all, as a handsome woman. Neither Hesselius nor Feke had the relaxed warmth of Johann Valentin Haidt (1700-1780), but he did not linger long enough in Philadelphia after landing in 1754 to be considered a member of the art circle. No American artist could match his credentials, for he had studied and worked in Dresden, Augsburg, Prague, Vienna, Florence, Sienna and Rome. He seems to have moved quickly to Bethlehem, where under his talented brush Biblical figures and his co-religionists alike smile good-naturedly for posterity. More than seventy of these vivacious portraits are extant, although curiously Haidt is almost wholly overlooked by critics, chroniclers and connoissseurs. Hesselius caught the attention of Philadelphians with a rendition of the Crucifixion he executed during his Moravian period. Only a few of his works remain.

Feke was the "society" artist, and in addition to the Willings, painted the Shippens and the Francis's. By 1748, ten-year old Benjamin West, born in nearby Swarthmore, was as good as most professionals in the city. His skill in drawing amazed visitors to his father's tavern and so impressed a Philadelphian that he took the youngster to meet William Williams, a Welshman, who resided at "The Sign of Hogarth's Head" off Chestnut Street. There West for the first time saw a brush, easel, and the various accouterments of the commercial artist. For his part, he had made his own brushes from fur plucked from his cat's tail and learned to mix colors from friendly Indians. Williams provided an entire spectrum of talent for Philadelphia. He taught drawing, painting, flute and oboe, voice—painted scenery for the Southwark Theatre, dabbled in landscape gardening, architecture, wrote poetry and in his old age turned out an adventure novel, concocted from strands of stories, professedly autobiographical, with which he regaled the wide-eyed West. The few pieces of his art that remain, reflect a stiff attempt to blend Hogarth with romanticism. If he contributed a mere mite to West's career, he opened new horizons for the uneducated boy with his vivid descriptions of shipwrecks, savages and flaming red flamingoes. West's talents were too strong to be mired by Williams' pedestrianism or his contemporary John Wollaston's "almond-eyed" styles. The incredible ability to transform a once-told tale into a remarkably accurate portrayal of the scene was displayed in his "Death of Socrates", done when he was scarcely eighteen. With no background of the era he costumed his characters so precisely, Dr. William Smith invited him to the College of Philadelphia for a crash course on the antiquities.

While there he became a close friend of young Thomas Godfrey and Francis Hopkinson along with the sons of leading Philadelphia merchants. It was through the latter that he was offered a free voyage to Italy, an opportunity for which he readied himself by traveling between Philadelphia and New York painting portraits. At twenty he sailed down the Delaware never to return. Lionized by the Italians as the living realization of Rousseau's "child of nature" he supplemented his natural abilities by close study of the great masters. As he prepared to come home, his father suggested he visit England and there he was befriended by George III, became the leading challenger to Sir Joshua Reynolds and succeeded him as president of the Royal Academy. Yet his attachment for the country and the countryside that one day would be the home of the "Brandywine Tradition" was so strong, that despite his close friendship with the King, he never foreswore America during the Revolution. Philadelphians acclaimed him in absentia, and aspiring young artists from the city were received in his studio with gentleness and encouragement. His Philadelphia fiancee, whose parents had objected to marriage when he was still in town, "eloped" to London to become his bride.

Years later, when the King became deranged and susceptible to stories whispered by his enemies that he was disloyal to the monarch, West lost his pension and the prospect of recovering large sums the Crown owed him for commissions. Even though his future was bleak, he responded to an appeal from the Pennsylvania Hospital for a contribution by offering to paint a scene of Christ healing the sick. Before it was completed the 73-year old West was offered 3000 guineas by the British Institution—the highest sum ever offered in England up to that time for the work of a living artist. Unable to refuse, he made a copy for the hospital where it still hangs. Philadelphians bought tickets to see it and the $25,000 thus raised was enough to endow thirty beds. Nathaniel Hawthorne said if West had done nothing else, this would "entitle him to an honorable remembrance forever." The aging artist received 2500 guineas in royalties from prints, and this single masterpiece, painted on the edge of despair, made him wealthier than he had ever been.

Immediately he began an even more massive canvas, "Christ Rejected," and when it was exhibited in Pall Mall, crowds lined the streets waiting to see it. He rejected 8000 guineas for it. This, together with "Death on a Pale Horse" are among his works in the Pennsylvania Academy of Fine Arts, which appropriately chose him in 1805 as its first honorary president. The Historical Society of Pennsylvania has many of his early drawings, numerous manuscripts and his idealized painting of Dr. Smith as "St. Ignatius." His choice of Smith as a model would have been vigorously challenged by Franklin who intensely disliked the college provost, and could see nothing resembling sainthood in him. West died in 1820, and is buried next to Reynolds in St. Paul's, his childhood wish to stand before kings granted, and his dream of returning to Philadelphia denied.

Fate dealt quite differently with another talented youth. John Meng (1734-1754) of Germantown, might never have made the "grand tour" student artists deemed indispensable to Italy and England. His father was vehemently opposed to a career in the two things his son loved most, art and music. Described as a "Kit-kat nicely painter," he seems to have had no formal training, although one scholar thinks the Hesselius—father and son—influence shines through. His untimely death in the West Indies at twenty, lends poignancy to a self portrait which shows a well-tailored teenager brightly anticipating a future that was to be all too brief. Clutched in his right hand is a sonata for violin, emblematic of his two loves, and conveying a respectful but firm challenge to his parent's position.

The peripatetic condition of Philadelphia artists immediately became apparent to young Charles Willson Peale in 1762. After a brief stint as a saddlemaker the Marylander journeyed to the city to look into the field of art. Only one artist, of nearly fifty, was available, and "Mr. Steele" graciously took Peale across a cluttered "painting room" and showed him a self-portrait which the visitor thought was well-drawn, but garishly-colored "purple red and the middle tints of blueish tinge." Fortunately, Peale took Steele's advice to call at the home of James Claypoole, and there saw some more proficient portraits. Claypoole was to forsake art for politics and become Sheriff of Philadelphia, but he had opened in 1743 a bookshop in Walnut Street that carried "most Sorts of Painter's Colours, ready prepar'd for Use and neatly put up in Bladders."

His portrait of Rebecca Doz, which has come down through the years, shows a stiffly posed girl holding a toy. A nephew, Matthew Pratt, a friend of West's, attained more skill and stature, but had the advantage of studying with West in London. He was there, however, at a period when West was going through an ostentatious stage in his painting, and it is believed that this negative influence, carried home, limited Pratt's concepts and consigned him to mediocrity.

Armed with a selection of paints he bought at Christopher Marshall's "Oil and Colour Shop at the Sign of the Golden Ball" in Chestnut Street, and a thick book, *The Handmaid of the Arts*, Peale returned to Maryland to prepare for still another career. Meanwhile he announced to the people of Annapolis that in addition to his "SADDLERS Business" he "MAKES, Cleans and Repairs CLOCKS, and Cleans and Mends WATCHES. . . ." This venture did not last long because an indignant, able watchmaker took issue with "the unskillful and injudicious Pretenders" against whom he felt it his civic duty to warn an otherwise unsuspecting public.

(Hist. & Museum Comm., Harrisburg; original in Hist. Soc. of Penna., Phila.)

BENJAMIN FRANKLIN—1789

Anticipating Franklin's death the Philosophical Society commissioned Peale to paint this portrait in 1789. Franklin, who was in the process of dying, was as obliging as possible—but suggested Peale work from one he had done in 1785 and he would try to sit for such changes as age made in the interim. But Franklin only managed to sit for 15 minutes at a time because he was in pain, and the compassionate Peale finished it without troubling him any further. The Society rejected the portrait, but was so impressed with the detailed lounging robe Franklin is wearing they ordered a portrait of David Rittenhouse, who turns up in the same robe.

"The Line of Beauty"

The resilient Peale became a permanent resident in Philadelphia in 1774, although as he progressed in his painting he frequently had come to the city in quest of commissions. He had been to London and studied under West, but came home embittered because the British derided his painting of William Pitt whom he unfortunately dressed in a toga. During his stay, however, he called on Dr. Franklin, still in London in 1767.

He was admitted to Franklin's residence and told by the maid to go up to the second-floor study. Reverentially tip-toeing up the steps he timidly looked into the study, and found him dallying with a chambermaid. He quickly sketched the intimacy in his notebook, then retreated to make a noisier approach giving the distinguished Philadelphian adequate time to assume a more formal attitude. The notebook with the sketch is among the Peale papers in the Philosophical Society, and for years the librarian banned it to even the staff. A more enlightened and younger librarian, Dr. Whitfield Bell, has made it available.

Peale was one of the first to paint Washington, traveling to Mount Vernon when he was still a colonel in the Virginia militia. Thereafter he would paint him at Trenton, Princeton and Valley Forge and through his years as President. A thoroughly delightful person, Peale had boundless energies which could not be denied. By two wives he had numerous children and christened some of them with names that virtually forced them into art, Rembrandt, Titian, Raphael included. Absorbed by war, politics and work, the ambitious Peale was active in various phases of Philadelphia life. Since painters had to depend upon cooperative shopkeepers to display their works, Peale, on July 18, 1786 opened his own gallery in "part of his House" at the corner of 3rd and Lombard, advertising it as a "Repository for Natural Curiosities." Interspersed with his paintings he displayed animals and birds he personally stuffed. Franklin contributed his pet Angora after its demise, but the taxidermy failed. Washington's deceased golden pheasants did better. Later as the collection expanded to mastadon bones, Peale took rooms in Philosophical Hall. He got the idea and some of his exhibits from Swiss-born Pierre DuSimitere, an erstwhile artist John Adams described as a "very curious man."

Convinced that the times were historic, DuSimitere painstakingly gathered newspapers, pamphlets and proclamations relating to the Revolution, and pleaded with other colonies to follow his example for the benefit of later generations. He was so dedicated to Philadelphia that he turned down an invitation for a short stay in the country with a statement he had not ventured beyond the sight of Christ Church's steeple in the ten years he was in town. A specialist in miniatures, he also did pencil and chalk portraits of public figures. Among the items displayed in his museum were some drawings by John Andre, who had studied under the same

131

teacher in Geneva, and whom he thought a "very great" talent. Andre's sketch of Peggy Shippen and a miniature of Rebecca Franks are some of the memorabilia of his stay in Philadelphia.

From Peale's Museum came the idea for an American counterpart of the Royal Academy which he called "Columbianum, or American Academy of Painting, Sculpture, Architecture, etc."

It attracted artists from the city's large foreign colony. Miniaturist Robert Field boasted to friends back in England that he expected to make

> a figure in an Academy of Arts and Sciences, now establishing here, the plans for which are the most enlarged, liberal and grand of any in the world. The President is much delighted with it, and will, when it is in a riper state, become the principal patron.

Such great expectations were not part of Peale's plan, and he protested he wanted nothing resembling monarchial support. A factional fight ensued and the idea came crashing to a conclusion. One of his objectives was to provide a school where his progeny could get a technical education in art. It was financially impossible to send them abroad, and with so many trained artists in Philadelphia it seemed logical to bring Mahomet to the mountain. With the disappointed foreigners going off to start an Academy of their own, Peale persisted in getting the school underway. He included in the curriculum a life class, but the baker who posed nude became so embarrassed under the scrutiny of the students, he pulled up his trousers and fled. Peale promptly stripped off his own clothes, but apparently was not an acceptable substitute. Nine years later, in 1805, the Pennsylvania Academy of Fine Arts opened and Peale, one of its founders, would have been amused that nearly a century later Thomas Eakins would quit its faculty because there was objection to his life studies.

Before the Columbianum closed in 1796 it held an exhibition. Thirty-seven painters were represented. Landscapes and still-lifes were almost as numerous as portraits, indicative of broadening tastes in art appreciation. Peale had tried to anticipate a trend in this direction back in 1787, when he experimented with perspective prints of Philadelphia. He began, and presumably ended, with Lombard Street, showing his home in the left foreground. To give it mobility and human interest, he depicted a little girl crying over a pie she had dropped, while some chimney-sweeps laugh at her misery. This field was soon to be preempted by William Birch, whose superbly detailed sketches of Philadelphia at the turn of the 19th century breathe life into its past.

The vain, hard-drinking Gilbert Stuart came to the city in 1795, carrying a letter of introduction from John Jay to President Washington,

LANSDOWNE HOUSE

Governor John Penn built this picturesque Italianate retreat on the west bank of the Schuylkill about 1773, and broadened its surrounding acreage to 200. The main building had recessed wings and a two-storied portico, with large bay windows to command the view of the carefully nurtured landscape. William Bingham leased it from Penn, now back in England, in 1789, and with a penchant for "country seats" to supplement the mansion house in town, bought in 1791 another place on Black Point in northern New Jersey, overlooking the ocean. Penn died in 1795 and his widow deeded "Landsdowne" to the husband of her niece, James Greenleaf. Greenleaf, driven into bankruptcy by the failure of Robert Morris, gave Bingham the opportunity to buy it at sheriff's sale in 1797 for $55,210. As with the town house, entertainment and culture at Lansdowne dazzled visitors, but a cold contracted on a sleighing party brought the beauteous Mrs. Bingham to a premature death, age 37, in Bermuda where she had been taken to recuperate, in 1801. Three years after, Bingham died at Bath, England, and "Lansdowne" descended to his daughter, Anne and her husband, Alexander Baring. They added a smaller house and spent intermittent periods here across the years, although in 1816-1817 it was rented by Joseph Bonaparte, Napoleon's brother, who still clung to briefly remembered reigns as king of Spain and Naples, as pretensions to royalty, and complained to all who would listen about the ill-treatment his more famous brother accorded him.

Gradually the place fell into an era of decline, cared for by one "Mr. Bones" who lived in the "hut", set afire by some youngsters celebrating July 4, 1854 with fireworks. For the next twelve years the damaged "Landsdowne" was neglected, and a group of philanthropic Philadelphians realizing it could be restored for a moderate sum, bought and gave it to the City. It was incorporated into the expanding Fairmount Park but had the misfortune of being on the site chosen for the Centennial Exposition of 1876. It was torn down to make way for Horticultural Hall, the city's answer to England's Crystal Palace which fell victim to depleted budgets during the Depression years and eventually to wind and weather, and was dismantled in 1954.

who, by this time was heartily weary of sitting for painters. So many of the Peale family worked on him at one time that Stuart quipped to an unamused Martha her husband was in danger of being "Peeled." Born in Newport in 1755, the son of an unsuccessful snuffmaker, Stuart sailed off for England on his second voyage on June 16, 1775, the day before Bunker Hill. He spent seventeen years in the British Isles and expensive tastes sent him scurrying back home in 1792, a step ahead of Irish and Scottish creditors whom he pledged to repay from the fortune he expected to make on portraits of Washington. Washington disliked the man intensely, and when Stuart tried to get him relax by suggesting he forget he was "General Washington and that I am Stuart the painter," got the cold reply, "Mr. Stuart need never feel the need of forgetting who he is, or who General Washington is." The President's face struck Stuart as extraordinary. "The sockets of the eyes . . . were larger than what I ever met with . . . and the upper part of the nose broader. All his features were indicative of the strongest passions." Had he been an Indian, Stuart felt, he would have been the fiercest in the forests.

While he was not wholly satisfied with his first effort, Stuart made fifteen copies, and then was commissioned by the wealthy William Bingham to do a full-length portrait of Washington for Lord Lansdowne. Working in his studio near the Library Company on the southeast corner of Fifth and Chestnut, Stuart found the taciturn subject challenging. Washington was troubled with new, ill-fitting false teeth, and Stuart was troubled by Washington's "aldermanic proportions," accentuated by the vest he was wearing. His shoulders were "high and narrow" and "his hands and feet remarkably large." Yet it was completed and Bingham assured the artist he would have the work copyrighted so that Stuart would get royalties on any engravings made in England. He apparently forgot, and when the mercernary artist discovered the fact, he was so infuriated he stopped in the middle of the beautiful Mrs. Bingham's portrait. It was a costly burst of anger, for the Binghams were the most influential couple in Philadelphia society. Banishment from Anne Bingham's salon was tantamount to excommunication. Still the loss was not one-sided. Stuart's sharp wit, his skill on the harpsichord and ability to match the graceful verse of the pretty Mrs.. Perez Morton, whose portrait he had done twice, added zest to a mansion frequented by Washington, Jefferson, Hamilton and scores of other prominent figures.

Stuart bought his "wine, brandy and gin by the cask" and his flushed face, red nose and liquored breath sometimes made it an ordeal for the sitter. "On one occasion he was seen kicking a large piece of beef

BEHIND THE STATE HOUSE

Across the gardens behind the State House at 7.55 A.M. on a summer's day the half-open door of Philosophical Hall can be seen over the little boy's shoulder. Peale's Museum was there. The original steeple on "Independence Hall" was dismantled in 1781 because the wood was rotting, and replaced with a hip roof. The famous bell hangs in the brick tower where windows have been replaced with "sounding boards." A smaller bell, in a cupola on the roof, tolls the hours recorded by the tall case clock. These both were sold to St. Augustine's Catholic Church when a new steeple, with its own clock, was put up in 1828. They were destroyed when the church was burned in the "Know Nothing" riots of 1848. Scars from the fire can still be seen in the church, preserved as a grim reminder of troubled times. One of the improvements made here in 1783 was the construction of "the new privy." The location, probably at 5th & Chestnut, was sufficiently well-known to legislators that the appropriation did not bother specifying the site.

across the street from his house to Diehl's, his butcher" in protest that it was not fit to handle.

During the summers from 1796 to 1799 Stuart had his studio in a small stone building behind his house at 5140 Germantown Avenue. It was here Washington grudgingly came at the behest of Martha who wanted a personal portrait for herself. Stuart claimed that he got Washington to relax by chatting about horses, but the President to relieve the tedium of the task and the painter, brought to the sittings General Knox and winsome Harriet Chew. Aware at last he had an animated Washington, Stuart stalled delivery until he had a chance to make copies which, somewhat coincidentally, he called his "hundred dollar bills." This was to be the most popular of all the Washington portraits, appearing on

135

the dollar bill and in countless classrooms. The delay irritated Washington and it was some time before Martha finally got one of the copies. She was not pleased, because she did not think it a "good likeness." Unperturbed, Stuart sold at least seventy and had to fend off many forgeries. In 1803 he took his easel off to the new Federal city on the Potomac, leaving Germantown with a grocer's bill of $216 unpaid.

Eighteenth century portraits are often suspect, unless the artist's ability and integrity has been well established. Historians today prefer to examine, whenever possible, several different artist's handiwork on a given subject before attempting a description of what the individual looked like. Philadelphians of the period, with becoming modesty, had their "heads" updated from time to time, so that a basic portrait supposedly grew with them.

Most cherished of all "likenesses," however, were the miniatures since they could be conveniently carried by a loved one, who often snipped a phrase from a letter or a lock of hair and tucked it in the frame to accentuate the association.

The earliest Philadelphia miniature seems to be that of Governor William Keith, done in India ink about 1723 by John Watson. Watson lived in Perth Amboy, New Jersey and appears to have made a tidy sum from his talent. His technique presaged the more translucent watercolors, oils and enamels subsequently used by Philadelphia artists. Peale, his sons Rembrandt and Raphael and his brother James were in the forefront of this media, along with Matthew Pratt and inventor Robert Fulton. The handsome Fulton came to Philadelphia from Lancaster, apprenticed to a silversmith and then a watchmaker. The first city directory in 1790 lists him as a painter and gives his address as the northeast corner of 2nd and Walnut, where it is believed he occupied quarters in the Old Krider Gunshop. A somewhat shaky tradition says as a child he was a student in an art class John Andre conducted while a prisoner on parole in Lancaster. Fulton studied under West, but experts say his portraits and miniatures are closer to James Peale's technique. Henry Benbridge, a Philadelphian whose early affluence permitted him to be a dilettante in art, was tutored in Italy by the same artists who instructed West. In London he exhibited a portrait of Franklin at the Royal Academy. An able miniaturist, he did not reach the height of his abilities until he settled in the South, and there his mature work compared favorably with Copley in the field of portraiture.

In the preoccupation with painters, the genius of William Rush is too little remembered in Philadelphia art. A wood sculptor of rare talent, he carved figureheads for ships, did a magnificent duplicate in wood of Houdon's life-sized Washington. He sculpted two classical figures for the New Theater's facade, and his rendition of "The Crucifixion" for

St. Augustine's Catholic Church was destroyed in the fire that damaged the church during the "Know Nothing" riots in 1848. His statue of Washington and an eagle, done for a tavern, are among the rare pieces that remain.

From Dr. Christopher deWitt's crude sketch of the mystic Kelpius in 1715, Philadelphia came far in the century. Of the triumvirate of artists associated with it who gained renown, only Benjamin West could be claimed, if one stretches the city limits a few miles, as a native son. Peale and Stuart, like Gustavus Hesselius, had been drawn by its position and power. By one of those curious quirks, West, whose affection for Philadelphia has been recounted, did Penn a disservice. In his imaginative portrayal of the founder's treaty with the Indians under the great elm, West depicted Penn as a squat, rotund man. Had he remembered that Penn was a striking-looking, strong thirty-eight year old who wore a blue sash that day, it might have helped the Proprietor's image considerably, for through this single painting, millions across the span of nearly two centuries have formed their image of William Penn.

9

INNER LIGHT AND EXTERIOR DARKNESS:

The Battle Between Good and Evil was Well Fought in Philadelphia

*   *   *   *   *

It is almost impossible to describe how few good and how many exceptionally godless, wicked people have come into this country every year. The whole country is being flooded with ordinary, extraordinary and unprecedented wickedness and crimes. Surely the rod of God cannot be spared much longer. Our old residents are mere stupid children in sin when compared with the new arrivals! Oh, what a fearful thing it is to have so many thousands of unruly and brazen sinners come into this free air and unfenced country!

—Pastor Henry Muhlenberg, Philadelphia, October 1750

*   *   *   *   *

Inner Light and Exterior Darkness

I t is doubtful whether the new arrivals brought any sin with which Philadelphians, with their plays and parties, were not already familiar. But when Henry Melchior Muhlenberg, a missionary sent from Halle, Saxony, arrived in Philadelphia in 1742, aged 31, to minister to the German Lutherans, he seems to have been in a state of shock from the moment he assumed his pastorate. The prospect of sin terrified him, and if he saw the city and its environs through a glass darkly, the stereoptic view was a bit illusory.

Like most seminary-trained clergymen, Muhlenberg had a hard time adjusting to the atmosphere in America. Accustomed to the authoritarianism which European churchmen enjoyed, he was jolted when one of his Philadelphia flock bluntly served notice: "I pay (the parson) by the year, but if his preaching does not please my taste, I'll go to another church where I can get it for nothing." Back home in Germany congregations were led by their pastors. Here he discovered "In religious and church matters each has the right to do what he pleases. . . . Everything depends on the vote of the majority."

The intrinsic beauty of Penn's phrase "Holy Experiment" made dogmas vulnerable, and the inability of the mother churches to get ministers to cross the ocean left the defense of a particular faith in the hands of laymen. Muhlenberg had some unChristian comments about his predecessor:

> Mr. Kraft now took off his hypocritical mask because it no longer yielded any returns in Philadelphia. He became the boon companion of some worthless, drunken schoolmasters who wander about the country as preachers and make money with the Lord's Supper, baptism and weddings. He got drunk with those fellows and carried on high.

Right or wrong, a considerable number of people wanted the old wine served in new vessels. Profound theology or stentorian strictures which sounded so comfortable in 15th century ornate churches on the Continent seemed impractical in the new society. Franklin, listening to Jedediah Andrews, pastor of the Presbyterian church in the city, summed it up this way:

> His discourses were chiefly either polemic arguments, or explications of the peculiar doctrines of our sect, and were all to me very dry, uninteresting, and unedifying, since not a single moral principle was inculcated or enforc'd, their aim seeming to be rather to make us good Presbyterians rather than good citizens.

Yet those who faithfully attended various services were not wholly

139

willing to settle for the gospel according to Poor Richard. The struggle was for some sort of a middle ground.

The Quaker influence was subtly profound. It demonstrated to Philadelphians of diversified creeds that ministers were not indispensable, and the warm glow of "inner light" with its doctrine of personal revelation, appealed to some who were not willing to take it with the limitations of Quaker tenets. Self-reliance, essential to survival in the business of material things, seemed to have a logical corollary in the spiritual world as well.

Pennsylvania, more than any other colony offered, thanks to Penn, the ideal conditions for religious individualism. Philadelphians might be puzzled by John Kelpius and his forty-two monks who lived in a cave along the Wissahickon, under the caption, "The Society of the Woman in the Wilderness," adapted from the Book of Revelations. Since their mysticism made it hard to determine whether they belonged to the "Inner Light" or "Outer Light" sector, the citizens were content to create a new classification, "Peculiar Light." The experiment did not endure much beyond Kelpius' death in 1708, after which the majority of the monks forsook solitude and celibacy for marriage, but Dr. Christopher Witt's translations of Kelpius' philosophy showed that the circle, of which Witt, "a skilled physician" was a member, were a well-educated group. Witt's many talents included one that was bound to fascinate— "casting nativities"—which susceptible Philadelphians agreed demanded "mathematical and astronomical learning."

On market days, around the year 1736, Michael Welfare, a "Christian philosopher of the Conestogoe" appeared with his "linen hat," prophet's beard and long staff to warn the populace about the need for "speedy repentance"—then did a brisk business selling copies of his "warning" for four pence apiece. Another "philosopher" declared he would walk on the Delaware. When his venture ended with a splash, he forsook the city and sailed for Londonderry, Ireland to preach repentance to the inhabitants thereof. Benjamin Lay, after acquiring some fame for being the first in Pennsylvania to call for the end of slavery, took up solitary residence in a cave on the York Road. When he emerged in 1741 he called himself "the singular Pythagorean, cynical Christian philosopher" and took a box of his late wife's china to the market, where he regaled a crowd with the evils of tea, and started to break, piece by piece, the costly set. His audience reacted in an unanticipated way. They "upset" him and ran off with the unbroken remainder. In 1742 the "eccentric and strange" Count Zizendorf came to town, seeking young women to join his daughter and him in a spiritual conclave in Germany. Parents who protested the taking of their daughters were termed "notorious children of the devil, and you, the woman . . . a twofold child of hell." Although Zizendorf did constructive work in establishing the Moravian communities at Bethlehem and Nazareth in Pennsylvania, Peter Kalm said "his uncommon behaviour here persuaded many Englishmen of rank that he was disordered in his head." Muhlenberg was chagrined to find, among the odd cults, the "Newborns" who, he said, "suddenly through inspiration and heavenly visions, through dreams and the like" claim to "receive the new birth" and then "they are God and Christ himself, can no longer sin, and are infallible."

The city's spiritual scene to 1750 was one of confusion, and not even the more organized denominations were free of difficulties. At the outset the Presbyterians and the Baptists worshipped together in "the Barbadoes-lot store," a small frame one-and-a-half story building with a peaked roof. When the Presbyterians outnumbered the nine Baptists by 1698 they unceremoniously evicted them, and they were forced to find a haven in Anthony Morris' brewhouse on Water Street, just above the Drawbridge. The Quakers in 1692 experienced a schism that shook them to their foundations. George Keith, a Scot convert, had been brought to Philadelphia as a schoolmaster, and his abilities led some to believe he would attain the eminence of the great George Fox, who had founded the sect. Then suddenly Keith, in the meeting house on the bank overlooking the Delaware, denounced participation in politics as an anathema to the Quaker creed and began to challenge some of their concepts of Christ. In an attempt to keep some sort of order a platform was built at the opposite end of the house where Keith could quietly preach to those who wanted to hear or share his views. It developed, however, into a shouting match between Keith and the conservative spokesman on the other platform. Peace-loving partisans of both factions came in with axes and dismantled the two platforms so that calm could be restored. Later the Keithians, or "Christian Quakers" built their own meeting house at the southwest corner of Second and Arch, and in 1707 the displaced Baptists left the brewhouse and joined them, sharing a more suitable setting.

Secular control of the congregations produced a curious byproduct. It turned the leading denominations into political parties. From the outset, Philadelphia Quakers disagreed with William Penn about letting non-Quakers share the privileges and responsibilities of government. They saw, particularly in the Church of England, a potentially dangerous foe. Up to the eve of the Revolution, there was a constant jockeying for position, with coalitions between the Quaker-German Reformed and the Anglican-Presbyterians struggling for political supremacy. Basically the Quakers and the German sects found a common cause in pacifism, while the Anglicans and Presbyterians grew increasingly concerned about an adequate defense against disenchanted Indians and the persistent threat of the French. In Philadelphia the differences were more sharply delineated, for the Anglicans saw in many Quaker policies a paralyzing effect on the city's progress. Quakers, for instance, felt a practical secondary education was sufficient for children. Anglicans thought the establishment of a college was essential. Quaker insistence on their moral precepts being written into law irritated Anglicans who enjoyed a more relaxed posture toward living. More and more, the Anglicans felt the only solution was to get rid of the Penn proprietary rights in Pennsylvania and change the province into a Crown colony. William Penn, just before his death, reached the same conclusion but for different reasons. Disillusioned by the heavy debt the intransigent Quakers forced upon him, and the constant bickering, he was ready to sell the "Holy Experiment" to the Royal government, but his strong-minded second wife, Hannah Callowhill Penn, taking the reins from his disabled hands, determined to preserve it for his heirs.

Against this background the appearance of a twenty-four-year-old Anglican clergyman in Philadelphia in October 1739 took on singular significance. George Whitefield was not merely a strong preacher. He was a phenomenon. David Garrick said he could reduce an audience to tears by simply pronouncing "Mesopotamia." He was in disfavor with his superiors in the Church of England because he railed against the indolence and luxury with which he felt it was engrossed. Christ Church, therefore, refused to let him use its pulpit, so he appeared on the balcony of a house at 177 South Second Street, at the corner of Little Dock Street. There he fired the opening salvos of what was to become in American church history, the "Great Awakening." A crowd estimated at 15,000 gathered to listen to him, and his dramatic, evangelistic style startled them, accustomed as they were to the dry rigidity of their own ministers or the dull indifference of lay preachers. Franklin came out of curiosity, and commented on the series of his sermons:

> The multitudes of all sects and denominations that attended . . . were enormous, and it was matter of speculation to me . . . to observe the extraordinary influence of his oratory on his hearers, and how much they admired and respected him notwithstanding his common abuse of them by assuring them that they were naturally half beasts and half devils. . . ."

As Whitefield moved to different locations around the city Franklin became intrigued with determining how far his voice carried:

> He preached one evening from the top of the courthouse steps, which are in the middle of Market Street and on the west side of Second Street, which crosses it at right angles. Being among the hindmost in Market

142

Inner Light and Exterior Darkness

(Hist. & Museum Comm., Harrisburg)

JEMIMA WILKINSON

This is hardly a flattering portrait of the attractive young woman who embarked on a "Holy Experiment" of her own. The dark hair, luminous eyes and fine teeth as well as other features Philadelphians admired do not come through too well in this drawing. Possibly it was made when she was somewhat older, but then again, the artist may not have been up to the challenge.

Street, I had the curiosity to learn how far he could be heard, by retiring backwards down the street towards the river; and I found his voice distinct till I came near Front Street, when some noise in that street obscured it. Imagining then a semicircle, of which my distance should be the radius, and that it were filled with auditors to each of whom I allowed two square feet, I computed that he might be heard by more than thirty thousand. This reconciled me to the newspaper accounts of his having preached to twenty-five thousand people in the fields, and to the ancient stories of generals haranguing whole armies, of which I had sometimes doubted.

143

Whitefield was ostensibly on a fund-raising tour for an "Orphan House" he had founded in Georgia. Franklin tried to convince him it would be cheaper to build the orphanage in Philadelphia, where labor and materials were plentiful, and bring the children to it.

> I happened soon after to attend one of his sermons, in the course of which I perceived he intended to finish with a collection, and I silently resolved he should get nothing from me. I had in my pocket a handful of copper money, three or four silver dollars, and five pistoles in gold. As he proceeded I began to soften, and concluded to give the coppers. Another stroke of his oratory made me ashamed of that, and determined me to give the silver. And he finished so admirably that I emptied my pocket wholly into the collector's dish, gold and all.

Franklin arranged to publish Whitefield's sermons, and the minister said he was praying for his conversion, "but" Franklin grinned, he "never had the satisfaction of believing that his prayers were heard."

The impact on Philadelphia was astounding. "From being thoughtless or indifferent about religion," Franklin said, "it seemed as if all the world were growing religious, so that one could not walk through the town in an evening without hearing psalms sung in different families of every street."

Annoyed at the discourtesy of Christ Church in refusing to allow Whitefield access to the premises, Franklin and some friends began a large building at Fourth and Arch Streets, which was almost completed when the young minister came back to the city in 1740. Franklin said it was

> expressly for the use of any preacher of any religious persuasion who might desire to say something to the people at Philadelphia; the design in building not being to accomodate any particular sect, but the inhabitants in general; so that even if the Mufti of Constantinople were to send a missionary to preach Mohammedanism to us, he would find a pulpit at his service.

The Quakers were delighted with the discomfiture of the Anglicans. Normally their arguments with each other were caustically tinged, as when a Quaker confronted a recently baptized Anglican, with: "Why didn't thee desire the Minister rather to piss upon thy Head . . . that would have been of more effect." Derision was a weapon that was often used throughout the city as sects sniped at each other. Now, the Quakers enjoyed the prospect of seeing Anglican fight Anglican, as the Reverend Archibald Cummings, pastor of Christ Church tried to refute Whitefield:

Inner Light and Exterior Darkness

Last First Day morning before Church time he preached a sermon on faith in opposition to good works ... And at church (so called) their parson Commings preached up works in opposition to Whitefield; and in the evening Whitefield again preached in opposition to him; So that those of the black robe sometimes display their different opinions.

Richard Hockley, a Quaker merchant appreciated the political value of Whitefield's crusade, and called him "a Shining Light."

Whitefield's denunciation of dancing and music as "devilish diversions" was consistent with Penn's teaching that they were "leaps to Hell." The high pitch of religious fervor during the crusade led dancing master Robert Bolton to consent to Whitefield's aide, William Seward, locking the room where the dancing assembly was regularly held—but Seward sent an article to Franklin's *Gazette*, saying the patrons accosted him "very roughly" and threatened to cane him, to which he allegedly replied: "What a Hurry Satan puts his *Servants* into when their darling *Idols* are opposed?" This was vigorously denied by the dancers who said they had none scheduled after April 22, 1740. Seward still maintained Whitefield had broken "Satan's strongest Hold in this City." Franklin published the denial:

I have often said, that if any Person thinks himself injured in a Publick News-Paper, he has a Right to have his Vindication made as publick as the Aspersion. The Gentlemen above mentioned have brought me the following letter to be inserted in my Paper, believing the Publication of it will be advantageous to their Reputation: And tho' I think there is a good deal of Difference between a *Vindication* and an *Invective*; and that, whatever Obligations a Printer may be under to publish Things of the former kind, he can be under none with Regard to the latter; Yet, as the publishing of this, will obviate a groundless Report (injurious to that Gentleman) that Mr. Whitefield had engag'd all the Printers not to print any Thing against him, lest his Doctrine and Practice should be expos'd, and the People undeceiv'd; I shall therefore print it as I received it: And when the Publick has heard what may possibly be said in Reply, they will then judge for themselves.

The citizens went back to their sinful ways after Whitefield headed for New England, but various denominations experienced reverberations. A Baptist lay preacher who denounced him for his "Enthusiastick Ravings" as not stemming "from the Spirit of God; for our God is a God of Order, and not of such Confusion," was driven out of the church and banned from the pulpit. The Presbyterians split in a bitter argument, and Whitefield's supporters, calling themselves the "New Lights," seceded and went off to hold services in the new hall at Fourth and Arch. When this building was turned over to the College of

145

Philadelphia in 1750, they erected a "New Meeting House" at the northwest corner of Third and Arch, and held a lottery to build a steeple. To some Philadelphians this brought the dissenting Presbyterians close to the Anglicanism that had raised, through the same method, the graceful spire on Christ Church. A jingle made the rounds:

The Presbyterians built a church, and fain would have a steeple
We think it may become the church, but not become the people.

In 1759 an attempt was made to reunite the divided elements, and showed some signs of success, but credal differences still simmered. The "Old Lights" in the Market Street Church provided funds to construct a "chapel of ease" in Pine Street, which called a "New Light" minister to its pulpit in 1771. He found the doors locked and guarded by a constable hired by the "Old Lights." With the aid of some friends he forced his way in, and a long legal battle between the Third and First Churches ensued. The case was on appeal in England when the Revolution broke out, and the matter was ultimately settled when the Pine Street congregation paid the Market Street group $4,250 and kept their minister.

Trouble was not confined to the Presbyterians. In 1742 the Lutherans forced the Moravians from a church they used in common, and indictments followed. In 1750 two ministers fought for possession of the German Reformed pulpit, one climbing into it on Saturday and spending the night to insure exclusive occupancy for the Sunday service.

Catholics encountered problems of a different kind. While Pennsylvania ignored the edict of William III prohibiting the public celebration of the Mass, as it was inclined to ignore most royal proclamations, the few Catholics first met in a small coffee house at the northwest corner of Front and Walnut Streets.

In 1734 they built a tiny chapel, St. Joseph's, back of Walnut Street below Fourth, although one of the members, certain the coffee house had been consecrated, still insisted on genuflecting when he passed it. Almost adjoining the Quaker Alms House, St. Joseph's was on the edge of the improved section of town, opening onto Shippen's apple orchards and the thickly wooded reaches of Walnut Street to the west. It was described as looking like an "out-kitchen." In 1757 it was razed and a somewhat larger building put up, made necessary by the influx of Acadians who had been expelled from Nova Scotia by the British, and were quartered by Anthony Benezet in a row of frame houses on Pine Street. Longfellow's *Evangeline* commemorates the "unknown and unnoticed" refugees who lie "Under the humble walls of the little Catholic churchyard"—a plot of ground St. Joseph's had acquired down Fourth Street for a cemetery. In 1763, the more elaborate St. Mary's was built there, and took over the burial ground. The pastor of St. Mary's, Father Harding, an English Jesuit, was active in civic affairs and exchanged visits with Protestant pastors. In 1768 he was elected to the American Philosophical Society. Before his death in 1772 he seems to have made his church popular with visitors to Philadelphia. John Adams and George Washington were among the delegates to the First Continental Congress who went there on the afternoon of October 9, 1774. Adams reported to Abigail that the altar was "very rich" with "little images and crucifixes about (and) waxed candles lighted up" and was impressed by "the paintings, the bells, the candles, the gold and silver." Washington merely jotted in his diary: "Went to the Presbyterian Meeting in the forenoon and Romish Church in the afternoon." In 1781 the Congress attended a Mass of Thanksgiving for the victory at Yorktown.

The French immigration to Philadelphia during the 1790's, along with additional Irish immigrants, raised considerably the Catholic population during that period, although many French returned to their homeland after the "reign of terror" ended. In 1757 there had been only 157 Catholics in the city. The British, during their occupation of Philadelphia, 1777-78 raised a Catholic regiment of 180 officers and men, commanded by a communicant of St. Joseph's. This high percentage is attributed to a remembrance of anti-Catholic sentiment that precipitated riots in 1740 and 1755. In the latter year Braddock's defeat by the French and Indians near Fort Duquesne raised fears that the small Catholic population might be a French "fifth column." Only the intervention of some courageous Quakers, citing the Charter of Privileges, quieted the mob. Members of St. Mary's congregation during the Revolution included Commodore John Barry, "Father of the American Navy," Thomas FitzSimmons, a signer of the Declaration, Stephen Moylan and George Meade, grandfather of the Civil war general who defeated Lee at Gettysburg, all four of whom are interred in the adjoining churchyard. As if in keeping with a Philadelphia tradition, turmoil came to St. Mary's in the celebrated "Hogan schism" which involved a highly-popular priest who, in 1821, delivered a sermon attacking his pastor. The case became a cause celebré, ultimately reaching the Pope and resulting in Father Hogan renouncing Catholicism and marrying a beautiful young, wealthy widow whom he reputedly treated badly, becoming a lawyer in Georgia and a whole sequence of events which ultimately led to his leading an anti-Pope, anti-Catholic movement in Massachusetts in 1842. In 1822, when his earlier controversy was at its height, rival factions in the congregation did extensive damage to St. Mary's during the election of trustees.

Life and Times in Colonial Philadelphia

Philadelphia's Jewish community alone seems to have escaped the struggles which, at one time or another, racked the other denominations during the 18th century. From 1740 they worshipped in several houses in the vicinity of Third and Cherry, and in that year consecrated the Mikveh Israel Cemetery on Spruce Street, across from where the Pennsylvania Hospital rose a short time later. In 1751 Franklin's *Pennsylvania Gazette* carried an item asking "sportsmen to forbear (for the future) firing" against the cemetery wall as it was damaging the tombstones. Haym Salomon is among the Revolutionary figures interred there. Born in Poland in 1740 he opened a brokerage and commission office in New York in 1772, became active in the Sons of Liberty, was arrested by the British in 1776 and upon his release married Rachel Franks, sister of Colonel Isaac Franks. In 1777 he was re-arrested by the British, charged with espionage, but managed to escape and come empty-handed to Philadelphia in 1778, forced to leave temporarily "his distressed Wife and a Child of a Month old at New York." Within seven years he not only recouped his fortune but had financed the Revolution to sums estimated at from $350,000 to over $500,000. In addition he helped James Madison, who in 1782 acknowledged this in a letter to Edmund Randolph:

> The kindness of our little friend in Front Street, near the coffee-house, is a fund that will preserve me from extremities, but I never resort to it without great mortification, as he obstinately rejects all recompense. The price of money is so usurious that he thinks it ought to be extorted from none, but those who aim at profitable speculations. To a necessitous delegate, he gratuitously spares a supply out of his private stock. . . .

Madison's description of him as "little" invites some question as to how tall he was, since Madison himself stood only 5'6". Salomon died in 1784, his entire estate consisting of unpaid claims against the government.

The cemetery attracts a number of visitors who come to pay tribute chiefly to Rebecca Gratz, believed to have been the inspiration for Sir Walter Scott's heroine in *Ivanhoe*. Born in 1781 into a prominent Philadelphia family, she was admired by both Washington Irving and Henry Clay. Her extensive philanthropy and great charm made her virtually a legend in the 19th century. Several portraits by Sully substantiate the frequent assertions of her beauty.

In 1769 the Methodists bore some resemblance to the Quakers in their attire, and to distinguish themselves made some slight modifications. Like the Quakers they believed in the "call" rather than ecclesiastical exegesis, and thus placed little emphasis on the education of their early ministers. Methodism gained impetus from Whitefield's preaching in 1739, but remained unorganized until an ex-British captain, Thomas Webb, came to Philadelphia in 1767 and formed a society with approximately 100 members. A sail loft on Dock Street provided their first place of worship, and thereafter they met at 8 Loxley Court in a house still standing. In 1769 they purchased the unfinished Dutch Presbyterian church at New and Fourth Streets, known as St. George's. Captain Webb, with a green patch over an eye lost in the Battle of Quebec, was a dramatic leader, who preached in his red regimentals with a sword sometimes laid across the Bible. From an unfloored shell, the little congregation transformed their church into a handsome edifice, and its unique hexagonal pulpit remains a cherished spot for Methodist ministers because it was occupied from 1771 to 1774 by the extraordinary Bishop Francis Asbury. A Scot, he became the driving force who built American Methodism, riding the rim of the frontier to form new congregations.

GREATER MEETING HOUSE

In deference to George Fox's distaste for "steeple houses" the first Quaker meeting houses looked like dwellings. But the thrifty Quakers salvaged materials as new structures replaced old, so that the Great Meeting House which served Philadelphians since 1699 at Second and Market was absorbed in this Greater Meeting House which was completed in 1755. 73 feet long, 55 feet wide, its peakroof and design marked a break from the Fox dictums, and was comparable in appearance to the building which later housed the American Friends Service Committee at 20 S. 12th Street. Like its predecessor it had a 50-year life span, giving way in 1804 to a still greater edifice on Arch Street, as the center of Philadelphia Quakerism. Across the street from the Old Court House and Jersey market, Greater Meeting House was occupied by troops from Maryland in 1776 under the command of General William Smallwood. While these were much better behaved than the Americans who took over the Lutheran church in Trappe, Penna. after the defeat at Brandywine the next year and played bawdy tunes on the organ, the presence of soldiers offended the peace-committed Quakers. Nonetheless they coexisted as some of Smallwood's unit attended services while others respectfully withdrew during them.

Perplexed visitors to Philadelphia may well have wondered why a plain sect would choose a patron so obviously Anglican. The explanation was that the Dutch Presbyterians had originally called it "Georg Kirchen," but when they requested the Bishop of London to be taken into the Church of England, changed it to honor that country's national saint. The Methodists adopted the name along with the building.

Benjamin Rush, inveterate foe of liquor, praised the lead taken by the Quakers and Methodists in 1788 "in rejecting spirituous liquors . . . from their harvest fields, their stores, and even from their houses." He credited both in 1787 for checking to "a great degree . . . the practice of Negro slavery in our state." The African Methodist Episcopal Church traces its beginnings to St. George's, since Richard Allen, a former slave who was to become in 1793 one of the heroic figures in the yellow fever epidemic, was licensed there in 1784 to preach. He went on to become the founder of the first black congregation at Bethel Church and the first Bishop of the African Methodist Episcopal Church in 1816.

Quaker Meeting Houses of the 17th century showed the influence of George Fox who disparaged "steeple houses." Thus they looked like dwelling houses with four-sided sloping roofs. The Bank Meeting House, built in 1684 on the west side of Front, north of Arch, was the scene of the Keith outburst and the ultimate feud which split that congregation. While the axe incident could hardly have helped the structure, its wooden frame decayed within a few years. Anticipating the westward expansion of the city a new brick building was completed in 1687 in Center Square at Broad and Market, but proved to be too far in the country. On Penn's second visit to Philadelphia the property was sold to him for £100 and then he was persuaded to give it back so the bricks could be used for a meeting house closer to the Delaware River. Some Quakers openly boasted of the "sharpness" of the deal which gave them money and the materials. While it is unlikely that Penn, in desperate financial straits, ever paid the purchase price, the attitude indicates the degree of strange hostility with which he was regarded.

With their spiritual philosophy deeply grounded in the doctrine of peace, the most formidable challenge Quakers faced was the recurrent threat of war. This was thrown into high relief by their insistence on keeping political control of the Assembly. They tempered their opposition to the appointment of non-Quakers as deputy governors in the early 18th century on the theory that they could take the necessary steps to defend the province, but they reserved the right to use their legislative prerogative to balk them when they chose. The issue of funding military expeditions brought them face to face with their conscience, and they

150

were unwilling to make a distinction between their private beliefs and their official responsibilities. Reality sometimes forced them to palliating compromises. Thus in 1693 when the province was temporarily in the hands of the Crown, they granted monies on the assurance "your money shall not be dipt in blood." In 1711 they voted £2,000 "for the Queen's use," knowing the Crown planned to use it for "the intended Expedition against Canada," and while "religious persuaded against War, and therefore cannot be active therein . . . yet (we) are as fully persuaded, and believe it . . . (our) bounden Duty to pay Tribute, and yield due Obedience to the Powers God has set over us."

The dilemma was divisive. Penn, in his First Frame of Government for Pennsylvania, stressed separation of Church and state, and liberty of conscience as imperative. Always in enunciating his political theories he drew a line between a person's religious and political obligations, premised on Christ's statement about God and Caesar. In challenging Quaker stubbornness in refusing to legislate funds for military objectives, the Anglicans repeatedly reminded them that they had a duty to be concerned about those whose consciences impelled them to fight to protect their homes— and they were not justified in pursuing policies fashioned in their personal tenets. A classic instance of the narrow legalisms which Quakers used is recited in Franklin's *Autobiography*. In 1745 the Crown demanded Pennsylvania's share of payment necessary to finance Colonel Warren's expedition for Nova Scotia's protection. The Assembly voted £4,000 "for the King's Use" but directed it be paid to two Quaker merchants for "Bread, Beef, Pork, Flour, Wheat or other Grain. . . ." Franklin chuckled over the words, "other Grain," and said Governor Thomas construed this to mean "Gun-Power" grains. Such sophistry wore thin the patience of the British Government, and they considered steps to exclude Quakers from the Assembly. The spring of 1748 brought Philadelphians face to face with an immediate crisis, when a "Spanish Privateer of fourteen Carriage Guns" was reported below New Castle, part of a French and Spanish operation in their war with England. The city fully expected an attack on its port, and had nothing to fight it off except an unseaworthy English man-of-war. The busy Franklin set to work organizing a voluntary militia, and got Reverend Gilbert Tennent, the Presbyterian leader to write a pamphlet stressing the "rightfulness of lawful defence." The pamphlet had a curious future. In July 1778 when Philadelphia was being combed for paper to make wadding for cartridges, 2500 copies of it were found in the garret of Franklin's old printing office, and most of them were used during the Battle of Monmouth.

But in 1748 the Assembly gave vague assurances they would support executive action "for the Good of the Province," and no sooner did this crisis pass than the towering French and Indian War come up. Realizing the implications to Crown, province and the population of Pennsylvania, suggestions were advanced that the Quakers withdraw from the Assembly for the duration, but not only did they remain, but voted a property tax to raise £50,000 to support the war. The appropriation caused anguish among the conservative Quakers. Some refused to pay such taxes, and to stiffen religious discipline it was decreed that reports on the conduct of Friends be read and answered at each Quarterly meeting. Complaints mounted for the next twenty years, many withdrew or were disowned, and by 1775 the membership had been decimated. As the war with France dragged on, Quaker members of the Assembly began to resign, caught in the interminable debates between their obligations as Quakers and legislators. Those who stayed levied more taxes and increased the penalties for nonpayment, thus ignoring the arguments of prominent Philadelphians like Anthony Benezet. Moreover, to furnish needed wagons for General John Forbes expedition to Fort Duquesne in 1758, they joined in legislation requiring the cooperation of all wagon owners, and Quaker magistrates along with non-Quakers were charged with enforcing the law. This introduced more striations in the Quaker church structure. Quakers who cooperated were haled before the meetings, and defended on the grounds they had been assured by Quaker magistrates the law was not in the sect's discipline.

All these difficulties were a mere prelude to the Revolution when Philadelphia Quakers underwent their most severe ordeal. The Society of Friends disowned those who took up arms on either side, but those who allied themselves to the American cause refused to surrender their spiritual identity, notwithstanding their expulsion. For a time they gathered for worship in private houses, and then in 1783 built the Free Quaker Meeting House, at the southwest corner of Fifth and Arch Streets, marking their cornerstone with this legend:

By General Subscription
For the Free Quakers, erected
In the year of our Lord, 1783
Of the Empire 8

The odd allusion to "Empire" is said to have reflected the belief that America was destined to become a great empire.

Those Quakers who endeavored to stay neutral in Philadelphia during the war were treated harshly by local Committees on Safety, who felt they were either British sympathizers or content to turn a profit by selling goods to the English during the occupation of the city. A number of men, some elderly, were led off to distant places such as Winchester, Virginia for internment during the war, without being permitted to make provision for their wives and families. Elizabeth Drinker stoically recorded her experiences in Philadelphia during this period, unemotionally noting the various pieces of furniture taken from her home by "assessors" who claimed them for taxes.

Christ Church, identified with Philadelphia history since 1695, made the transition from Crown to Continental Congress with comparative ease. The present church was virtually completed in April 1744, and the steeple, financed by a lottery managed by Franklin and some others, was added ten years later. Its bells, cast in the Whitechapel Foundry in London, where the Liberty Bell had been cast earlier, were described by a visitor in 1783:

> Christ Church has a beautiful chime of bells, which makes a complete octave and is heard especially on evenings before the weekly markets and at times of other glad public events. The bells are so played that the eight single notes of the octave are several times struck, descending, rapidly one after the other—and then the accord follows in tercet and quint, ascending; and so repeated. On certain solemn days, there is repetition to the 13th time, that sacred number. At Philadelphia there is always something to be chimed, so that it seems almost as if it was an Imperial or Popish city.

Both the fact that the bells were chimed, and their holier location, appears to have spared them from the protests made in September 1772 by "divers Inhabitants of the City of Philadelphia, living near the State-House" to the General Assembly. They complained

> they are much incommoded and distressed by the too frequent Ringing of the great Bell in the Steeple of the State-House, the Inconvenience of which has been often felt severely when some of the Petitioners Families have been afflicted with Sickness, at which Times, from its uncommon Size and unusual Sound, it is extremely dangerous, and may prove fatal. . . .

Like the Liberty Bell, the bells of Christ Church and those in its "chapel of ease" St. Peter's, were removed by order of the Executive Council of Pennsylvania as the British approached in 1777, to prevent being melted into bullets. Reverend Jacob Duche, then pastor of Christ Church and chaplain to the Continental Congress, protested "the great risque that would attend the taking down the bells, the improbability of ever meeting with a Person capable of putting them up again," Not-

153

withstanding, they came down and were re-hung a year later, October 1778, "at publick Expence."

Duche had been selected to open the session of Congress on September 7, 1774 at Carpenter's Hall. Philadelphia was tense with rumors that Boston had been bombarded. On the night of the 6th Silas Deane wrote to his wife:

> This City is in the utmost confusion, all the bells toll muffled, and the most unfeigned marks of sorrow appear in every countenance . . . the people run as in a case of extremity, they know not where nor why. . . .

In this tense atmosphere Duche began with the thirty-fifth Psalm, "Plead my cause, O Lord, with them that strive with me, fight against them that fight against me. . . ."

John Adams said:

> I never saw a greater effect upon an audience. It seemed as if Heaven had ordained that psalm to be read on that morning. After this Mr. Duche, unexpectedly to everybody, struck out into an extemporary prayer . . . as pertinent, as affectionate, as sublime, as devout, as I ever heard offered up to Heaven. He filled every bosom present.

Silas Deane wrote it was

> worth riding one hundred miles to hear. (He) prayed without book about ten minutes so pertinently, with such fervency, purity and sublimity of style and sentiment, and with such an apparent sensibility of the scenes and business before us, that even Quakers shed tears.

Other delegates echoed these praises.

Three years later, on October 8, 1777 Duche wrote a long letter to Washington urging him to negotiate for peace, and the general, as was his wont with such communications, sent it on to Congress. Now the minister was denounced by Congress as a "Judas," an "apostate," "a traitor," "the first of villains," and John Adams sighed, "Poor man! I pity his weakness and detest his wickedness."

The ill-starred minister had first been assigned to St. Peter's Church on the southwest corner of Third and Pine Streets when it opened in 1761. His father three years earlier had built a house for the young minister, patterned after one of the wings of Lambeth Palace. After his defection to the Tories the property was confiscated and became the residence of Governor McKean.

The interior of St. Peter's, with its high box pews, has had only minor changes since it was originally constructed, and presents a clear picture of what a Philadelphia church of the period looked like. Christ Church, while still retaining much of its colonial charm, moved the center-altar wine-glass pulpit to the north end of the sanctuary and lowered the height of its pews. Washington, during his seven-year residency in Philadelphia as President attended services there irregularly, although Mrs. Washington was usually in the pew designated as the "President's" every Sunday. Washington's spasmodic attendance was not due to a lack of devotion but a distaste for clergymen in general and lengthy sermons in particular.

Most of the notable personages in Philadelphia during the 18th century, whether residents or visitors, came to services in Christ Church on occasions, but its churchyard abounds with celebrities. Seven signers of

(Keun Archives, Phila.)

FIRST PRESBYTERIAN CHURCH

Although this handsome First Presbyterian church building was just five years old when Birch etched it, the congregation dated back to 1692. It stood on the corner of High Street and White Horse Alley (now Bank Street) and was opened for worship in 1794. The way in which the expanding public markets narrowed the one-hundred foot wide High Street is graphically illustrated, and a meat hook projecting a butcher's stall suggests the dismal view worshippers might have had on market days since butchers left scraps and cuttings lay where they fell to be devoured by the numerous homeless dogs. Sanitary conditions might have improved somewhat as a result of tougher enforcement of city ordinances during the Yellow Fever epidemic of 1793. In any case the Presbyterians moved the First Church in 1825 to its present location at 7th and Washington Square, where the lofty Corinthian columns shown here grace the portico.

the Declaration, the largest number in any single place, are buried there, Franklin, Morris, James Wilson, Benjamin Rush, Francis Hopkinson, Joseph Hewes and George Ross. One Continental Army general is buried along the south side of the church very much against his will. General Charles Lee, the strange ex-British officer Washington regarded as second in command until he cursed him out at Monmouth for dilatory tactics, had died in disgrace at "The Sign of the Conestogoe Wagon" on the south side of Market between Fourth and Fifth, "badly attended, except by two faithful dogs, who frequenty attempted in vain to awaken their dead master. He lies buried in Christ's church yard. No stone marks his head. Indeed, those who saw his open grave can scarcely mark the site, as it is continually trodden by persons going into and coming out of church. Behold the honor of the great!" Lee's grave has since been compassionately marked with a tablet gently describing him as the "knight errant" of the Revolution. Bitter and forgotten, he declared in his will he did not want to be buried

> in any church or churchyard, or within a mile of any Presbyterian or Anabaptist meeting house. For since I have resided in this country, I have had so much bad company when living that I do not choose to continue it when dead.

Church history in 18th century Philadelphia came to a colorful close with the arrival of lovely Jemima Wilkinson, a "women's liberationist" of first rank. Since she billed herself as "the Universal Friend" preaching a doctrine of universal love and universal peace, she was welcomed by the Free Quakers, although they may have had some misgivings about her splendid carriage, and her unisex attire, a woolen robe that looked seamless and a broad-brimmed "shiningblack beaver hat." An eyewitness could not remember what she said, but was obviously impressed when he saw her

> standing up and speaking from the south end of the gallery to a staring audience. . . . She appeared beautifully erect, and tall for a woman, although at the same time the masculine appearance predominated; which, together with her strange habit, caused every eye to be riveted upon her. Her glossy black hair was parted evenly on her pale round forehead, and smoothed back beyond the ears, from whence it fell in profusion about her neck and shoulders, seemingly without art or contrivance—arched black eyebrows and fierce looking black eyes, darting here and there with penetrating glances . . . as though she read the thoughts of people; beautiful acqueline nose, handsome mouth and chin, all supported by a neck comfortable to the line of beauty and proportion. . . . She spoke deliberately, not 'startingly and rash' but resting with one hand on the banister before her, and using her occasional action with the other, nev-

ertheless she seemed as one moved by that 'prophetic fury' which 'sewed the web' while she stood uttering words of wondrous impact, with a masculine-femine tone of voice, or kind of croak, unearthly and sepulchral.

Jemima claimed to be reincarnated, a delusion that could have come from a thirty-six-hour coma during a prolonged bout with fever in 1776 when she was about eighteen. A story circulated that she had arisen from the dead, raising up in her coffin while friends and neighbors were paying their respects. Given the medical ineptitude of the times, it is probable she was thought dead. Born and raised in a prosperous Rhode Island family—the eighth of twelve children, she was intrigued with the "New Light" Baptists and Mother Ann Lee, founder of the Shakers. Her own mother, a Quakeress, died when she was young, and Jemima grew into young womanhood a headstrong, beautiful and intelligent person. She claimed she had been reanimated possibly with Christ's spirit and talked of being "swept to Heaven in a cloud of glory" after a thousand years. Her doctrine was a composite of many popular at the time, and she indicated that while she regarded the Sabbath as Saturday she felt Sunday should be a day of rest. Going forth to preach the gospel brought a number of prominent and wealthy men in her wake, and ultimately she persuaded them to pool their talents and contributions to assist her in obeying the command to "go into a strange country", which proved to be western New York. With their financial assistance, she bought a 15,000 acre tract near Lake Seneca and called it "New Jerusalem", where women who would renounce marriage could live with her in celibate bliss, while men, residing away from the mansion house, could perform the chores. Between two and three hundred accepted the invitation, but Pennsylvania got officially concerned when she became a threat to the stability of marriages. The Quakers quickly disowned her, but she had established a branch congregation in Worcester, just beyond Philadelphia. The Duc de la Rochefoucauld Liancourt visited her in "New Jerusalem" in 1799, noticed all the furniture had the emblem "U.F." on it and watched Jemima in a discourse with about thirty people—men, women and children. She

> stood at the door of her bed-chamber on a carpet, with an armchair behind her. She had on a white morning gown, and waistcoat, such as men wear, and a petticoat of the same color. Her black hair was cut short, carefully combed, and divided behind into three ringlets; she wore a stock, and a white silk cravat, which was tied about her neck with affected negligence. In point of delivery, she preached with more ease than any other Quaker I have yet heard; but the subject of her discourse was an eternal repetition of the same topics, death, sin, and repentance. She is

said to be about forty years of age, but she did not appear to be more than thirty. She is of middle stature, well made, of a florid countenance, and has fine teeth, and beautiful eyes, Her action is studied; she aims at simplicity, but there is something pedantic in her manner.

Eventually the inevitable rumors of Jemima's morals and arguments with the trustees led to court. She was acquitted of blasphemy and managed to retain her property, but when she died in 1819 her followers buried her in some secret corner of the extensive property at a place said to be known only to the descendants of those who placed her there.

10

TAVERNS IN THE TOWN:
Pleasure was Where They Found It, and Often in a Noggin

*   *   *   *   *

There is a cry come over into these parts against the number of drinking-houses, and looseness, that is committed in the caves. I am pressed in my spirit, being very apt to believe too many disorders . . . strictly . . . require . . . speedy and effectual care be taken. . . . To reduce the number of ordinaries or drinking-houses. . .;—Such are (to be) continued, that are most tender of God's glory, and the reputation of the government . . . let virtue be cherished. . . .

—Penn's order from England to his Philadelphia magistrates, 1688

*   *   *   *   *

E xactly one hundred years after William Penn wrote these words, "The Three Jolly Irishmen" achieved the reputation of being the roughest tavern in town. To accomplish such a feat took quite a bit of doing, but its location at the northeast corner of Race and Water Streets helped considerably, insuring that it would be "a primary resort for newcomers." It was "at times one continued scene and sound of daily riot, and night brawl, making it dangerous to meddle with." Young blades teasingly urged "a little old German watchman, who stood in his box hard by" to go in and stop the fighting. "His shoulders bending under the pressure of the years, and his chin and nose almost in contact," he answered, "Bless my soul, gentlemen—bless my soul, wass can I do wid dem?"

Penn's appeal to virtue was more than the most idealistic magistrate dreamed practical. In 1688 the path of righteousness was rigidly prescribed for the tavernkeeper. His prices were regulated—molasses beer one penny per quart, and malt beer for two pence. Credit for familiar patrons of "publick houses" was limited to twenty shillings, but no credit could be extended to seamen unless the ship's master guaranteed payment. Negro servants could not be served unless they brought permission from their owners. Meticulous records, for tax purposes, had to be kept on all imported liquors and wines. To prevent "cutting" of liquor, the law dangled a reward of half the fine for informers. The tavern owner was required to provide, for not more than seven pence, an "ordinary" meal of good beef or equally good meat of another kind, and he could charge up to six pence for furnishing hay to the traveler's horse, but not a penny for tethering.

All these were not prompted by piety, but experience. The tavern was a quasi-public institution and, left to their own devices, unscrupulous innkeepers could gouge strangers. Other shops could display signs if they chose, but long English custom decreed that taverns must. The illiterate wayfarer learned to find the roads he wanted by being directed to look for inns bearing specific symbols. The practice still prevails in rural Britain.

In 1685 Philadelphia had seven licensed ordinaries, the oldest being "The Blue Anchor," the first building Penn saw when his barge landed on the "low, sandy beach" at the mouth of Dock Creek. A timbered structure, faced with small brick, it sat amid pines and whortleberries, a hundred yards from the Delaware. It measured only twelve feet along the roughly delineated Front Street, but its creekside prospect was twenty-two feet. With an eight-and-a-half foot ceiling, the small dimensions made the place easier to heat. Various dates are assigned for its origin. Some say it had been started in 1671, others that it was still under construction when Penn sailed into the wide cove. Whatever, the Quaker who kept it in 1682 not only served food and drink, but operated a ferry over Dock Creek for those whose business carried them from the north side of town to the south. Later, when a public mill was built on Windmill Island, people wishing to grind grain could get a boat at the Blue Anchor to transport them.

For the first few years after the settlers began to arrive in 1681 the Blue Anchor found its situation ideal. As the only inn, overlooking the harbor with its constantly increasing ship traffic, it was filled with lucrative promise. But when the boats from New Jersey were shunted upriver to a suitable landing at Vine Street, a two-story brick tavern was built, Penny Pot House, its name pragmatically reflecting the price of its beer. Both places, situated on Front Street, eventually became victoms of neglected road maintenance. Grand juries repeatedly represented the hazardous conditions, and by 1740, almost as if they had despaired of overland customers, the two changed their names, the. Penny Pot becoming The Jolly Tar, and the Blue Anchor to the more pretentious Boatswain and Call.

Legitimate operators soon discovered, as did Penn, that virtue offered no shield against unlicensed rivals. Most of these were in the Caves where smuggled wine, rum, and beer from the malt houses on Swedish farms reduced the overhead, while in the semi-darkness of the extensive dugouts customers had more privacy to taste other forbidden fruits. Penn had a dual concern about these dens of iniquity—he could breathe fire and brimstone at the "looseness" of morality, and lament the loss of revenue. The "cry" that came to him in London hardly stemmed from the sailors who were the beneficiaries of lower prices and entertainment. It could only have been voiced by Quakers who felt the moral fibers of the "Holy Experiment" might be endangered. Penn ordered the caves purged. The first one seized was Joseph Knight, whose underground establishment was obviously the most notorious. But no practical Philadelphian thought his arrest would eliminate the spectre of sexual laxity, or "Two Swedish women drunk," or the cards and dice. Banished from the good earth, the "tippling houses" burgeoned brazenly to such a degree that, in the mid-18th century a whole section of Race Street, from Third to Front, was called "Helltown." The Assembly fulminated and frothed and enacted stiffer laws and penalties regarding ordinaries, without even denting the "Nurseries of Vice and Debauchery." In 1721 when considering a complaint about "gaming in Publick Houses—particularly by the young," they concluded that a Parliamentary study of similar problems in London ended in futility, and thought there was not much sense in retracing those steps in Philadelphia.

Most Europeans brought to the city an antipathy to drinking water. Sludge-filled pipes and contaminated supplies had instilled a fear of malaria and a host of other diseases. Thus the taverns were looked upon as a sort of health spa, as well as centers for convivial conversation. Dr. Nicholas More, who was president of the Free Society of Traders, earnestly believed Pennsylvania would produce finer wines than France. In 1686 a Frenchman living in Philadelphia, had made from his vineyards a "Mador" which More pronounced superior to any he had tasted, and reported to Penn that the proprietor's vignon at Pennsbury had made a barrel to celebrate the founder's next visit, but it had leaked down to two quarts. It took a while before Philadelphians realized they were not destined to be the wine capital of the world, but disappointment in their over-optimism was tempered by the abundance of pears, apples and peaches which yielded excellent brandies. The "great brew house" on Walnut Street improved the quality of the beer by 1685, and the large influx of Scotch-Irish around 1726 introduced a thirst for whiskey, but this traveled westward with the new arrivals. Penn in 1685 sent word to his friends in England.

> Our Drink has been Beer and Punch made of Rum and Water. Our Beer was made mostly of Molosses, which well boyld, with Sassafras or Pine infused into it, makes very tollerable drink; but now they make Mault, and Mault Drink begins to be common, especially at the Ordinaries and the Houses of the more substantial People. . . .

Philadelphians began to lose their taste for beer when some merchants in 1726 petitioned the Assembly to deal with the "intolerable frauds . . . of large Sediments, with mixtures of Dirt and Filth" in beer made by "Cheats, not fit to commerce with." The legislature pondered the problem for four years and finally decided to empower city judges to regulate prices and quality. At the same time they launched a new drive to close down illegal pubs, with the usual lack of success. In 1728 it was estimated that at the elections, 4,500 gallons of common beer were "drunk or thrown away" and Franklin offered the "surprizing tho' authentick" news that Pennsylvania had imported 212,450 gallons of rum in the same year. "Cyder Royal," new cider fermented with applejack, became a favorite in Philadelphia taverns. In 1736 Thomas Apty walked into the Red Lion Inn in Elbow Lane and "laid a wager of Half a Crown that he would drink within the space of one hour and a half, a Gallon of Cyder Royal; which he had no sooner accomplished, and said 'I have finished' but he fell down . . . and then expir'd." He was a plasterer by trade.

162

Taverns in the Town

Robert Proud noted in 1760 that "Cyder is the common drink . . . and very plentiful. . . . West India rum and spirits are much drank by people in general . . . Malt liquor . . . now (is) made in small quantity." In an interesting survey he conducted in the various colonies, Reverend Israel Arelius tabulated forty-five kinds of drinks. The South Carolina delegation to the Continental Congress in 1775 were intrigued with a "julep" served at Frye's Tavern in Philadelphia, asked the Irish bartender for the recipe, added a sprig of mint and gave it to the South. John Adams expressed a distaste for it, and Franklin preferred Madeira.

The amount of drinking in the Philadelphia area caused considerable alarm among the Quakers. In 1724 the Chester Monthly Meeting reported:

> At our Quarterly Meeting it was desired ye friends take care at Burrialls not to make great provision as to provide strong Liquors & hand it about; but lett Every one be free to take it as they have occasion and not more than will doe them Good.

In Franklin's *Pennsylvania Gazette* in 1733 this item appeared:

> It is now become the practice of some otherwise discreet women, instead of a draught of beer and toast, or a chunk of bread and cheese, or a wooden noggin of good porridge and bread, as our good old English custom is, or milk and bread boiled, or tea and bread and butter, or milk, or milk and coffee, etc., they must have their two or three *drams* in the morning, by which their appetite for wholesome food is taken away.

But Franklin never lectured. In 1736 when his competitor Andrew Bradford threw the editorial weight of the *Pennsylvania Mercury* behind the temperance movement, giving five fundamental reasons for moderation, the *Gazette* carried this rejoinder:

> There's but one Reason I can Think
> Why People ever cease to Drink
> Sobriety the Cause is not
> Nor Fear of being deam'd a Sot,
> But if Liquor can't be got.

A few years later, he listed five positive reasons:

> If on my Theme I rightly think
> There are Five Reasons why Men drink:
> Good Wine, a Friend, because I'm dry,
> Or lest I should be by and by
> Or any other Reason why.

163

Life and Times in Colonial Philadelphia

Franklin loved the conviviality of taverns and composed a few drinking
songs, of which these verses give a sample:

> T'was honest old Noah first planted the vine
> And mended his morals by drinking its wine;
> And thenceforth justly the drinking of water decried;
> For he knew that all mankind by drinking it died.

> Derry-down

And one that debated the merits of love and wine:

> Fair Venus calls; her voice obey
> In beauty's arms spend night and day.
> The joys of love all joys excel
> And loving's certainly doing well.

> *Chorus*

> Oh! no!
> Not so!
> For honest souls know
> Friends and bottle still bear the bell.

> Then let us get money, like bees lay up honey;
> We'll build us new hives and store each cell.
> The sight of our treasure shall yield us great pleasure;
> We'll count it and chink it and jingle it well.

> *Chorus.* Oh! no! etc.

> If this does not fit ye, let's govern the city;
> In power is pleasure no tongue can tell.
> By crowds though you're teased, your pride shall be pleased,
> And this can make Lucifer happy in hell.

> *Chorus.* Oh! no! etc.

> Then toss off your glasses and scorn the dull asses
> Who, missing the kernel, still gnaw the shell;
> What's love, rule, or riches? Wise Solomon teaches
> They're vanity, vanity, vanity still.

> *Chorus*

> That's true!
> He knew!
> He'd tried them all through;
> Friends and a bottle still bore the bell.

THE SLATE ROOF HOUSE

William Penn lived here 1699-1701 when it was inconvenient to go upriver to his estate near Bristol. On Second, between Walnut and Chestnut, at what later was called Norris Alley and still later Sansom Street, on the east side, it was here that his second wife, Hannah Callowhill Penn gave birth to John Penn, the only American-born member of the Penn family. Later it became a boarding house.

The names tavernkeepers chose were sometimes adapted to the kind of signs they could afford, and the building often became better known than the proprietor. Mrs. Jones, living in Jones' Alley between Front and Second Street, just north of Market, opened The Pewter Platter about 1700. The simplicity of the sign, just a large pewter platter, and the alliterative rhythm not only consigned Mrs. Jones to obscurity, but took over the alley as well. The Crooked Billet by Chestnut Street wharf, identified by a gnarled piece of firewood, was in operation twenty-three years before young Franklin made it his first stop in Philadelphia:

> Walking down again toward the river, and, looking in the faces of people, I met a young Quaker man, whose countenance I liked, and, accosting him, requested he would tell me where a stranger could get lodging. We were then near the sign of the Three Mariners. 'Here', says he, 'is one place that entertains strangers, but it is not a reputable house; if thee wilt walk with me, I'll show thee a better.' He brought me to the Crooked Billet in Water Street. Here I got a dinner; and, while I was eating it, several sly questions were asked me, as it seemed to be suspected, from my youth and appearance, that I might be some runaway.

> After dinner, my sleepiness returned, and being shown to a bed, I lay down without undressing, and slept till six in the evening, was called to supper, went to bed again very early, and slept soundly till next morning.

165

Then I made myself as tidy as I could, and went to Andrew Bradford the printer's.

The Crooked Billet stood in Crooked Billet Alley.

In 1760 Franklin's Junto met to discuss philosophy, politics and science in the Pewter Platter.

As the city grew and the number of taverns increased, more elaborate signs appeared. Young Benjamin West, sitting in a yet unnamed pub at 18 Strawberry Alley, saw a bull poke its head through the open window, painted the scene on a board and the place became "The Bull's Head." The Bear, The Rattlesnake, The Blue Lion, Ewe and Lamb, Boar's Head, Red Cow, Hen and Chicks, Black Horse and the Golden Sawn were part of a menagerie from which the less imaginative took titles. Those with aristocratic leanings chose The Queen's Head, The Queen of Hungary, King of Prussia, King of Poland and the like, but somewhat poetically, The Indian Queen on Fourth Street ranked far above these, numbering among its patrons Thomas Jefferson in 1776. Stars, the moon and mariners, in a variety of forms, were favorites. A Mr. Sober managed the ancient double-hipped-roofed Cross Keys at Fourth and Chestnut while a block away Israel Israel operated one with the same name. His perfect Hebraic name notwithstanding, Mr. Israel was a Protestant, and became one of the heroes during the yellow fever epidemic in 1793.

Duplication did not seem to disturb patrons or proprietors. Within a single square two bore the exotic name Kouli Khan, but as the fame of that conqueror dwindled, one changed to Turk's Head. The Centre House, which had a "Billiard Table and a Bowling Green" in 1744, was alternately known as The Indian Queen before its celebrated namesake was built. Franklin, Washington and Wayne had taverns named in their honor, and without too much impact on their egos, for none of the three inns amounted to much. Noah's Ark and The Struggler, together with The Butcher's Block show some effort to break out of the conventional mold, but "The Quiet Woman" took its inspiration from the French Revolution and showed a decapitated female. Even Philadelphia's Francophiles were not ready for this macabre sign, and the loss of business led the owner to choose a more palatable name.

Tun Tavern on the east side of Water Street was the birthplace of American Masonry in 1732 and the United States Marines in 1775. While it was noted for its food, gourmets preferred Pegg Mullan's "Beef-Steak House" nearby, where "rump steaks, cut with the grain, and only one brought in at a time was the order—always red hot and no detention." Race horses brought to town for the frequent races at Center Square were stabled in a "long house of two story brick" which served customers of the Indian Queen on Fourth Street. The weathervane atop the cupola bore bullet marks from the Paxton Boys who stopped at the Inn after Franklin dissauded them in 1755 to abandon their mission of murder against friendly Indians.

Philadelphia had its share of coffee houses. Before 1750 most of these were run by widows down by the waterfront, and over bitter coffee, importers and exporters discussed trade with their sea captains. John Shubert opened the London Coffee House on Water Street near Carpenter's Wharf in 1734, and his facilities drew a steady stream of patrons. Auctions were held there, and those seeking passage to foreign or coastal ports made arrangements with ship masters. Country people bringing produce and poultry to markets relaxed over beverages in the coffee room. Governor John Penn "made a very handsome entertainment" in 1735 for the Pennsylvania General Assembly at Shubert's, and Thomas Lawrence gave his mayoralty dinner for the City Corporation there. A larger London Coffee House was built at the southwest corner of Front and Market Streets in 1754, raised by subscriptions from principal businessmen. The public drank coffee on the ground floor, while a large hall upstairs featured the King's portrait and shared space with smaller meeting rooms. Merchants met at noon each day to hear ship reports, check commodity prices and learn the latest news. With its rack of English and American newspapers and magazines supplemented on "Post Days" with word from special correspondents elsewhere, it lived up to its claim of giving "latest Advices both Foreign and Domestick."

This kind of financing marked a departure from the traditional family-affair public houses, and served as a model for The City Tavern when it was built in 1773 on Second between Chestnut and Walnut. Supervised by a board and managed by Daniel Smith, Philadelphians perversely called it "Mr. Smith's" rather than by its formal name, a sharp contrast to the Pewter Platter and its owner, Mrs. Jones. Its decor and furnishings were expensively patterned after "the latest London mode." Two stories high, it advertised widely throughout the colonies, a "Genteel Coffee-Room . . . properly supplied with English and American papers and Magazines" and boasted of its "Long Room divided into boxes, fitted with tables and elegantly lighted." John Adams arriving "dirty, dusty and fatigued" in Philadelphia, on August 29, 1774 "could not resist the Importunity to go to the Tavern, the most genteel in America . . . after some Time spent in Conversation a curtain was drawn, and in the other Half of the Chamber a Supper appeared as elegant as ever was laid upon a Table." During the British occupation of Philadelphia many colorful balls and banquets were held there and beautiful Rebecca Franks, a Tory belle who attended most, if not all of them, later went to dances staged by the "Whigs" and sniffed haughtily, "Not a Lady present."

Entertainment posed more problems for middle class taverns than those higher or lower in the customer scale. The latter left it up to their patrons to manage with a deck of cards, or dice or frequent fist fights. After the Quakers began to lose their grip on the control of the city about 1742, bull baitings and cock fights appeared in the back streets of Helltown. Until the Revolution, the sedate places kept things on a high level. The City Tavern expected its patrons to find pleasure in erudite and quiet conversations or enjoyment in the music drifting in from private parties in the Long Room. In 1781, however, a drunken brawl involving American officers led to the murder of a waiter, and General Anthony Wayne shielded the suspect from the searching constabulary. No such misadventures would have been likely at the Indian Queen when Quaker John Biddle presided. In 1754 a visitor wrote Ezra Stiles of Yale how pleased he was with the service, the moderate prices of the finest liquors, and the nightly custom of "civilly" acquainting guests at 11 p.m. that no more drinks would be served "that night to any Body." He hastened to add "tho agreeable to me [it] may not perhaps be so to all People."

Unless one could get in with Franklin and his fellow singers, or similar groups, there was not much excitement to be found in the better taverns. In the 1740's, one could admire "The Great Hog's portrait" at the Indian Queen, if one was disposed to interest in an American-bred swine "near Nine Hundred Weight." There were Punch and Judy Shows, which were not much improvement over the 1723 display of a "curious and exact Modell of the Czar of Muscovia's Country Seat." David Lockwood's Musical Clock and Camera Obscura, and "A Christian Nobleman from Syria" with his Arabian Camel or African leopard quickened pulses a bit, but the 1760's brought a 17-foot model of the City of Jerusalem carved by two Germantown men, and the wax figures of Biblical characters and the late George Whitefield, the evangelist, or the solemn shape of The Pennsylvania Farmer.

The "fine bowling Greens" John Adams found at the Library Tavern may have looked even better over the "fine Turtle and admirable Wine" on which he dined, but the Centre House was generally regarded as having the best bowling in town. In the late 1760's attempts were made in several large cities to create Vauxhall Gardens, presumably without the elements that made the English prototype famous. Thomas Mullen experimented with one "on the agreeable Banks of the Schuylkill" but it was a pale replica of the original. During hot summers it was fashionable to drive to Germantown for tea and cakes, or to patronize John Dudley's Mead House on Society Hill. Duchemine's Lebanon, in the thickly wooded vicinity of Pennsylvania Hospital was another favorite spot.

"In order to better accomodate Strangers," the City Tavern "fitted up several elegant bed rooms, detached from noise, and as private as a lodging house." As a rule, however, strangers preferred boarding houses. The better Philadelphia inns escaped the chronic complaints registered against their country counterparts. "It was the dirtiest House, without exception in the Province," a 1773 traveler from Bethlehem to Reading wrote, "every Room swarming with Buggs. . . . If I did not pray all Night, I surely watched, as Sleep was entirely banished from my Eyes; tho I enclosed myself in a Circle of Candle grease it did not save me from their devourations."

Philadelphians, like everyone else, then and now, were not immune to flies and mosquitoes, but unscreened windows admitted them in droves. Peter Kalm in 1748 found the latter particularly sinister:

> When the people have gone to bed they begin their disagreeable humming, approach nearer and nearer to the bed, and at last suck up so much blood that they can hardly fly away. . . . The old Swedes here said that gnats had formerly been much more numerous; that even at present they swarmed in vast quantities on the seashore near the salt water, and that those which troubled us this autumn in Philadelphia were of a more venomous kind than they commonly used to be. The last quality appeared from the blisters, which were formed on the spots where the gnats had inserted their sting. In Sweden I never felt any other inconvenience from their sting than a little itching, while they sucked. But when they stung me here at night, my face was so disfigured by little red spots and blisters that I was almost ashamed to show myself.

The nearby livery stables generated flies, and the hordes increased when houses were located near the markets, where waste meat from butchers' cuttings was left for dogs. Few wanted to follow Hector St. John's method of ridding his home of flies in 1782:

> In the middle of my new parlour I have, you may remember, a curious republic of industrious hornets; their nest hangs to the ceiling, by the same twig on which it was so admirably built and contrived in the woods. Its removal did not displease them, for they find in my house plenty of food; and I have left a hole open in one of the panes of the window, which answers all their purposes. By this kind usage they are become quite harmless; they live on the flies, which are very troublesome to us throughout the summer; they are constantly busy in catching them, even on the eyelids of my children. . . . By their assistance, I am but little

troubled with flies. All my family are so accustomed to their strong buzzing, that no one takes any notice of them. . . .

Despite the confident assurance of the City Tavern, it was almost impossible to insulate guests from noise. The rumbling of heavy Contesoge wagons, and the clatter of stages were supplemented from dawn till dusk by the incessant clang of the carpenter's hammer. Philadelphia, according to one observer, was forever tearing down or putting up.

It was both economical and more private to take rooms in a lodging house. Adams and some of the Massachusetts delegates stayed at Mrs. Yard's "Stone House opposite the City Tavern" in 1774-75, but the thrifty New Englander was always comparing rates at different boarding houses, and moved briefly away from Mrs. Yard's before deciding her accommodations outweighed the savings. Washington, deKalb, Hancock and the Tory journalist James Rivington stayed at one time or another in the old Slate Roof House Widow Graydon operated. She also numbered among her boarders Lady Moore and daughter, Sir William Draper and the comedian O'Brien and Lady Susan, his wife—all from London. As Vice-President, Adams lodged at Francis', 11-13 South Fourth Street. Eventually post-war inflation in Philadelphia took its toll. The cost of living bothered many Congressmen when the Federal Government moved from New York to Philadelphia in 1790, and there were repeated threats to move back. Before it relocated at the new "Federal City" in the muddy lowlands along the Potomac, government officials did have the pleasure of patronizing for dinners, at least, the magnificent Oeller's Hotel.

In a sense, it was an extension of the French influence that already had led some tavernkeepers to put tables on the sidewalks in imitation of the Parisian cafes. Since the State House was first opened for the Assembly and Courts about 1747/48 those within looked across the three-foot deep defile of Chestnut Street to a small two-story tavern, surrounded by piles of bleached oyster shells, redeemed only by tall walnut trees "rising above the open and cheerless lots which served to guide the stranger to the State House, itself beyond the verge of common population." Its rough-dashed construction bore the date "1693," and William Penn was said to have stopped and "refreshed himself with a pipe" when he was out that way, for which "Black Alice" recalled, "she always had his penny."

In 1745, "Clarke's Inn," as it was then known, advertised it had "for sale several dogs and wheels, much preferable to any jacks for roasting any jount of meat." The little "spit dogs," bowlegged from running in "a hollow cylinder, like a squirrel" to turn the jack which kept the meat rotating over the fire, were conversation pieces, for "at cooking time . . . it was no uncommon thing to see the cooks running around the streets looking for their 'truant labourers.' " Then it became the State House Inn, and after the Revolution was renamed the "Half Moon" by the new proprietor, Mr. Hassel, whose only daughter Norah drew many admirers including Aaron Burr.

Oeller's ended its happy isolation. Just across the street from the new Congress Hall, at Sixth and Chestnut, and next to Rickett's Circus, it dazzled Philadelphians. Some Senators and Congressmen took rooms, and virtually all, during recesses, stopped in for punch or dinner. Talleyrand and other notable French emigres adopted it, and the German waltz was introduced to America in its sixty-foot square Assembly room, "with a handsome music gallery at one end, papered after the French taste, with the Pantheon figures in compartments, imitating festoons, pillars and groups of antique drawings, in the same style as lately introduced in the most elegant houses in London." Citizen Genet was the guest at a gala banquet upon his arrival in Philadelphia, and the Society of Cincinnati was one of many organizations which met there. Washington much preferred the equestrian acts at Rickett's circus, and that edifice was a marvel in its own right since it could be transformed from a tanbark arena into a gigantic stage. Throughout the 1790's, however, Oeller's perfectly complemented the New Theatre as a monument to Philadelphia's progress.

The City Tavern desperately tried to hold on. It hastily added some more rooms and as early as 1789 took the title of "hotel." But even this French touch could not save it, and it was in a state of marked decline as the '90's opened, a victim of the strange twenty-year life cycle which haunted so many of Philadelphia's inns and taverns. Then on December 17, 1799 a fire devastated Rickett's and destroyed Oeller's. Amid all the excitement, on December 18 a rumor of Washington's death reached Philadelphia, and was soon confirmed. The great man of the century had died on December 14th at Mount Vernon, but some of the Philadelphians who were such staunch partisans of France mourned the passing of Oeller's more, especially those, perhaps, who found in the city's taverns the courage required to embark on that sometime companion of liquor, romance.

11

"REFLECTIONS ON COURTSHIP AND MARRIAGE": Love Wasn't Always Brotherly In Philadelphia

* * * * *

Let us survey the morning dress of some women. Down-stairs they come, pulling up their ungartered, dirty stockings; slipshod, with naked heels peeping out; no stays or other decent conveniency, but all flip-flop; a sort of clout thrown about the neck, without form or decency; a tumbled, discoloured mob or nightcap, half on and half off, with the frowzy hair hanging in sweaty ringlets, staring like Medusa with her serpents, shrugging up her petticoats, that are sweeping the ground and scarce tied on, hands unwashed, teeth furred, and eyes crusted.

—From a pamphlet published by B. Franklin, 1746

* * * * *

"Reflections On Courtship and Marriage"

Scholars are divided on whether Franklin wrote this Hogarthian description. His puckish habit of pretending he found controversial items on the doorstep of his print shop, gave him a measure of anonymity when he preferred. Unlike some of the dour essays on marriage that proliferated in Philadelphia in the 18th century, the mission of this piece was to eliminate marital problems.

> What fermentations and heats often arise from breaking of china, disordering a room, dinner not being ready at a precise hour, and a thousand other such impertinent bagatelles

the author asks, giving us in the process vignettes of life in the city's kitchens and dining rooms.

Not all romances had marriage in mind, as Franklin illustrates in his advice to a young man purportedly debating that course or choosing a mistress. His crisp bluntness so shocked the staid historians of the 19th century they banned its publication as "unhappily too indecent to print," and no one ventured to publish it until 1926. Thomas Paine, who forsook his bride and creditors in the British Isles and fled to Philadelphia in late 1774, not as a fugitive but as a searcher after freedom, gloomily wrote the following June:

> . . . the young, the rash and amorous, whose hearts are ever glowing with desire . . . dote on the first amiable image that chances throws in their way, and when the flame is once kindled, would risk eternity itself to appease it. . . . Thus for a few hours of dalliance, I will not call it affection, the repose of all their future days are sacrificed.

He quoted with approval the comments of an "American savage" (whom he may have invented) when responding to a suggestion he "marry according to the ceremonies of the church, as being the ordinance of an infinitely wise and good God:"

> . . . either the Christian's God was not so good and wise as he was represented, or he never meddled with the marriages of his people; since not one in a hundred of them had anything to do either with happiness or common sense. Hence . . . as soon as ever you meet you long to part; and not having this relief in your power, by way of revenge, double each other's misery. Whereas in our's, which have no other ceremony than mutual affection, and last no longer than they bestow mutual pleasures, we make it our business to oblige the heart we are afraid to lose; and being at liberty to separate, seldom or never feel the inclination. But if any should be found so wretched among us, as to hate where . . . [there] . . . ought to be love, we instantly dissolve the bond. God made us all in pairs; each

173

has his mate somewhere or other; and 'tis our duty to find each other out, since no creature was ever intended to be miserable.

In 1788 Philadelphians could re-read this essay in Matthew Carey's pocket-sized *American Museum,* prefaced with ruminations by "The Old Bachelor":

> As badly off as I am, I had rather be a solitary bachelor, than a miserable married man. . . .

But to counterbalance this negativism, Carey inserted a testimonial by "Philander" which extolled the writer's good fortune in the "Five years . . . since I was enrolled in the list of married men," and then went on to blame the increased "number of bachelors and maids" on the high cost of living.

The Quakers, staunch believers in the sanctity and worth of marriage, as early as 1683 pondered a suggestion that all single men be fined for each year they remained unwed after their 21st birthday. It was dropped, but bachelors were, for a time, taxed on a separate basis, more for revenue than as a spur to marriage. No one endorsed the impetuous approach of John Rambo who, according to a complaint of Peter Cock, was charged with having criminal intercourse with Peter's daughter, Bridget, "about the time of Christmas, 1684.

> The said John Rambo came at midnight to the house of her father, and by pulling off a plank of the house, on the loft, near the chamber, he jumped down to the floor, and directly after got into the bed wherein said Bridget, and her two sisters (aged 16 and 19) were also laying; saying he was resolved to be the husband of Bridget, (even as his brother had before taken another sister), and must therefore lie there. Whereupon, there being a crowded place, the two sisters, with strange submission, withdrew and lay upon the floor all night in a cold December! The court, after the verdict of the jury, adjuged John Rambo to marry Bridget before she be delivered or then maintain the child. Both to be fined £10 each. . . . Afterwards said Rambo was fined £150 for noncompliance.

Before the Revolution it was next to impossible to get an absolute divorce. Only the unwitting victim of a bigamous marriage and a couple wed in violation of the prohibited degrees of blood relationship could be freed from the bonds of matrimony. Others whose spouses had committed bigamy, adultery or the various crimes against nature, could, after the conviction of the offender, apply for a divorce from bed and board, tantamount to a legal separation. The problem was further complicated by the uncertainty as to where the aggrieved party could go. for such a decree, since the 1705 statute was murky on the point. In 1766 John Goggin, a mariner, petitioned the Assembly to give him more than a mere separation:

> ... he had the Misfortune, in the Year 1756, to be married to a certain Catherine O'Brien, whom he then took to be an honest industrious Woman, but in some Time afterwards ... to his inexpressible Grief and Misery, found the Reverse:—that he used all moderate Means, for a considerable Time, to reform her Evil Habits—his Pains proved ineffectual, she notoriously abandoning herself to a lewd and dissolute Course of Life, and by her Extravagant Fondness for strong Liquors, run the Petitioner very much in Debt; that unable to lead a tolerable life with his said Wife, after publishing a Notice in the Gazette, forewarning all Persons not to credit her on his Account, and obtaining a Writing obligatory from her never to challenge or trouble him on Account of said Marriage, the Petitioner gave her a good Sum of Money, and went to Sea; that he continued abroad ... about Fourteen Months, in which Space of Time she got and brought forth a Bastard Child, and became a Burden to the City;—that the Overseers of the Poor attached the Petitioner for the Maintenance of her and the said Child, and that he, to avoid Contention, paid down every Demand;—that ... being grievously afflicted at the frequent Scandals of the said Woman, [he] went again beyond Seas, and continued abroad these two Years past, and on his late Arrival here, found the said *Catherine* was become a Prostitute to Negroes, and in the Month of *January* 1765, was delivered of a Bastard Mulattoe Child ... ; that in this unhappy Situation the Petitioner is again called on by the Overseers of the Poor, to pay the Expences attending the Birth, &c. of the Mullatoe Child ... and the distressed Petitioner can find no Relief under Abuses and Oppressions of this most unhappy and wicked Woman. ...

A divorce from bed and board would hardly help, since his wicked wife could still "sue for Alimony and Support." Moreover he could not remarry if he was so inclined. The General Assembly merely tabled the petition, probably because it was uncertain whether it had the power to give him an absolute divorce.

In 1769, however, the legislators granted a similar request from Curtis Grubb, a Lancaster ironmaster whose wife Ann, after deserting him, had a "Bastard-Child" and then "married ... a certain Archibald Neale." The governor signed the measure and when, with other provincial laws, it was sent to London for the Crown's approval, it engendered discussion whether colonial legislatures should be exercising power beyond that already given. The divorce was allowed to stand without a formal opinion. Encouraged by this tacit approval four more divorce actions were considered by the Assembly in 1772 but only one was granted and sent on to England. George Keehmle offered proof of his wife's conviction for adultery. This time the Board of Trade was leary. Elizabeth Keehmle had not married her lover, as had Ann Grubb, and hence did not add bigamy to the complaint against her. So the Board referred the matter to the Privy Council with the observation that it thought the governor and Assembly action was "either Improper or Unconstitutional" and voiced concern that, unless disallowed, it might become "a Precedent and Example." On April 27, 1773 the Council nullified Keehmle's decree, and directed all colonial governors to withhold consent from any provincial bill of absolute divorce.

After the Declaration of Independence, the Assembly was unfettered, and granted absolute divorces in eleven of the thirty-five cases it considered between 1777 and 1785. Catherine Summers was freed from her husband Peter because he

> beat her in a most cruel and inhuman manner and hath estranged his affections from her and placed them on other women and hath frequently committed the heinous sin of adultery and hath boasted of such his crimes.

In 1783 Mrs. Keehmle asked the Assembly to reinstate its decree of ten years before granting a divorce to her husband, but just as the legislators were ready to act favorably, the husband intervened and asked that it be done in his, rather than her name. The lawmakers washed their hands of the whole matter. Nor did they give relief to Elizabeth M'Farren Shanks in 1777 when she said her husband James deserted her "about seven years ago" and she had "never since . . . seen, and very seldom heard of him." The Reverend Nathaniel Irwin, however, was given his freedom from Martha, after he produced "authenticated copies of the records of two several courts of justice" that his wife had been convicted of adultery. Jane Bartram in 1784, got no satisfaction in her divorce suit when she claimed her husband "joined the British forces and departed with them without leaving a maintenance or support for her and her son, and previously to his departure used her very cruelly."

A form of veteran's preference seemed to prevail. In 1779 James Martin won his decree when he averred that during the British occupation of Philadelphia when he was absent from town, his wife Elizabeth "resorted among the British soldiers" and had taken "one serjeant Havell . . . into his . . . house and bed and cohabited." Moreover she proclaimed the sergeant was her husband and adopted his name, and went off with him when the British evacuated the city, "taking with her the said James Martin's effects, and leaving him to pay sundry debts of her contracting." Giles Hicks, a captain in the 10th Pennsylvania Regiment got swift satisfaction in 1780. He contended that in 1776 when he was but fifteen "and . . . intoxicated" he was "seduced by . . . Hester McDaniel and her relations" into marriage against "the consent of his guardians and other friends." At that time Hester was "a common prostitute" and since the marriage "hath . . . lived separated from (him) in open adultery with divers other men

> by means whereof she became so diseased of the lues venera as to be declared incurable after seven months continuance in the Pennsylvania Hospital.

One incident of bigamy had political overtones. In June 1783 Mrs. Henry Osborne arrived in Philadelphia, fresh from Ireland. She found her husband had acquired another Mrs. Henry Osborne since leaving her several years before. An engaging Irishman, Henry had in the comparatively brief interval charmed his way into a wealthy marriage, high places in the Radical Party and was Escheator General of Pennsylvania. The Republicans expressed shock at Henry's action, but took the occasion to denounce George Bryan, "the grand old lady" of the Radical Party.

In so doing they ushered in a new phase in Pennsylvania politics by introducing the art of abuse on a state-wide scale, smearing Bryan with everything from sadism to smuggling. Osborne quickly vanished and his marital saga seems to have passed into osbcurity with him, but not before Bryan—and perhaps the political art—suffered irreparable damage.

The Assembly, after two years study, agreed in 1785 to vest the courts with authority to handle divorce cases and established grounds for absolute decrees: adultery, bigamy, desertion for four years and, in certain instances, impotence or sterility. Far broader than either England or the other twelve states, the new code was modeled to a large extent after the Scottish law. One of the legislators who sat on the committee which drew up the bill was Anthony Wayne. While he contributed little or nothing to the legal discussions, there is a tinge of humor in his mere presence for no prominent American of the times could match his accomplishments in extra-marital affairs. So extensive was his range and conquests that it would be safe to eliminate the qualifying adjective "prominent" and concede the title.

War gave Wayne a much wider theatre than he might otherwise have enjoyed, and the Revolution produced a profound change in the attitude of many Philadelphians. As in any conflict soldiers took advantage of the dramatic circumstances with which fate vested them. Washington's naked, freezing army on the slopes of Valley Forge during the winter of 1777-1778, was visited by prostitutes from Philadelphia until the general, fearing either espionage or venereal disease, or both, ordered the women driven out of camp under a threat of lashing. Within the occupied city Sir William Howe set the tempo by proudly displaying his beautiful blonde mistress, Mrs. Joshua Loring. Any objections Mr. Loring might have had seem to have been settled by his appointment as Commissary of Prisoners.

The Lorings from Massachusetts had been friends of Sir William for some time, and the exotic arrangement by which she accompanied him during his American campaign intrigued Philadelphia Tories and Rebels alike. Howe's apparent lethargy in attacking the depleted and demoralized forces of Washington at Valley Forge was not altered by Loyalist jibes like

> Awake, arouse Sir Billy
> There's forage in the plain
> Ah, leave your little filly
> And open the campaign.
>
> Heed not a woman's prattle
> Which tickles in the ear
> But give the word for battle
> And grasp the warlike spear.

Neither was he moved by taunts like that composed by Francis Hopkinson from the Patriot's side:

> Sir William he, as snug as a flea
> Lay all this time a-snoring
> Nor dreamed of harm, as he lay warm
> In bed with Mrs. Loring.

A congenial, handsome man who was as tall as Washington, Howe acted resolutely to quiet the fears Philadelphia mothers had that their daughters might be raped by the Hessians. American propagandists had circulated tales of terror about the German mercenaries who in turn had been terrified by English propaganda that if captured they would be eaten by the Americans. Propagandists apart, the Hessians, accustomed to the European theory of spoils going to victors, had demonstrated their adherence to that concept in New Jersey the year before. Howe directed that any of his troops convicted of rape were to be hanged, and made it clear that any officer who got a young woman pregnant might be forced to marry her. He had required Major Lord Cathcart, a friend of André, to marry the daughter of a New York Tory. If this had any chilling effect on British ardor it was not noticeable. The officers assured everyone that they had not come to despoil America and promised to leave a bastard for every slain American soldier. Captain Oliver DeLancey, highly popular with Philadelphia girls, fathered two without being required to marry either mother. To the complete shock of the Quakers some British openly advertised their lust:

> Wanted to hire with two single gentlemen, *a young woman,* to act in the capacity of housekeeper, and who can occasionally put her hand to *any*

thing. Extravagant wages will be given, and *no character* required. Any young woman who chooses to offer, may be further informed at the bar of the City tavern.

As winter and the lack of food, blankets and other necessities immobilized General Washington twenty miles away, Philadelphia settled down to "a frolicking Winter" under the auspices of the British. Fortunes were won and lost at faro, and the stunned Quakers, content to take English gold, watched in silence as the merriment gathered momentum. One British officer had a set of regimentals made for his mistress and let her review the troops "like a Queen." Even girls whose sympathies were with the Continentals were lured by the excitement. One later criticized "the censure thrown on many of the poor girls for not scorning the pleasures that courted them" and urged that "proper allowances" be made "for young people in the bloom of life and spirits after being so

STATE HOUSE—1778

When C. W. Peale made this sketch after the British had left Philadelphia, a contemporary complained about "the offensiveness of the air in and around the State House, which the Enemy had made an Hospital and left it in a condition disgraceful to the Character of civility. Particularly they had opened a large square pit near the House, a receptacle for filth, into which they had also cast dead horses and the bodies of men who by the mercy of death had escaped from their further cruelties." Another observer said they left the building "in a most filthy condition & the inside much torn to pieces . . ." The Assembly room was repaired and the Congress returned from York, Pa., to resume residence, having fled there to avoid capture. In 1783 they vacated the premises and went to Princeton to escape a confrontation with irate soldiers demanding redress for a list of grievances. Peale's perspective shows the original steeple and the wooden sheds at either end of the complex. Congress Hall on the 6th Street side, and the new City Hall on the 5th were not built for several years after the Revolution.

long deprived of the gaieties and amusements of life which their ages and spirits called for. . . . Plays, concerts, balls, assemblies court their presence. Politics were never introduced. . . ." Pretty Rebecca Franks tried to entice a close friend, the recent bride of a Maryland congressman, William Paca:

> You can have no idea of the continued amusement I live in. I can scarce have a moment to myself . . . and most elegantly am I dressed for a ball this evening at Smiths [City Tavern] where we have one every Thursday. . . . No loss for partners, even I am engaged to seven different gentlemen for you must know 'tis a fixed rule never to dance but two dances with the same person. Oh, how I wish Mr. P. would let you come in for a week or two. . . . I know you are as fond of a gay life as myself. You'd have an opportunity of raking as much as you choose, either at plays, balls, concerts or assemblies. . . .

Ever alert, merchants advertised products like Dr. Yeldall's "Antivenereal Essence" which claimed it could either protect or cure, "Hannay's Preventive," and for the more semantically sensitive, "Keyser's Pills," professedly famous throughout Europe for efficacy against "a certain disease." A poem in Towne's *Evening Post* in February 1778 purportedly described the mood of some Philadelphian belles:

AFTER SUPPER

Twas ten o'clock; the cloth removed
The servants all retreated
Two tapers blaz'd; his fair beloved,
On Damon's knee was seated.

By love conducted, Celia's cheek
On Damon's bosom lay;
He gaz'd—he sighed—and wish'd to speak—
And knew not what to say.

His arms, twin'd round her taper waist,
Explain'd his wishful sighs;
And well were Celia's thoughts exprest—
They glistened in her eyes.

But soon these mutual looks of love
Their mutual silence broke;
And thus (his lips were seen to move)
The trembling Damon spoke:

'When will my Celia make me blest?
Oh when, my charmer! When?—'
The fair one leer'd, his hand she prest
'Put out the lights—and THEN!

"Reflections On Courtship and Marriage"

General Charles Lee, then a British prisoner of war, caustically summarized Howe as one who "shut his eyes, fought his battles, drank his bottle, and had his little Whore." But Lee was hardly one to talk. When he was exchanged in the spring of 1778 and rejoined Washington at Valley Forge, the overjoyed American commander invited him to spend the night at the Headquarters, and gave up the back bedroom to Lee, moving into the front with Martha. Elias Boudinot who had arranged for Lee's return, described the eccentric officer the next morning:

> . . . he lay very late and breakfast was detained for him. When he came out, he looked dirty, as if he had been in the street all night. Soon after I discovered that he had brought a miserably dirty hussy with him from Philadelphia (a British sergeant's wife) and had actually taken her into his room by a back door, and she had slept with him that night.

This classic demonstration of double-occupancy, within a few inches of the Washingtons, may have been Lee's finest hour. Within a few weeks at Monmouth he would be suspected of treason.

To honor Sir William Howe's impending departure for England and their own departure from Philadelphia, the British staged a "Mischianza" at Duke Wharton's estate at Front and Christian Streets, "Walnut Grove." Guests were transported by water from center city aboard gaily furbished vessels, followed by a barge with a band. A mock tournament between two sets of "knights" vying to prove their ladies fairest of all ended in a tactful tie, while fourteen of Philadelphia's prettiest wore outfits designed by André and described by him

> . . . gauze turbans spangled and edged with gold or silver, on the right side a veil of the same kind hung as low as the waist, and the left side of the turban was enriched with pearl and tassels of gold or silver and crested with a feather. The dress was of the Polonaise kind and of white silk with long sleeves. The sashes which were worn around the waist and were tied with a large bow on the left side hung very low, and were trimmed, spangled, and fringed according to the colors of the knight. . . .

A Hessian officer noted that the English firm of Coffin & Anderson took in £12,000 sterling for the silks and other materials. Two triumphal arches were erected in the gardens, and through these the knights and their ladies led the way to "a spacious hall . . . painted in imitation of Sienna marble" where "cooling liquors" were served—the knights on bended knees received the compliments of their ladies and dancing began. At 10 p.m. the windows were thrown open and "a magnificent bouquet of rockets began the fireworks," which ended with the interior of a triumphal arch being "illuminated amid an uninterrupted flight

181

of rockets and bursting balloons." At midnight "supper was announced, and large folding doors, hitherto artfully concealed, being suddenly thrown open" revealed "a magnificent saloon of two hundred and ten by forty, and twenty-two in height, with three alcoves on each side, which served for sideboards. . . ." Hundreds of candles lit the room, some affixed to branches, some suspended in clusters from the ceiling and three hundred "disposed along the supper tables." There were 430 covers, 1200 dishes and "twenty-four black slaves in Oriental dresses, with silver collars and bracelets, ranged in two lines. . . ." After supper, toasts were offered to the King and Queen and royal family, the army and navy, their respective commanders and the knights and their ladies. Then "we returned to the ballroom and continued to dance until four o'clock."

Peggy Shippen was not allowed to attend when her father at the last minute yielded to a Quaker delegation's protest against the flimsiness of the dresses. She was inconsolable. One of the belles said wistfully, "we never had, and perhaps never shall have so elegant an entertainment in America again." But some older Tories were appalled at the "folly and extravagance." And the resolute Quaker Mrs. Henry Drinker told her diary,

> This day may be remembered by many for the scenes of folly and vanity. . . . How insensible do these people appear, while our land is so greatly desolated, and death and sore destruction has overtaken and impends over so many.

Even the English newspapers in the city thought it was a bit much for a commander who had not won a war. Writing an epitaph on the British stay in Philadelphia, one loyalist lamented:

> Our officers were practising at the dice-box, or studying the chances of picquet when they should have been storming towns, and crushing the spirit of rebellion; and the harlot's eye glistened with wanton pleasure at the general's table when the brightness of his sword should have reflected terror in the face of the rebels.

The most unsophisticated observer could hardly reconcile the platitudes of pulpit and law with the events taking place under anyone's nose, and the impact on impressionable minds was inevitable. Not that Philadelphians were naive. Prostitution along the waterfront had been strongly entrenched since Penn's time and flourished in face of intermittent raids and fines. Philadelphia's prisons, where men and women were thrown into common cells, were hotbeds of promiscuity and the General Assembly periodically had to cope with complaints that women were getting themselves arrested on fictitious debt charges so they could be reunited with their lovers. In nearby New Jersey there were tragic overtones to a British experiment undertaken in 1776 when they still occupied New York. An English colonial trader, Captain Jackson contracted with the British War Office to transport 3,500 women "whom England felt it could dispense with, to become the intimate property of the army quartered in New York City," designed to relieve "the tensions" of enlisted personnel. Although one of the ships sank enroute with 50 of the women, Jackson put into the West Indies and acquired fifty black women to fulfill his contract. They became known as Jackson's "Whites" and were maintained with their companions in a stockade. But when the British departed in July 1777 for their long circuitous voyage to conquer Philadelphia, they opened the gates and let the whole company of girls shift for themselves in the strange and alien countryside. Some managed to get aboard London-bound ships, others were absorbed into the American stream, but many wandered through New Jersey. Driven off by local farmers, desperate with hunger, they managed to survive by raiding orchards and gardens and finally entered Ramapo Pass in the Saddle River Valley. There they were treated hospitably by some Indians, Dutch and ex-negro slaves, along with Hessian deserters. Sheltered by their fears, they remained secluded in those parts for generations and eventually inbreeding produced a varicolored race with physical defects such as 12-toed feet, webbed fingers and toes. An estimated 6,000 descendants of these original sex slaves are scattered today through New York's Rockland and Orange counties, and Passaic, Morris and Sussex counties in New Jersey. What is left of their community life is based at Ringwood, New Jersey.

Women who took up with the British in Philadelphia and who accompanied them on their march back to New York may not have been aware of the Jackson episode, but the more knowledgeable sympathizers who were forced to flee unquestionably wondered whether they would be subjected to the same callous treatment. Mystery envelops the destiny of those who had neither the money nor the social status to become expatriates in London. In July 1778 Ann Robinson offered a $20 reward "for a servant Negro woman, named DINAH, about five feet eight or ten inches high, tawny complexion, about nineteen or twenty years old; had received a cut on the forehead from one of the soldiers shortly before she went away; was big with child and near the time of her lying in" when she "ran away with the last of the British troops from the city of Philadelphia."

In June 1778 when the Americans occupied Philadelphia once more a returning civilian appraised the period of British rule:

... the morals of the inhabitants have suffered vastly. The enemy introduced new fashions and made old vices more common . . . The females who stayed in the city . . . cut a curious figure. Their hats, which are of the flat, round kind, are of the size of a large, japanned tea-waiter . . . their hair is dressed with the assistance of wool, etc. . . . I cannot yet learn whether the *cork rumps* have been introduced here, but some artificial rumps or other are necessary to counterbalance the extraordinary natural weight which some of the ladies carry before them . . . most of the young ladies who were in the city with the enemy and wear the present fashionable dresses have purchased them at the expense of their virtue. It is agreed on all hands that the British officers played the devil with the girls. The privates, I supposed, were satisfied with the *common* prostitutes. Last Saturday, an imitation of the *Mischenza* . . . was humbly attempted. A noted strumpet was paraded through the streets with her head dressed in the modern *British* taste, to the no small amusement of a vast crowd . . . She acted her part well; to complete the farce, there ought to have been another lady of the same character (as General Howe had two). . . .

Richard Henry Lee saw this:

Woman of the Town with the Monstrous headdress of the Tory Ladies. . . . Her head was elegantly and expensively dressed, I suppose about three feet high and of proportionable width, with a profusion of Curls, &c &c &c—the figure was droll and occasioned much mirth—it has loosened some heads already and probably will bring the rest within the bounds of reason.

But Anthony Wayne got reports from his friend Walter Stewart:

'Tis all gaiety. Every Lady and Gentleman endeavours to outdo the Other in Splendor and Show . . ." As to the girls, "They have lost that native innocence in their manners which was formerly their characteristick, and supplied in its place with what they call an Easy Behavior. They have really got the art of throwing themselves into the most wanton and Amorous Postures which their free manner of speech adds not a little to. By Heaven, it is almost too much for a young Soldier to bear."

As the church bells pealed in the New Year of 1779, a citizen who signed himself Philanthropos surveyed the scene in Philadelphia:

I see nothing but extortion, a love of pleasure, madness and dissipation . . . Public virtue is a standing jest, religion no longer respected, while avarice and extortion are universally contaminating the morals of the people, and destroying all confidence in government and laws . . . It is high time for the virtuous few to step forward and endeavour to do something towards repelling the rapid and alarming torrents of vice and corruption. . . .

Relishing the prospect of returning to the "madness and dissipa-

184

tion" Anthony Wayne would not have qualified for Philanthropos' "virtuous few." Borrowing a familiar line from the *Beggar's Opera* he summarized his personal philosophy, "Like the bee, I move from flower to flower and sip the honey from each rose." A thoughtful friend cautioned him about possible thorns in some roses, saying that a mutual acquaintance lost his sweetheart "on account of his getting the C——p last campaigne." The sweetheart did not have "quite so horrid an idea" about the ailment, but her mother broke up the romance by denouncing it as a "crying and unpardonable sin." If Wayne was disposed to be particularly careful, it was not due to concern for any mother's reaction, but from his fastidious sense of cleanliness. Like Gouverneur Morris he never slept with any woman below, what he felt, was his social station. This, of course, was hardly a guarantee against infection.

Washington had placed Philadelphia under the military protection of Benedict Arnold, whose undisclosed ambitions made him a natural ally of the Tories. Far removed from the political feuding between Congress and the Supreme Executive Council of Pennsylvania, and Arnold's private war with both, Philadelphia's ambassador of good will, Franklin was delighting the French with his infinite bag of tricks. He told one young matron that earlier in life when women bestowed sexual favors upon him he never suffered from gout, and attributed his present plight to the lack of "Christian charity" among them. To another he explained he had too much regard for her husband to force a divorce, but exacted a promise that she be his wife in the next world because he could not be content with just bussing her on the cheek. Since he thought he would die forty years before her, he assured her he would practice on his harmonica so he would be sufficiently skilled to accompany her superb singing when she arrived to share Paradise with him.

Arnold, who courted Peggy Shippen with affectionate notes and letters he copied almost verbatim from an earlier and unsuccessful correspondence with a Boston belle, married the 19-year old Philadelphian in February 1779. She persuaded him to forego his dream of a manor in New York, and buy instead Mount Pleasant, as part of the marriage contract.

Neither the return of Congress nor the state government to Philadelphia changed the moral atmosphere. Congress was threatening to move out of the city because the astronomic rise in the cost of living was staggering, and the Supreme Executive Council was doing its best to encourage the move. One Congressman asked his state to relieve him so he could get out of this "land of bondage," but Benjamin Harrison, writing to his fellow Virginian, General Washington, said he would not mind staying longer, particularly if his date with "little Kate, the washerwoman's daughter across the way" turned out as he hoped. He described her as "rosy, clean and fresh as the morning." The Marquis de Chastellux, touring the city in 1780 was startled to see prudish Samuel Adams having a "tete-a-tete" with a pretty young girl who was preparing his tea. Since Adams was nearly 60, the young Marquis generously dismissed any notion of scandal. In any case word came to Adams that the Devil was loose in Boston and he hurried home, leaving Philadelphia to fend for itself.

Charles Willson Peale could not fathom such promiscuity. He puzzled over a conversation with a colonel who kept "boasting of his victories in the arms of Venus," and wondered why a married man did not look to his wife for "domestick Bliss" instead of running around with a "Sett of Prostatutes."

Hardly had the British influence begun to wane than the French arrived in Philadelphia. The French minister, Gerard, entertained lavishly at his new residence, and twice a week it was the scene of balls, concerts and parties where the more influential Philadelphians got a chance to see the latest French fashions and hear the latest from Paris. Among the ladies "French hair dressers, milliners, and dancers are all the *tone*," one correspondent wrote; "The Virginia-Jig has given place to the *Cotillion* and minuet-de-la-cour."

In September 1781, Rochambeau led 6,000 French troops up Front Street and down Vine to the Center Square, enroute to join Washington in the ultimate triumph at Yorktown. Coming in behind a long lean line of homespun Continentals, the King's soldiers paused a mile out and changed into dress whites—the several regiments being distinguished by facings of blue, rose, green and pink. The Soisonnais wore pink plumes in their caps, and Gouverneur Morris thought they looked like "effete aristocrats." Philadelphia women were delighted, the French observers said, and watched the precision drills from windows, decked out in their finest gowns. At dusk some of the crowd of 20,000 went over to the French legation where the Minister hosted a banquet for the notables, and chanted, "Long Live King Louis." Since 1779 Philadelphians had been accustomed to saluting "His Most Christian Majesty" on his birthday, August 23, with fireworks, concerts and ships in the harbor booming out thirteen rounds. When the army finally got back on the road, it paused at Valley Forge to survey the site where the Americans struggled to survive the hard winter of 1777-78, thus becoming the first in an endless procession of pilgrims.

With the victory at Yorktown, the contagion of enthusiasm for France almost overwhelmed Philadelphia. When the new minister, Luzerne, held a gala on July 15, 1782 at the legation to honor the birth of an heir to the French throne, the grounds were transformed by the renowned engineer Pierre L'Enfant into groves, elaborate gardens and walks with a

186

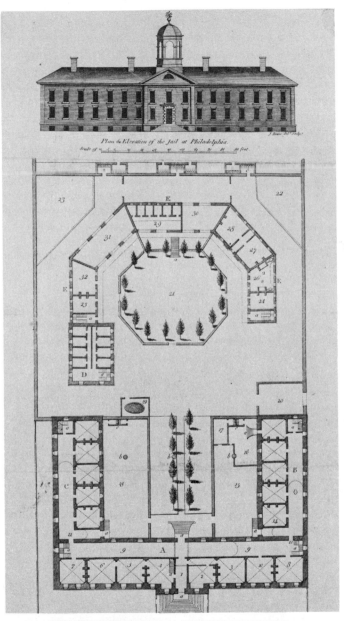

Plan & Elevation of the Jail at Philadelphia.

WALNUT STREET JAIL—A VIEW FROM THE TOP

Like most penitentiary blueprints the symmetry is more attractive on paper than in actuality. Brutal jailers, dissolute prisoners naturally are not included. Its yard, depicted here with trees, served occasional civic purposes such as the balloon ascension in 1793. Presumably the debtors in the "apartments" at the top of the plan had a better view than the "felons" who could, if correctly situated, gaze wistfully at "Independence Hall."

pavillion in the center. Luzerne had the board fence torn down so the 10,000 people outside could see the elect dining and dancing and suggested to city officials that he distribute 600 livres among them or two pipes of Madeira. He was thanked, but told either gesture would likely cause a riot. The fete created much excitement. Hairdressers had to schedule appointments as early as 4 a.m. to accommodate anxious women. The considerate Luzerne even had a room set aside for "the several Quaker ladies whose dress would not permit them to join the assembly" and they "were indulged with a sight of the company through a gauze curtain." A farmer whose son witnessed the affair was startled by his changed appearance:

> His hair is besprinkled with powder so that it looks as white as that of a man eighty years old. A pair of ruffles reaches from his waistband to the extremity of his nails. A strip of gold lace encircles his hat. A huge stock is worn around his neck containing muslin enough to be his winding sheet. A long piece of cold iron, called a sword, hangs at his side. He looks like a baboon!

Duelling, that perennial companion of romance, became fashionable. In one week there were nine "affairs of honor" reported, but the participants were poor shots and fatalities were rare. A young, lovesick French officer killed himself because an attractive Philadelphia widow rejected him. His superiors were at pains to explain that the unfortunate fellow was really German, implying that any failure in amour by Frenchmen was an impossibility.

A rural clergyman dolefully summed up his reaction to the Philadelphia scene:

> Thus calico and silk and sin
> By slow degrees kept coming in—

Frenchmen bent on conquests, however, found Philadelphia matrons, on the whole, were scrupulous about their marriage vows. Brissot de Warville thought the city was admirable, but far from exciting:

> The men are grave, the women serious. There are no finicial airs to be found here, no libertine wives, no coffee-houses, no agreeable walks.

But Prince de Broglie thought it would "vie with the first Courts in Europe for dissipation, luxury and extravagance. . . ." Accustomed to a code where married women enjoyed utmost freedom in matters of love, the Duke of Liancourt discovered the rules reversed. "Unmarried women enjoy the same degree of liberty which married women do in

France," he wrote, "and which married women here do not like." Rochambeau found the same thing. "American women once they have entered matrimony give themselves to it." Talleyrand, the French bishop, politician and philanderer, was disgusted to find that French wives in America deserted their native traditions. Madame de la Tour du Pin, a Dillon beauty, was actually sleeping with her husband every night. "It is essential," he grimaced, "to have a good reputation in this country." Nancy Shippen, forced by her physician-father to marry a wealthy scion of the Livingston family in New York, although her life-long love was a French attache in her home city, tried desperately to make her marriage work in spite of her husband's open maintenance of two mistresses and two families. When she gave up and came back to Philadelphia she was snubbed, and when she tried to get a divorce, her father and mother sided with her tyrannical spouse.

Bigamy most often occurred in the "back country" where the law was not quite as evident, but Mary Dicks, whose husband John failed in 1773 to win a divorce, set some sort of record. She left Dicks in 1764 after a year of marriage to live with William Ford "in a state of Adultery for a Number of Years having by him . . . Six Children." In 1780 she married William Pearce, "well-knowing" her husband to be alive. Pearce was lost at sea in 1781, and Mary "giving out that she had inter-married with him . . . cohabited with William Walter Humphries" and was living with him "as his Wife" when, after twenty-three years, John Dicks renewed his efforts to get a divorce. Peter Pfeiffer and his wife, Mary, decided to resolve their "divers unhappy differences" by con-tract, but when Peter married Anna Maria Bauer, Mary accused him of bigamy. The nonplused Peter told the court that he had consulted with "Ministers of the gospel," all of whom assured him he was free to remarry, and the "bans of matrimony" to Anna were "published from the pulpit of the church in Germantown three several Sundays and no ob-jection thereto made." The Supreme Executive Council refused to prosecute Peter for bigamy, and new articles of separation between Mary and him were approved.

Religious scruples, as well as social position, forced some couples to weather difficult times in marriage. Others surmounted touchy situations with common sense, as did Elizabeth Hamilton when Alexander Hamilton, then Secretary of the Treasury, got involved with a black-mailing prostitute, Mrs. Reynolds. The incident, more an episode, began in 1791 shortly after the Federal Government moved to Philadelphia. James Reynolds, the woman's husband, was the architect of the extortion scheme, and when he demanded and was flatly refused a position in Hamilton's department, carried the story to the Jeffersonians, who were

189

the bitter enemies of the secretary. An embarrassed Congressional delega-
tion was deputed to investigate and Hamilton met the nasty mess head-on.
Subsequently the sordid story came into the full glare of publicity.
Philadelphians were titillated by the details, and the pious shock
Hamilton's political foes professed was brushed off as hypocritical.
Promiscuity was hardly a novelty. In the August issue of the *American
Museum* for 1787, the monthly poetry section, in successive verses,
carried these captions: "The injured husband's complaint";
"Seduction—An Elegy"; "The dying prostitute—An elegy." Even
the omnipresent spectre of death during the yellow fever epidemic of 1793
failed to discourage some people. The sanctimonious Dr. Rush noted that
some patients, as they recovered, experience "a sudden revival of the
venereal appetite" which sparked numerous weddings, twelve of them
among the survivors at Bush Hill. "I wish I could add," he said sadly,
"that the passion of the sexes for each other, among those subjects of
public charity, was always gratified in a lawful way. Delicacy forbids a detail of the scenes of debauchery which were practised near the hospital, in
some of the tents which had been appropriated for the reception of
convalescents."

The high incidence of illegitimate births throughout the 18th century
was more of a problem to the overseers of the poor than a social disgrace
to the unwed mother. Franklin's illegitimate son had an illegitimate son,
thus preserving to a third generation the grandfather's proclivities.
Around 1746 Franklin concoted a fictional news story about a "Miss Polly
Baker," prosecuted "at Connecticut . . . the Fifth Time, for having a
Bastard Child." As with most of Franklin's tales, it had a happy end-
ing, for Polly's eloquent defense "induced one of her Judges to marry her
the next Day." In essence the imaginary Miss Baker explained she was
a good mother, worked hard for her little brood, and maintained them
"without burthening the Township, and would have done it better, if it had
not been for the heavy Charges and Fines." She thought "it Praisewor-
thy, rather than a punishable Action" that she added "to the Number of
the King's Subjects" and suggested "the great and growing Number
of Batchelors in the Country" who "leave unproduced (which is little
better than Murder) Hundreds of their Posterity to the Thousandth Generation" were guilty of "a greater Offence against the Publick Good than
mine." She suggested they be compelled either to marry or "pay double
the Fine of Fornication every Year." As for any transgression against
the Almighty, how "can it be believed, that Heavan is angry at my having
Children, when to the little done by me towards it, God has been pleased to
add his Divine Skill and admirable Workmanship?" She reminded her
judges of the Biblical admonition to "Encrease and Multiply"—"A

Duty, from the steady Performance of which, nothing has been able to deter me; but for its Sake, I have hazarded the Loss of the Publick Esteem, and have frequently endured Publick Disgrace and Punishment; and therefore ought, in my humble Opinion, instead of a Whipping, to have a Statue erected to my Memory."

Five English newspapers reprinted the story as factual and a French priest included it in a book on moral theology. When Franklin later met the Abbe and told him he invented the tale, the clergyman laughingly said he preferred it, even as fiction, to some of the duller real examples he had cited.

Color constituted no real barrier to romance or relationships. Both the Quakers and Germans had a strong distaste for slavery, although in the former, the greed for gold sometimes prevailed, and a few Quakers were involved in the slave trade. While Philadelphia was not spared the inhumane sights attendant upon an inhumane system such as seeing slaves auctioned "like so many bullocks," or occasionally being taken to the city prison by masters for a preventitive whipping of a dozen lashes to "keep them submissive," the attitude toward blacks was considerably better than in most other parts of America, and much better than that displayed toward many indentured white servants, working off their passage money through periods up to seven years. The maximum slave population in Pennsylvania was reached in 1751 when it was estimated at 11,000—a ratio of about one to fifteen. By 1780 when the state's population was over 300,000 and Pennsylvania became the first to enact a gradual emancipation law, there were about 6,000 and ten years later, when the initial United States census fixed the number of inhabitants at 434,373, slaves had declined to 3,737. Of these Philadelphia County had 387, Bucks 261 and Chester 145. Economics as much as humanitarianism contributed to the dissolution of the institution, since it was more expensive to maintain a slave than to either hire unskilled freemen or acquire an indentured servant. Slaves in Philadelphia were most often employed in household duties and often attained more gentility than a good percentage of the whites. When they were freed, as frequently they were as a mark of affection or for other reasons, they became part of the Philadelphia scene. Penn, in 1700, had urged the Yearly Meeting of Friends to take a position against slavery, a step proposed in Germantown in 1688 by the German-Dutch Quakers. He provided in his will "that my negroes John and Jane his wife shall be set free one month after my decease" and bequeathed to "Old Sam" one hundred acres of land. Coupled with the Quaker-German philosophy about equality of men, a theme which gathered added force after the phrase was written into the Declaration of Independence, the indentured servant system had done much to curb prejudice, since

191

forced servitude by whatever name had given blacks and whites involved a common experience. Intermarriage reached such an extent at various times before 1750 that the General Assembly was importuned unsuccessfully by some narrow minded whites to prohibit future weddings. Frenchmen fleeing to Philadelphia from the black insurrection in the West Indies in the latter part of the century brought with them their negro wives or mistresses who commanded much admiration, and Talleyrand proudly escorted a beautiful black woman during his stay in the city.

In the raucous year 1799 when the Federalist party under President John Adams was fending off the Jeffersonians with the highly unpopular Alien & Sedition Acts, the countryside around Philadelphia was seething with indignation. Rumors were rife in every tavern—a reported plan to wreck a Republican printing press brought Jefferson supporters to stand guard over it. Then the Germans of Northampton County were reported to be marching on the city with pitchforks. Some pirates, awaiting execution, slipped out of the Walnut Street Prison and were chased through the night by mounted troops. The clatter brought night-capped Philadelphians to their windows, thinking it was another chapter in the political furor. But when they searched the *Aurora* for details, that newspaper pronounced Philadelphia calm and quiet: "Nothing more serious than the disturbance of love-making."

12

TEMPER OF THE TIMES:
Philadelphia's Press Reflected the Growing Colonial Metropolis

*   *   *   *   *

30 Sept. 1713. — William Hill, the Beadle of this city, having lately in a heat broke his Bell, and given out that he would no longer continue at the place, but now Expresses a great deal of Sorrow for so doing, and humbly Desires to be Continued therein During his Good Behaviour And the Premises being Considered, And the Vote put, whether he Should Continue the Place any Longer or no, It past in ye affirmative.

*   *   *   *   *

Open-hearted though he was, Penn was pragmatic enough to realize the diversified population of his "Holy Experiment" could be a breeding ground for trouble. As a veteran of protest movements he was well aware how a frontal assault against governmental policies could be mounted. While in Britain the establishment proved too strong for his theories, history demonstrated in 1649 how a king could be struck down, and within a few years would show how James II could be driven from his throne. The government of Pennsylvania stood on much shakier ground, for it had no armies to suppress rebellion and, being privately-owned, could not expect military assistance royal governors in some other colonies could invoke. So when he came to compile the Great Laws of 1682, Penn the Proprietor inserted provisions similar to those under which a younger Penn, the Militant Quaker, had suffered. It was made illegal to write, say or do anything "Tending to Sedition or Disturbance of the peace" or to "carry" one's self "abusively against any Magistrate or person in office."

As if to emphasize this, in 1683 when Anthony Weston and his wife were fined for selling liquor without a license, Penn and the Council rejected some "Proposalls" he offered by way of appeal, as being "of great presumption and Contempt of this Government" and ordered him to "be Whypt at the Market place on Market daye three times. Each time to have Tenn Lashes, at 12 of the Clock at noone, this being the first daye." "Tho. Hooten" and "Tho. Wynn," who helped the unfortunate Weston draft his proposals were admonished, and the freemen who subscribed their names to it were put under £50 bond not to repeat the offence.

But apart from the merrymakers in the caves and the tippling houses, Penn's principal problem was not with his citizens, but with the government itself. The Assembly, chafing under restrictions that denied it the power to suggest laws, became almost psychotic in defense of prerogatives it claimed to have. His Council was rife with personal jealousies. If the "Holy Experiment" was apt to come apart at the seams, the Proprietor had reason enough to think the split would first appear at the top. In the biting winds of January 1684 as he stood glumly surveying the frozen Delaware and the bleak woods that even game had deserted, it was said his prayers were mingled with "strong and impressive sighs . . . because the true Philadelphia and brother love is not to be met with as freely in this our Philadelphia as he on his part desires." The next year when he was back in England, his Assembly impeached his newly-appointed chief justice, Nicholas More, and arrested the court clerk, Patrick Robinson, for refusing to produce the court records. They also voted Robinson "a publick Enemy . . . and a Violator of the Privileges of the Freemen in Assembly met." From across the ocean Penn pleaded, "For the love of God, me, and the poor country, be not so *governmentisi,* so noisy, and open, in your dissatisfactions: some folks love hunting in government itself."

When 28-year-old William Bradford brought his printing press to the area in 1686 "to set up the trade of printing Friends' books" and various legal forms, he found the people more concerned about calendars than government, "complaining . . . they scarcely knew how the time passed, nor . . . hardly knew the Day of Rest." With the help of Samuel Atkyns, he produced an almanac with apologies for any "irregularities" in type, "for being lately come hither, my materials were misplaced and out of order, whereupon I was forced to use Figures and Letters of various sizes." What annoyed the council, however, was the reference to the Proprietor as "Lord Penn," and they ordered Atkyns to "blot out the words," and warned Bradford "not to print anything but what shall have lycence from ye Council."

In 1688 when Penn's close friend, James II was forced to flee England, the Proprietor was worried about the reaction in Philadelphia to the news that James' daughter Mary and her Dutch husband William now occupied the throne of England. Already under suspicion in an alleged plot to restore James, Penn sent word to his commissioners, "Have a care of printing there, for it may cost me and the Province Deare." A pamphlet containing Penn's Frame of Government for Pennsylvania began circulating through Philadelphia, and the deputy governor, John Blackwell summoned Bradford. Despite the fact he was the only printer within a hundred miles Bradford would not admit he had printed the document, but added he would print what he pleased. The bold assertion for freedom of the press led Blackwell to threaten the printer with a heavy bond if he dared to put anything on his press that was not first approved by Blackwell. This crisis passed when Penn eased the governor out of office because the Quaker-dominated council complained "he hath rather watched us for evill and takes downe every word wee say in short hand whereby to insnare or over awe . . . us wch wee looked upon very hard."

Bradford had a more dramatic setting in which to assert his avant garde notions of a free press in 1692. In the heat of the battle George Keith was waging within the Quaker Meeting, Keith wrote a tract condemning his opponents, including one Jennings, who also happened to be a judge. Bradford printed it, and since Keith's foes controlled city and state government, a series of indictments were handed down by the Grand Jury. Bradford was arrested, and with him James McComb who had delivered two of the pamphlets. Poor McComb had a singular lack of success in door-to-door activities. Earlier he tried his hand at collecting taxes, but the abuse heaped upon him in the first few houses where he called made him resign. Now he was arraigned as a scandal-monger, seditionist and potential enemy of the state. He was not without a sense of humor, for when he and Bradford were brought before the justices at the preliminary hearing they kept their hats on, and one judge denounced them for "standing so before the court." Recalling a pertinent incident in Penn's career, McComb jibed, "You can order our hats taken off," and the embarrassed bench ruled that defendants could decide the hat question for themselves. Bradford refused bail. When his case came to trial, he argued that since the pamphlet was incident to a religious dispute, not a governmental matter, it could not be seditious. Then he put forward an argument that the eminent Philadelphia lawyer, Andrew Hamilton would assert forty-two years later when he was defending a New York newspaperman, John Peter Zenger against a charge of criminal libel and sedition—the case that would become the American classic in the struggle for freedom of the press. Bradford contended it was for the jury, not the judges, to decide whether he was guilty of sedition. Under existing English law, juries in such cases were only to find whether the defendant did the printing, and the judges determined whether the subject matter was seditious. Bradford's case went to the jury with those instructions. There seemed to be no problem, for Bradford obviously was the printer. While the jurors were conferring "without meat, drink, fire or tobacco"—the English custom of forcing a quick decision—the prosecution sent Bradford's printing frame into the ice-cold room, never having bothered to introduce it during the trial. They deliberated for forty-eight hours, then returned to ask the judges a question. Later they announced they could not agree on a verdict, and Bradford was discharged. Weary of these repeated brushes with the authorities, the only printer in Philadelphia decided to go to New York.

He did not cut all ties with the Philadelphia scene. His paper still came from David Rittenhouse's mill in which he had the foresight to invest. His son, Andrew, on December 22, 1719 published the first newspaper in Philadelphia and the middle colonies, *The American Weekly Mercury,* offering it for sale "at the Bible in the Second Street and (by) John Copson in High Street." It was a drab little sheet, sustained more by its novelty than intelligence. Ten years later, the brash young Franklin, under the pseudonym "Busy Body" wrote Andrew, "I have often observ'd with Concern that your *Mercury* is not always equally entertaining. The Delay of Ships expected in, and want of Fresh

Advices from Europe, make it frequently very dull. . . ." Franklin offered to liven Bradford's columns with extracts from "a good Author" "when I happen to have nothing of my own to say that I think of more Consequence . . . perhaps I may sometimes talk of Politicks. . . ."

This was the last thing Andrew Bradford needed. He had already been in trouble with the city officials for publishing Francis Rawle's pamphlet *Some Remedies for restoring the Sunk Credit,* and an innocuous item in 1721 which had simply said

> our General Assembly are now sitting and we have great expectation from them . . . that they will find some effectual remedy to revive the dying credit of the Province and restore us to our former happy circumstances.

The Council regarded the mere mention of the subject a reflection on the government and apt to excite the inhabitants, and Bradford escaped with warnings not to mention public affairs again.

Young Franklin was not very charitable toward the Bradfords, even though father and son, not having employment for him when he sought a job, went out of their way to get him associated with a rival printer, Samuel Keimer. Franklin thought Andrew "illiterate" and Keimer an "odd Fish, ignorant of common Life" and "slovenly to extream dirtiness. . . ." He and Hugh Meredith, an apprentice of Keimer's decided to publish a newspaper, and opened their own shop on Market near Second. Another employe of Keimer's a German, learned of their plans and informed his boss, who quickly made up his mind to put out a paper of his own. In a prospectus he announced:

> Whereas many have encouraged me to publish a Paper of Intelligence; and whereas the late *Mercury* has been so wretchedly performed as to be a Scandal to the Name of Printing, and to be truly styled Nonsense in Folio . . . I shall begin in November next a most useful Paper, to be entitled, *The Pennsylvania Gazette or Universal Instructor.* The Proposer having dwelt at the Fountain of Intelligence in Europe, will be able to give a Paper to please all and to offend none, at the reasonable Expense of Ten Shillings per annum. . . .

Frustrated at Keimer's preemption of possible subscribers he needed to make his own plans a reality, Franklin decided to use Bradford's *Mercury* as the vehicle for destroying the *Gazette.* The first issue appeared on December 24, 1728, but like Bradford, Keimer had no nose for news, and soon was publishing generous extracts from Chamber's *Dictionary of the Arts and Sciences* he imported from London. Apparently he simply handed the book to one of his printers and told him

197

to start with "A" and keep going alphabetically within space limitations. Eventually he printed the selection on "Abortion," and Franklin composed two irate letters from two women he quickly invented for the occasion and sent them to Bradford, who dutifully "thought fit to Publish" them. "Martha Careful" expressed outrage

> In behalf of my Self and many good modest Women in this City (who are almost out of Countenance) . . . as a Warning to Samuel Keimer; That if he proceed farther to Expose the Secrets of our Sex . . . my Sister Molly and myself, with some others, are Resolved to run the Hazard of taking him by the Beard, at the next Place we meet him, and make an Example of him for his Immodesty. . . .

"Celia Shortface," affected a Quaker visage in asking "Friend Andrew Bradford" to please insert her letter to "Friend Samuel Keimer" "in thy Next Mercury" and "perhaps save Keimer his Ears."

> I was last Night in Company with several of my Acquaintance, and Thee, and *Thy Indecencies,* was the Subject of our Discourse, but at last we Resolved, That if thou Continue to take such Scraps concerning Us, out of thy great Dictionary, and Publish it, as thou hath done in thy Gazette, No. 5, to make Thy Ears suffer for it. And I was desired by the rest, to inform Thee of our Resolution, which is That if thou proceed any further in that *Scandalous manner,* we intend very soon to have thy right Ear for it . . . if thou canst make no better Use of Thy Dictionary, Sell it at Thy next *Luck in the Bag;* and if Thou hath nothing else to put in Thy *Gazette,* lay it down. . . .

Keimer claimed a circulation of two hundred and fifty with No. 13, but it steadily dropped, and within seven months he had less than a hundred subscribers. Franklin continued to use the *Mercury* as "Busy Body" to mock and ridicule Keimer, but the "odd Fish" was hurt more by his own lack of style and content. Tales of English life and slices of Defoe's "Religious Courtship" did nothing to bolster his readership and, in 1729, the debt-ridden publisher sold the *Gazette* to Franklin and Meredith. They assumed control with issue No. 40 on October 2, 1729.

Andrew Bradford was probably glad to see the end of "Busy Body" in his paper, since one of Franklin's philosophical pieces said that men in authority should be invested with a public spirit and a love of country. The observation offended the Governor and Council, and Bradford was sent off to jail. The stay was brief, and the publisher gained some popularity in the process.

Temper of the Times

For all his joviality, Franklin could be ruthless. His ambitions now centered on two posts Bradford held, that of public printer and local postmaster. He achieved the first by printing the Assembly's address to the Governor in an exceptionally neat format, so that it could be compared with Bradford's official version. He smugly noted the members "were sensible of the difference; it strengthened the hands of our friends in the House; and they voted us their printer. . . ." He got rid of Meredith "who . . . was often seen drunk in the streets, and playing at low games in alehouses, much to our discredit" by buying him out. Franklin did not dislodge Bradford as postmaster until 1737, patiently building his prestige and paper in the interim. By 1734 he had become public printer for Delaware and New Jersey and subsequently was to be appointed by Maryland. He became clerk to the Pennsylvania Assembly in 1736 and held the post until 1751. Privy to "hot" news his *Gazette*

STATE HOUSE—1790

When the Federal Government moved from New York City to Philadelphia in 1790 to begin a ten-year stay this is how the State House appeared. The building to the east (far left of the picture) had been erected as a city hall, and the one to the west (far right) as a county courthouse. The latter had been completed by 1789, but the former was not finished until 1791. Tradition fixes the second floor of the east building as the United States Supreme Courtroom, although there are indications it may have occasionally used the large room on the first floor intended for the Mayor's court. The first session was held on August 1, 1791 with Chief Justice John Jay presiding and four associate justices present. Before the Congress occupied the county building on the west end alterations had to be made, including the construction of galleries. Neither the House which occupied the first floor, nor the Senate which occupied the second, waited until the galleries were finished for Congress convened here on December 6, 1790. Washington was inaugurated for his second term in the Senate chamber on March 4, 1793, and delivered his last formal message to Congress downstairs in the House on December 7, 1796. This is not to be confused with the Farewell Address which he never personally delivered. Congress Hall was the scene of other historic events, including Secretary of the Treasury Alexander Hamilton's remarkable reports and proposals on establishing credit for the new government. The first Bank of the United States and the Mint were created here as a result of Hamilton's recommendations; Jay's Treaty with England was ratified; Vermont, Kentucky and Tennessee were admitted to the Union; and Congress and the Administration faced the challenge of the Whiskey Rebellion in Western Pennsylvania. John Adams was sworn in as second President in the House chamber on March 4, 1797, and Congress got word in December 1799 of Washington's death. Just before closing out its Philadelphia period, prior to moving to Washington to begin business in 1800, Congress passed a resolution recommending a solemn observance of Washington's birthday.

quickly gained recognition as one of the leading papers in America. In his *Autobiography* he tells of the reasons he needed the postmaster job:

> As he (Bradford) held the post office, it was imagined that he had better opportunities for obtaining the news, and his paper was thought a better distributor of advertisements than mine, and therefore had many more; which was a profitable thing for him and a disadvantage to me, for tho' I did receive and send papers by the post, yet the public opinion was otherwise; for what I did send was by bribing the riders, who took them privately, Bradford being unkind enough to forbid it, which occasioned some resentment on my part; and I thought so meanly of the practice that when I afterwards came into the position, I took care never to imitate it.

Much of the *Gazette's* popularity stemmed from Franklin's wry humor and homespun philosophy. Even his advertisements were tinged with wit:

> Taken out of Pew in the Church some months since, a Common Prayer Book, bound in red, gilt, and lettered D.F. [Deborah Franklin] on each cover. The Person who took it is desired to open it and read the eighth Commandment and afterwards return it into the same Pew again, upon which no further Notice will be taken.

The sheer joy of Franklin was his ability to moralize without being stuffy. Writing letters to his own paper under such outrageous names as "Alice Addertongue," kept his readers entertained while they were being subtly lectured. Alice, for instance, describes herself as "a young Girl of about thirty-five, and live at present with my Mother." As a child she "had a violent Inclination to be ever talking in my own Praise, and being continually told that it was ill Manners" she "began to speak for the future in the Dispraise of others.

> This I found more agreable to Company, and almost as much so to my self; For what great Difference can there be, between putting your self up, or putting your Neighbour down? *Scandal,* like other Virtues, is in part its own Reward, as it gives us the Satisfaction of making our selves appear better than others, or others no better than ourselves.

"Alice" found her mother's insistence on talking about the good qualities of people inordinately dull, and slipped away from a circle of family friends to the kitchen with an "Acquaintance" and there discussed "a ridiculous Story of Mr. -----'s Intrigue with his Maid, and his Wife's Behaviour upon the Discovery; at some Passages we laugh'd heartily," and one by one the parlor guests who had been nodding in agreement that this woman had "a fine Set of Teeth" or that "one is very kind to her poor Neighbours, and besides has a very handsome Shape" "got up to go see what the Girls were so merry about" and were soon plunged into the saltier conversation. "Alice" suggests to Franklin:

> I have long thought if you would make your Paper a Vehicle of Scandal, you would double the Number of your Subscribers. I send you herewith Account of 4 Knavish Tricks; 2 crackt M----n---ds, 5 Cu----ld-mns, 3 drub'd Wives, and 4 Henpeck'd Husbands, all within this Fortnight; which you may, as Articles of News, deliver to the Publick; and if my Toothach continues shall send you more. . . .

Franklin replies to his alter ego, thanking "Mrs. Addertongue for her Good-Will, but desire to be excus'd of inserting the Articles of News she has sent me; such Things being in Reality No News at all."

To critize the *Mercury*, he wrote himself a letter under a fictitious name complaining about stale news in the Gazette in "Numb. 669," and then Franklin gently answered by noting that the letter was misdirected and should have gone to the *Mercury* since it was the only paper in town to have reached that number of issues. Sometimes he poked fun at himself. "Celia Single" criticizes him for "severe Reflections upon us Women, for Idleness and Extravagance, but I do not remember to have once seen any such Animadversions upon the Men."

> If I were dispos'd to be censorious, I could furnish you with Instances enough: I might mention Mr. Billiard, who spends more than he earns, at the Green Table; and would have been in Jail long since, were it not for his industrious Wife; Mr. Husselcap who often all day long leaves his Business for the rattling of Half-pence in a certain Alley; Mr. Finikin, who has seven different Suits of fine Cloaths, and wears a Change every Day, while his Wife and Children sit at home half-naked; Mr. Crownhim, who is always dreaming over the Chequer board, and cares not how the World goes, so he gets the Game. . . .

The *Gazette* was not a model of good printing. Franklin, absorbed in so many other activities, was plagued by the wooden type which colonial printers used. It wore down easily and lost its sharpness. New figures had to be constantly whittled or ordered from abroad. Christopher Sauer, Jr., of Germantown, publisher of the *Germantauner Zeitung,* in 1750 began to manufacture the first American hand presses and in 1772 started to cast type at his foundry, but had to import his raw material from Germany. Franklin, profiting from this pioneer effort, and the earlier experiments of Michelson in Boston, in 1775 established the best type foundry in the colonies, and put his son-in-law, Benjamin Bache in charge.

If the technical improvements were slow, more far-reaching achievements in American journalism were occurring. The tight grip of government was loosened by the eloquence of Andrew Hamilton in the *Zenger* case. Although this was a New York case, Hamilton was called in as defense counsel, after the Crown-dominated court disbarred New York lawyers who attempted to plead Zenger's cause. The poor Palatine printer had published items written by critics of the arrogant royal governor, William Cosby. Under existing English law Zenger's guilt was quite clear, and truth was no defense. The jury was simply to find—as in Bradford's case—whether Zenger had printed the newspaper. The judge quoted English Chief Justice Holt's statement, which succinctly summed up the attitude of government toward publishers:

> To say that corrupt officers are appointed to administer affairs, is certainly a reflection on the Government. If people should not be called to account for possessing the people with an ill opinion of the Government, no Government can subsist; for it is necessary for all Governments that the people should have a good opinion of it; and nothing could be worse to any Government than the endeavor to procure animosities.

Hamilton took a bold approach. He admitted the publication, and thus technically there was nothing left for the jury to decide, but he drew a distinction between the English law and its concern about the "sacred person" of the king, and lesser officials who sought to presumptively try to cloak their misdeeds with a royal mantle. It was for the jury to determine, said he, whether Zenger's paper carried a seditious libel

> It is a right which all freemen claim, and are entitled to, to complain when they are hurt; they have a right publicly to remonstrate against the abuses of power in the strongest terms, to put their neighbours upon their guard against the craft or open violence of men in authority and to assert with courage the sense they have of the blessings of liberty, and value they put upon it, and their resolution at all hazards to preserve it, as one of the greatest blessings heaven can bestow.

Franklin quickly published in 1736 a pamphlet giving an account of the trial and a number of copies were sold. The verdict of acquittal was celebrated in New York City in a variety of ways. Hamilton, on August 18, 1735 was entertained by "About forty of the Citizens . . . at the Black Horse . . . at dinner, and at his departure next day was saluted with the great Guns of several ships in the Harbour, as a public Testimony of the glorious Defense he made in the cause of Liberty in this Province." On September 16th the Common Council of New York City, "presented . . . the freedom of this Corporation" and later sent him a gold snuffbox duly inscribed. Although the verdict did not change immediately English law, the publicity given it throughout America and in London made a marked change in attitudes.

Philadelphians had developed a sense of individualism which Hamilton's words confirmed. The Quaker majority in the Assembly were pulling away from Penn's heirs who had switched their religious affiliations to the Anglicans. The people were the beneficiaries in the contest for control, as each side sought to build strength with the citizenry. The Courthouse in Market Street across Second from the Jersey market was the polling place for Philadelphia County, which then embraced all its present bounds plus the area later to become Montgomery and Berks counties. From 1738 elections involved a "trial for the stairs," since voters filled out their tickets, walked up one flight to deposit them on the balcony and then descended the steps on the other side. The Quaker party between 1738 and 1741 kept the stairs crowded with their own people, permitting favorable electors to cast their ballot on the balcony, and blocking the opposition. Printers, who just a few years before would have risked prison for their temerity, now were kept busy turning out political propaganda. In 1742 the Proprietary Party distributed leaflets extolling the actions of the governor, and charging incumbent Assembly members with being "Enemies to the publick Peace, Enemies to the Publick Welfare" who put "Gratification of their private Resentments . . . over all other Considerations . . . so Artful as to cover their real Designs under a pretense of Zeal for the publick Good. . . ." The Quakers responded with pamphlets reminding "the Freeholders" that "Unity and Peace are indeed desirable, but not at the Expense of Liberty. . . ."

Angry charges and counter-charges heated the atmosphere to fever pitch. The city had become used to fist fights since the "trial for the stairs" was introduced into local politics, but girded itself for mass violence on October 1, 1742 because the Proprietary Party promised the Quakers "a surprise." Mayor Clement Plumsted issued a meaningless appeal for everyone to keep calm, and not to bring sticks or canes to the polling place, but this was made even more meaningless when word got around at dawn on October 1 that some sailors were seen "at Andrew Hamilton's Wharf with Clubbs in their hands." The Quaker Party, supported by large crowds of Germans, milled around the City Hall to dominate the voting, when between fifty and eighty sailors appeared. Quaker spokesmen appealed to William Allen, the Recorder, to send the sailors away, but being a Proprietary man, Allen announced they had as much right to be there as "the unnaturalized Dutch." Thomas Burgess, a merchant, said to the sailors, "Brothers, you'd better go on board your Ships or you'll be in bad Bread before Night." "Damn you," one of the sailors retorted, "we have nothing to say to you, but to the Broadbrims and Dutch dogs." Near Second and Chestnut one of the ship's masters called to the sailors, "Damn you, go and knock those Dutch Sons of Bitches off the Steps." One sailor shouted, "There goes a Parcel of Quaker Sons of Bitches; they are the Men we want, Men with broad Hats and no Pockets."

Franklin's *Gazette* reported the scenes with relish, noting that in the melee several people were "carried off for dead." While there were no fatalities—"a Miracle," Richard Peters said—"They took up great stones and bricks ... and broke the Court house Windows all to pieces." Sticks and clubs were passed to the Quakers and Germans, and eventually the intruding sailors were driven off—fifty-four of them hauled off to jail. There were other curious features, since one of the ship captains involved was associated with the Mayor, and a ship owned by Plumsted, along with others belonging to Allen and other Proprietary party people were in port. Governor Thomas wanted the sailors brought to trial in the city court where the judges were friendly towards the Proprietors, but the Assembly demanded the proceedings be held in the county court. In the end all the sailors were released since it "appeared that (they) had been privately employed in this work by some party leaders . . . to divert the established form of the constitution from its *peaceable* order and course." Mayor Plumsted, Recorder Allen and others were charged with laxity in permitting a riot to occur, and the Assembly began an investigation. Eventually, when both sides made all the political capital they could of the "Bloody Election of 1742," the matter was quietly dropped.

Political leaders, however, now began to realize the value of having newspaper support. Andrew Bradford's *Mercury* had been tilted toward the Proprietors for some time, but Franklin kept his *Gazette* free of any political overtones. Even in the accounts of the election riots, he hewed to straight reporting and nowhere editorialized on the topic of blame. He continued this policy until 1766 when he sold his interest in the paper to his partner Hall, who shifted his support immediately to the Proprietors. William Bradford, grandson of the original, and a nephew of Andrew started a third Philadelphia paper on December 2, 1742, the same day the *Mercury* with inverted column rules and black borders was mourning the death of Andrew on November 23. His widow carried on until 1747.

To survive, a newspaper had to count on between eight hundred and twelve hundred paying subscribers, and collections throughout the 18th century were difficult. Yet Franklin, in the sixteen years he published the *Gazette,* showed a £12,000 profit from sales, and £4,000 from advertisements. Despite this impressive competition, young William Bradford's *Pennsylvania Journal and Weekly Advertiser* did well, subsidized partially at the outset by influential members of the Proprietary party. Except when it was suspended during the British occupation, the *Journal* lasted until 1797, surviving its founder by six years. Even then it merely changed its name to *The True American* and did not lose its identity until it merged with the *United States Gazette* in 1818. Bradford shrewdly published on Wednesday, thus avoiding conflict with the publication days of the *Gazette* and *Mercury*. This technique was adopted by papers that followed, so that in 1776 when Philadelphia boasted seven weekly newspapers, each came out on a different day giving the citizens, in effect, a daily paper.

The long running battle between the Proprietors and the Assembly continued unabated through the Stamp Act crisis. While both factions opposed the British revenue package it was for different reasons. The Assembly group saw in it a setback for their efforts to make Pennsylvania a crown colony, and to regain ground lost, Joseph Galloway and Thomas Wharton founded, in 1767, the *Pennsylvania Chronicle and Universal Advertiser*. Through this controlled newspaper they expected to marshal public opinion behind their drive to oust the Penns. They chose William Goddard as publisher, and thus brought to Philadelphia the best newspaperman in America. The 27-year old Goddard, a native on New London, Connecticut, had started a paper in Providence, R.I., but left it in charge of his mother and sister when it was moving too slowly to suit his quick-paced drive. A meticulous editor, he insisted on a clean-lined format, and the superior quality of the *Chronicle* soon outdistanced in appearance any publication Philadelphians had ever seen. He set up a network of twenty-two sales agents in various sections of Pennsylvania to build subscriptions, and had them double as correspondents. When he became incensed at the high rates the post office was charging for carrying the *Chronicle* he hired his own post riders, and these too were used as reporters. This challenge to the monopoly of the postal system endeared him to editors in other colonies, but it was also characteristic of the fierce independence upon which he insisted. In 1768 he first published John Dickinson's fourteen "Letters from an American Farmer," scholarly analyses of the relationship Dickinson felt England should maintain with America. Galloway was alarmed because while the tone was temperate he was afraid Dickinson's critical appraisal of Britain's policies would hurt his cause at home and abroad. Goddard, blunt and egocentric, was not inclined to trim his sails, and the breach between him and his patron widened to a point where by 1770 he felt impelled to write a small pamphlet, "*The Partnership: or the History of the Rise and Progress of the Pennsylvania Chronicle.*" By September 1771 he turned the paper against Galloway in a savage attack, and in 1773 left Philadelphia for Baltimore where his *Maryland Journal and Baltimore Advertiser* carried an account of the Boston Tea Party, brought to him by his own post-riders.

The high percentage of Germans in the Philadelphia area led to several attempts to start a paper that would break the Sauer hold on the many hundreds who spoke and understood no language other than German. Even Franklin, who was seriously concerned that German might supersede English as the predominant language in Pennsylvania, was instrumental in founding the short-lived *Philadephische Zeitung* in 1755 to checkmate Sauer's opposition to one of his pet projects, the "charity" schools. Not until 1762 was a successful rival launched when Henry Miller, a highly skilled German printer began *Der Wochetliche Philadelphische Staatsbote*. Miller had a cosmopolitan background, having worked at his craft in Germany, Holland, France and England. By 1764 he proudly reported his paper was reaching most of the colonies, Nova Scotia and the West Indies.

Such claims were made frequently on the basis of a single subscriber in distant parts, for publishers were confident that one copy would be read by possibly a hundred people, particularly if it wound up in a well patronized tavern.

In Pennsylvania Miller's importance was self-evident to the political factions, since by 1750 Germans were estimated to number between a third and a half of the population. There were repeated unfounded rumors that they might try to create a state of their own within the boundaries of the province, something they had neither the inclination nor organizational ability to do. Even as a political force they had to be approached on something of a piecemeal basis, usually through their churches. Miller's as well as Sauer's support was deemed essential to win their backing. The Quakers particularly courted Sauer.

The selection of Philadelphia as the meeting site for the Continental Congress gave the city's newspapers an enviable edge which would continue through most of the last quarter of the century. It was frequently possible to cover national, state and local governments by walking a distance of four blocks.

During the Stamp Tax furor in 1765, newspapers in America not only alerted the people to the dangers implicit in the legislation, but refused to purchase or affix the required stamps. While some in other colonies suspended publication rather than comply, the Philadelphia *Journal* and *Gazette* were among those openly defiant. The *Gazette* dusted off the cartoon of the severed snake which Franklin devised in 1754 to push his plan for colonial union with the legend, "Join or Die." It ran the cut in two issues. The *Journal* revised its format dramatically, and with wide coverage of events about the fate of the tax elsewhere, commanded widespread attention. When a stamped paper arrived in Philadelphia from Barbados it was "exposed to Public View at the Coffee-House," then suspended from an iron chain and burned. Franklin's famous snake was subsequently to be used in 1774 by New York and Massachusetts papers, and ironically the *Journal* virtually made it a fixture in its editions between July 27, 1774 and October 18, 1775.

Americans picked up their pens with enthusiasm in the wake of the repeal of the unpopular tax, having found non-importation an effective weapon in the mounting debates between Britain and America. Aware that the reversal of its stand on the stamp tax was a temporary strategic retreat by Parliament and the Ministry, lawyers, merchants and ministers

(Kean Archives, Phila.)

THE PRESIDENT'S HOUSE

Just why Pennsylvania built this "President's House" is not quite clear. Both the Federal and State governments were planning to move out of Philadelphia so its days as an executive mansion were numbered before construction on Ninth below Market was even begun. To make matters worse it was not completed during Washington's term of office, and it was too expensive for President John Adams' pocketbook. He rejected the offer of rental on March 3, 1797, preferring to stay in the house Washington had occupied between 5th and 6th on Market, known in the confused numbering system as 190, High Street. Even this was costly. Abigail Adams summed up the family headaches: "House rent at twenty-seven hundred dollars a year, fifteen hundred for a carriage, one thousand for one pair of horses, all the glasses, ornaments, kitchen furniture, the best china, settees, plateaus, &c., all to purchase . . . and not a farthing probably will the House of Representatives allow, though the Senate have voted a small addition. All the linen besides . . . " Washington told Adams he was going to have to auction some of his own furniture to raise money for the move back to Mount Vernon. At any rate this pretentious property here pictured did not go to waste, for the University of Pennsylvania bought it in 1800.

207

wrote scores of letters to editors on the pros and cons of English policy. Oddly, William Bradford, now in partnership with his son, Thomas, either missed the significance or wholly avoided these trenchant essays, and the *Journal* printed no political piece of any moment from March 1768 to January 1769—leaving the field entirely to the *Gazette.* Still Bradford was both astute and inspired enough to become active in the Sons of Liberty and serve as secretary of its Philadelphia chapter, and on February 1, 1775 the *Journal* boasted that more Sons of Liberty read it than any other newspaper. The slogan was obviously intended for the eyes of the Continental Congress which named the Bradfords the official printers. The high percentage of neutral Quakers and Tories in town were not likely to subscribe to the *Journal* on that basis. Most Philadelphians, including the liberal elements, seemed to prefer the *Gazette,* whose publishers, Hall and Sellers, were sensitive not only to the international political scene, but to such issues as complaints about apportionment in the Assembly, the protest of small merchants about new markets being built in the city, and scores of state and local topics. Even the "Mechanics," beginning to emerge as a political power turned to the *Gazette* to voice their sentiments, and while the Bradfords could glory in the title of "printer to the Congress" Hall and Sellers eventually got a large share of that business.

Other newspapers began to appear. In 1771, John Dunlap from his print shop at 134-136 Market Street, began publication of *The Pennsylvania Packet, or the General Advertiser,* most famous now for having been the first to print the text of the United States Constitution in its issue of Wednesday, September 19, 1787. Dunlap made such rapid strides that, after moving his press to Lancaster to continue publication during the British occupation of Philadelphia, he stepped it up on his return to the city in July 1778, to three times a week, and on September 21, 1784 converted it to a daily—the first successful in America. As printer to the Continental Congress in 1776 he set up and printed the official broadside copy of the Declaration of Independence from Jefferson's original manuscript. Signed by John Hancock, this broadside carried the official word to each of the colonies and friendly countries abroad.

Dunlap had the added distinction of first putting Washington's Farewell Address in print. His progress from an apprentice to his printer uncle to one of the wealthiest men in Philadelphia, and a founder of the First City Troop in whose service he saw some action at the battles of second Trenton and Princeton, offers an interesting chapter in the city's journalistic history.

Benjamin Towne, a more nimble figure, published *The Pennsylvania*

Evening Post in 1775, the same year James Humphreys began *The Penn-sylvania Ledger*, and Enoch Story and Daniel Humphrey, the *Pennsylvania Mercury*. The latter two were Tory papers and had brief careers. The *Mercury*'s first issue was April 17, 1775 and its last December 27, 1775, the demise being due to the printshop's destruction by fire. Its distinguishing feature was the unusual number of "female" contributors. Towne was responsible for the end of the *Ledger*, which ran continuously from January 28, 1775 to November 30, 1776. Although his own political sympathies were suspect, he managed to cast enough suspicion on James Humphreys that he fled the city.

Towne, who printed "in Front street near the Coffee-House," boldly embarked upon an evening paper which was published every Tuesday, Thursday and Saturday. Ostensibly a Whig, and the first in America to venture a tri-weekly, Towne devoted much of his ample space to commerce, politics and literature and, as an inducement to inventors, offered free advertising to publicize new and worthwhile machines for agriculture or manufacture. With the arrival of the British in the fall of 1777, he suspended publication for two weeks, but then was back with a pro-English look which he retained until the enemy left the city in June 1778. During that interim James Humphreys returned to revive his *Ledger*, from October 11, 1777 to May 23, 1778 but left when the British army pulled out. The *Royal Pennsylvania Gazette* had an even shorter run, March 3 to May 26, 1778.

Despite the vigilantes who went to extremes in rooting out suspected Tories when Philadelphia once more reverted to American control, Towne blithely went on with his *Evening Post* now wearing a Patriot mask. Even when he was proscribed as a loyalist, he succeeded in surmounting the charge, and died in 1782 in "very comfortable circumstances."

Throughout the Revolution the city's newspapers were low-key in propaganda, content to publish the few proclamations or orders to civilians a reluctant Washington issued as Commander-In-Chief in somewhat larger type face than other news items. The *Packet* occasionally carried significant London items, but these were so delayed they were almost historic. Letters from officers describing encounters with the British constituted most of the battle reports, while some of the jealousies which permeated the Continental Army over officer promotions—a constant headache to Washington—spilled into the columns. Pious letters, tedious dissertations always signed with a classical Latin or Greek name—a practice extensively used to make opinions seem profound—and a mercifully sparse collection of noble, pep-talk type pieces—took up a good part of the papers. When hard news was lacking spirited, argumentative letters between two correspondents gave vitality to the paper. General Charles Lee who unsuccessfully tried to charm Rebecca Franks at a ball in Philadelphia was turned off by her with a remark that his breeches were patched. He then wrote her a masterful letter, enclosing the breeches, and told her to "turn them, examine them, inside and out" and if she found them not to be genuine *sherry vallies*, ankle-length breeches with a broad stripe of leather on the inside of the thighs for riding comfort, he would "submit in silence to all the scurrility" which she could "pour out." In a subtly suggestive paragraph he concluded:

> You have already injured me in the tenderest part, and I demand satisfaction . . . I insist on the privilege of the injured party, which is, to name his hour and weapons; and as I intend it to be a very serious affair, I will not admit of any seconds: and you may depend upon it, Miss Franks, that whatever may be your spirit on the occasion, the world shall never accuse General Lee with having turned his back upon you. . . .

The fiery Miss Franks sent him scurrying in confusion, and he wrote her an abject letter of apology. As frequently happened, the "breeches" letter was published—in this instance, *The United States Magazine* proudly put it in its first issue, and Rivington's *Gazette*, a formidable Tory paper in New York, carried the purported reply from Rebecca. Lee turned to the *Gazette*, denouncing the magazine publishers for their "impertinence and stupidity" and "for salaciously emphasizing certain aspects." He said if the letter had just "made a noise in this town (which is not an Athens)" he would not bother with explanations, but it got into the "New York papers" and is "giving much uneasiness to an amiable young lady, for whose character, in every respect, I have the highest regard." He confided to readers of the Packet:

> I have just now had a sight in Mr. Rivington's *Gazette* of Miss Franks's pretended answer . . . I declare solemnly that Miss Franks never did write, nor can any body who is acquainted with that young Lady, think her capable of writing, a single syllable of such abominable Grub-street. It is probably the production of some grasping expectant for an office, who has absurdly flattered himself that he should recommend himself to his Excellency (Washington) by any scurrility on me. . . .

The *Packet* made a serial of the whole business, promising its readers further developments. Rebecca Franks, beautiful and tart-tongued was regarded as good copy by Dunlap. When another American officer came to a ball in the fall of 1778 dressed in a scarlet tunic to please her, the *Packet* reported her reaction:

> Hey day, says she to some other officer standing near her, I see certain animals will put on the lion's skin.

Temper of the Times

It provoked a response from her:

> Mr. Printer, There are many persons so unhappy in their disposition that, like the dog in the manger, they can neither enjoy the innocent pleasures of life themselves, nor in others without grumbling and growling, participate in them; hence it is, we so frequently observe hints and anecdotes in your Paper respecting the Commanding Officer, Head-Quarters and Tory Ladies. This mode of attacking characters is really admirable, and equally as polite as carreying slander and defamation by significant nods, winks and shrugs. Poor beings indeed who plainly indicate to what species of animals they belong by the badness of their conduct.

While the Army was at Valley Forge the *Packet* carried numerous advertisements for the apprehension of deserters who were described in colorful language

> LAZARUS CARMADY, American born, about five feet seven inches high has very sore eyes ... JAMES DRIGASS, a yellow looking scoundrel ... RICHARD SWIFT, American born, about five feet nine inches high ... he is a great coward ... JOHN M ELVAIN, born in Ireland, five feet ten inches high, sandy complexion, very talkative and drunken....

A Delaware sheriff searching for one William Gray, who escaped and was last seen heading for Philadelphia, was more temperate in his description:

> He is an ill-looking fellow with remarkable red hair, about five feet three or four inches high, a talkative, insolent fellow fond of liquor and frequently boasts of his honesty (though a villian he is a great singer)....

Vignettes of domestic life appeared:

> WHEREAS Rachel Buchanan, wife of William Buchanan, of New Castle, hath eloped from her home, without any reason, and lodges at the House of James Rushbottom, bricklayer, of Philadelphia, who encouraged her last winter, and received of her 5¾ yards of black satin, a bonnet and gown, of my property, of which I made a lawful demand, but refused delivering them to me ... if he does not deliver the same to me, and send me child, I shall take such steps as the law directs....
>
> WILLIAM BUCHANAN
>
> N.B. Was taken from said Buchanan, by one of the enemy, a silver pint, marked in cypher W.R.B. and two table spoons of the same mark, supposed to have been sold in Philadelphia. I will give the person that purchased them 20£ for the same.

211

Rushbottom a week later put the record straight "In justice to my Character," explaining that while Buchanan

> was a prisoner in the city Last Winter, his wife came up from New Castle to see him, and she being a sister to my wife, was invited out of kindness ... to make her home with me, which she did during her stay in town. Since the death of my wife, her mother came to live with me, and was visited by Mrs. Buchanan and her child, but neither she, her child or cloathing, but for anything within my knowledge, may be at Mr. Buchanan's. As this is a true state of facts I trust no unfavourable opinion will take with any reasonable person, from a scurrilous publication, occasioned by envy and malice alone. . . .

One correspondent objected to the manner in which words were bandied about by other correspondents:

> I have heard the *public* mentioned, and the *opinion of the public*, when I knew very well there was nothing more in it than the opinion of the speaker, or writer, and half a dozen of his acquaintances. Just so the *people* is frequently used, to signify nothing more, than the company present; that is to say, if the company present are of one opinion; if not, *the people* are such of the company present, as are of opinion with the person that uses the expression. *The better part of people* is an expression which is frequently used to signify such persons as are pleased to concur with us ... and the *low, dirty fellows* are generally those who are opposed to us.
> ... if I had time to study languages, I would learn Dutch and French; but to have my own native tongue to learn over again, when I thought I was pretty well master of it, is cruel. . . . Lord have mercy, Sir! a plain man may not be able to keep up with it. The word *gentleman* may in time come to mean a cut-throat, and a *man of honour* a public plunderer.

The *Packet* carried a story in 1778 about a Good Samaritan who took time and trouble to visit American prisoners of war in the Walnut Street prison:

> A free Negro woman (who is in the service of a gentleman of the city of Philadelphia, now ... in the country) having received two hard dollars for washing, and hearing of the distress of our prisoners in the gaol, went to market and bought some neck-beef and two heads, with some greens, and made a pot of as good broth as she could; but having no more money to buy bread, she got credit of a baker for six loaves, all of which she carried to our unfortunate prisoners, who were much in want of such a supply. She has since paid the baker, and says, she never laid out money with so much satisfaction—Humanity is the same thing in rich or poor, white or black.

Temper of the Times

The Philadelphia press, located close to the largest supply of paper in the colonies, suffered only minor inconveniences from the critical shortage of that commodity. In most states, prior to 1765 paper was imported from England, and the non-importation policies adopted in protest against the Stamp Tax, forced them to look to the few mills in America, most of which were located in Pennsylvania. By 1775 there were fifty-three in operation, but their inability to keep up with the demand was further aggravated by the outbreak of war. Newspapers in some cities suspended operations, many reduced the size of their sheets, and most experienced delays in publication dates. Notwithstanding the favorable situation Philadelphia papers enjoyed, steps were taken by both the Continental Congress and the State Committee of Safety to keep production maintained. The Congress ordered in 1776 that no papermakers were to be inducted into military service in Pennsylvania, and specifically prohibited those in militia units from going to the relief of the beleagured American forces in New Jersey. On January 30, 1776 state officials asked newspapers to inform the inhabitants of Philadelphia "that in the course of next week persons properly authorized . . . will call at their houses to receive the rags that are so greatly needed by the papermakers. . . ." Elsewhere appeals were made to women. The North Carolina *Gazette*, November 14, 1777, tried a touch of southern romanticism, assuring "Young Ladies . . . that by sending to the Paper Mill an old Handkerchief, no longer fit to cover their snowy Breasts, there is a Possibility of its returning . . . in the more pleasing form of a Billet Doux from their Lovers. . . ." The Massachusetts *Spy* in 1779 asked "the fair Daughters of Liberty . . . to serve their country, by saving for the paper-mill . . . all Linen & Cotton and Linen Rags, be they ever so small." This, however, was not a public service advertisement. It was inserted by a paper supplier, who suggested "A bag hung up in one corner of the room, would be a means of saving many which would otherwise be lost." For clean, unused linen he was willing to pay cash. There was little danger in Pennsylvania of men escaping the draft by pretending to be papermakers. These were usually recognized by their red hands and stooped shoulders, acquired in the agonizing process which required three months or more to turn rags into paper. On July 14, 1779, the Pennsylvania *Gazette* had an advertisement from a Trenton man seeking journeyman papermakers, offering exemption from military duty and the highest wages to successful applicants. Apart from a resolution of the Council of Safety, August 27, 1776, asking politely that "Printers of this State . . . spare a quantity of paper . . . for the purpose of making Cartridges", the impact was minimal. Recognition that the press was an important ally in the struggle for independence

213

spared it from more stringent restrictions in the use of paper. Editors were quick to respond to requests such as one made by the State when the Americans reoccupied Philadelphia in June 1778, that they publish urgent pleas to the citizens to send any scraps or waste paper to the nearest military post.

13

"... THIS ALL PERVADING (PARTY) SPIRIT ..."

Politics, as Everywhere, Consumed the "Holy Experiment"

*   *   *   *   *

"... in the present unhappy state of the community there is ... not a place (in) the pulpit or forum, the theatre or the tea-table, that is not contaminated with this all pervading (party) spirit; we have heard it in our streets and in our houses, in the public prints and on the floor of the legislature, even within the walls of the National Councils; it has obtruded ... into every class of society. ... Unless an end is speedily put to this dreadful evil, no man will accept a situation in the public councils, it will be no longer safe, no longer honorable. ..."

—A. J. Dallas, before a State Senatorial Committee
investigating Israel Israel's election—1797

*   *   *   *   *

Within the broader spectrum of the Revolution against George III, Pennsylvania was immersed in a political revolution of its own, and Philadelphia was the hub.

It had been brewing a long time. Since the 1760's the Assembly, a tight-knit coalition of propertied interests, ruled the province, turning a deaf ear to demands from the western counties for adequate representation, and stifling similar protests from the middle and lower brackets in Philadelphia by giving their spokesmen meaningless posts in the city government.

As the crescendo of cries "taxation without representation" became the battle cry against Britain, Pennsylvanians discovered they had precisely the same problem on their own doorstep. Concerned citizens like Franklin could picture what might happen. Only a few years before, in 1764, he had been called by a frightened governor to head off an armed mob of "Paxton boys" marching on Philadelphia to seize some Indians in protective custody. If a few hundred men with sticks and rifles could throw a city into panic, what would happen if thousands of restless, poor and belligerent Scotch-Irish came out of the west, gathering other dissentients enroute, descended on a city where a majority of the citizens shared their discontent? Fired with a national spirit of revolution they could, without much imagination, see in their pro-British Assembly the image of King George.

In February 1776 the Assembly grudgingly made a gesture of reapportionment, but contrived it so that thirty hand-picked representatives from Philadelphia, Bucks and Chester counties would offset twenty-eight from the others, where two-thirds of the population lived. The ploy deepened the anger.

Then on May 10, 1776 the Continental Congress recommended that states establish new governments to replace their colonial governments. Franklin and others who shared his views saw in this the opportunity to right the balance. Their movement was carefully orchestrated. The Philadelphia city committee called a mass meeting on May 20, 1776 to consider the question of a provincial convention. More than four thousand crowded onto the grounds around the State House, listened to the oratory and shouted approval. The next step was to invite county committees to convene in Carpenter's Hall on June 18. There they solemnly endorsed the Congressional recommendation, and agreed that each county and the city of Philadelphia should, if the voters approved, send eight delegates to a Convention which would draft a constitution and organize a government. A special election was called for July 8. Fortuitously, this proved to be the day the Declaration of Independence was publicly announced. The electorate voted "Yes" and the delegates convened at Philadelphia on

July 15 to begin work. They did more. They constituted themselves an interim government. Caged in the crossfire of popular emotions, the old Assembly found itself powerless. At its session on September 26, its members thought their prospects so hopeless not even a quorum showed up. Those who did denounced the arbitrary actions of the convention and adjourned forever. Pennsylvania, for all practical purposes, was now in the hands of a revolutionary tribunal.

They called themselves "Whigs", but sharp differences arose between the extremists and the moderates, and it was the radical faction that controlled the writing of the State Constitution. Advice and objections from such able men as John Dickinson, James Wilson, Robert Morris and Thomas Mifflin, were shouted down.

The Constitution consisted of two parts—a Declaration of Rights and a Frame of Government. In both, newspapermen could find a measure of satisfaction. Section 12 of the former provided:

> That the people have a right to freedom of speech, and of writing and publishing their sentiments; therefore the freedom of the press ought not to be restrained.

Section 35 of the latter declared:

> The printing presses shall be free to every person who undertakes to examine the proceedings of the legislature, or any part of government.

None quarreled with provisions like these. The debates took place on the structural phases of the new government and, disregarding the experience and scholarship of the Pennsylvania delegation to the Continental Congress serving as members of the Convention, the radicals rammed through a monstrous and unworkable plan. The legislative concepts were sound enough—a single assembly to be elected annually, with membership apportioned on the basis of the number of taxables in each county and the city of Philadelphia. But in lieu of a single governor there was to be a twelve-man executive council, one from each county and the city of Philadelphia. From this number, the council and Assembly were to choose ·a president and vice-president, yet their offices were to confer no additional powers. Every seven years a committee of censors, two from each county and Philadelphia, were to be elected by the voters for a term of one year, during which they were to appraise the operation of the Constitution and laws. If two-thirds felt changes were needed they were empowered to call a constitutional convention to revise them. The Constitution of 1776 was never put to the electorate

217

for ratification. It was simply proclaimed, and the new government was inaugurated in Philadelphia on November 28, 1776.

Two new political parties emerged. The moderate Whigs, upset by the hydra-headed executive and the one-chambered legislature, started immediately to clamor for revision—through speeches, letters to editors and wherever they could find a forum. They acquired the name, "Anti-Constitutionalists" or "Republicans." The radicals also sent communications to the press and, in addition, enlisted the clergy in western Pennsylvania to warn that the "Republicans" were actually Tories who wanted to impose a "House of Lords" on the people. Off and on, at every election, and until a new Constitution was adopted in 1790, the bitter battle raged, across the pages of newspapers, in taverns, at polling places, and sometimes exploded in violence.

One such incident occurred in Philadelphia on Monday, October 4, 1779. Some two hundred militiamen, mostly Germans, gathered at Paddy Burn's tavern on the Commons. Over their morning ale they were muttering threats against Tories, profiteers and the inflation. Rumors quickly spread they were out to "get" James Wilson, one of the most successful lawyers in the city, signer of the Declaration and destined to be a key draftsman of the Federal Constitution. His incisive and learned attacks on the new State constitution nettled the radicals. When he heard the news, Wilson alerted the City Troop and rounded up twenty of his fellow Anti-Constitutionalists—two of whom ran to Carpenter's Hall and drew bullets from the arsenal. Armed with pistols and muskets, under the hasty command of General Thomas Mifflin, they marched up and down Second Street near Walnut. Eventually the drum and fife were heard, and the Wilson group scurried to his brick home at the southwest corner of Third and Walnut. The militiamen, heated up with the liquor, had collected a mob along the way. Captain Campbell of the Wilson contingent threw open a window and ordered the militia and the crowd to disperse. He was shot dead. Then the barricaded men opened fire, and it was returned. A few of the militiamen went to bring up a cannon, while others got a sledge and hammered at the back door. When they broke it down, Colonel Chambers standing on the stairs, fired point blank, wounding a soldier. Chambers was grabbed before he could reload, dragged down the steps and bayoneted. President Joseph Reed, summoned by the frightened Charles Willson Peale, came racing down the street with two mounted dragoons. Pistol in hand, he commanded the militia to withdraw. The sight of their militant leader caused them to pause, and then the City Troop, swords flashing, rode their horses into the crowd. Four militiamen and a Negro boy were killed and fourteen others wounded. The militia scattered, but the troopers seized twenty-seven and hauled them off to the Walnut

Street Prison. Wilson was advised to get out of town until things calmed down. The German community thought the arrests were discriminatory and marched on the Executive Council, demanding their neighbors be released on bail. The defenders of Fort Wilson posted bail for themselves, between £5,000 and £10,000. But the case never came to trial. In March 1780 the Council passed "an act of free and general pardon" for all. Despite their apprehensions about the election on October 11, the Constitutionalists won. Philadelphians, oblivious to the sound and fury, settled down to the prosaic business of shooting pigeons which flew over the city in such large flocks "they darkened the sun for two or three hours."

Until the mid-1780's newspapers in the state were all published in Philadelphia, and their offices were concentrated in the vicinity of Front and Market. Shops like Hall & Sellers, Dunlap and the Bradfords were not wholly dependent upon the success of their papers for survival. Printing of books and pamphlets were prime sources of revenue. Schoolbooks were in increasing demand, and Franklin's accounting of his partnership with Hall shows 36,100 copies of a primer printed between 1749 and 1766, while Dunlap in 1772 had one printing of 10,000 for the perennially popular Dilworth's speller. The lack of international copyright laws allowed pirated editions of English best sellers to be reprinted without royalties, an inequity about which Charles Dickens vehemently complained on his 1842 American tour. This sort of a bulwark allowed established houses to maintain a degree of editorial independence in their newspapers, a luxury fledgling papers were not apt to enjoy. When, after 1785, a few weeklies began to appear in other Pennsylvania towns, publishers were often advised to get themselves adopted by a political party. William Spotswood, determined to "steer an impartial line" in his *Pennsylvania Herald,* found it impossible and shut down rather than compromise his principles.

Since editorial comment before 1785 was extremely rare, there were few criteria by which partisanship could be judged. A preponderance of letters on one side of an issue might indicate that the publisher favored a particular view. Positioning of a story could mean the editor's reaction to it or indifferent layout.

Two papers came on the scene in the early 1780's that bolted this reserved attitude, and introduced a scurrility that led Franklin, in France, to write, "I am afraid to lend any of them (American newspapers) here, till I have examined and laid aside such as would disgrace us." Francis Bailey began the *Freeman's Journal* in April 1781 and hired Philip Freneau as editor. Freneau, a classmate of Madison's at Princeton, came from a wealthy New Jersey family, but aspired to fame as a poet, a feat which some literary experts believe he accomplished. For most of the war he was studying law, teaching school, dabbing in journalism, writing poetry and serving as a secretary to a plantation owner in the West Indies. In 1780 he quit this last post which he held for three years, and built and commanded the privateer, *Aurora,* which he appears to have sailed with more enthusiasm than consummate skill, since after several narrow escapes from the British in its brief career, the *Aurora* was captured, and Freneau wound up on a prison ship. After his release in 1781 he came to Philadelphia and *Freeman's Journal.* Highly sympathetic with the radical Constitutionalists, his satirical pen provided them with a sharpness new to Philadelphia journalism. He was soon matched on the opposite side by Colonel Eleazer Oswald, who began the *Independent Gazetteer.* Oswald had come to America from England in 1770, starting off in Connecticut, and fast became a staunch patriot. He was a private at Lexington, took part in the capture of Ticonderoga and went on Arnold's march to Quebec, where he was wounded and captured. After his exchange he developed into an outstanding artillery officer, distinguishing himself in a number of battles including Monmouth. Chagrined at not being promoted to higher rank, he resigned his commission in 1778, and joined William Goddard and his *Maryland Journal.* His *Gazetteer,* begun in April 1782, produced the direct editorial attack technique. In 1783 he added the monthly *Price Current,* "the earliest commercial paper in the United States" and simultaneously revived in New York the *Independent Gazette.* Freneau went back to sea in 1784, where a series of shipwrecks, hurricanes and other catastrophes added realism to his poems about the ocean, but would return to Philadelphia in October 1791 as editor of the *National Gazette.* Oswald went off to the French Revolution in 1792 after fighting a duel with Matthew Carey and unsuccessfully challenging Alexander Hamilton. He also spent a month in jail for contempt of court. Between them, Freneau and Oswald changed the whole tone of journalism.

It was Philadelphia's good fortune that Carey survived the duel with Oswald. The young Irishman offered much to his adopted city, and became one of its leading men of letters. He first came to know of it through Franklin, at whose private press outside Paris, he worked briefly. Frustrated by the limitations on free speech in his native Ireland, he arrived in Philadelphia in 1784, fleeced of his savings by shipboard "sharpers." An unsolicited gift of $400 from Lafayette enabled the 24-year old Carey to start the *Pennsylvania Herald* on January 1, 1785, but he was more interested in producing a magazine. *The American Museum,* a pocket-sized monthly, lasted only until 1792, yet its compendium of pieces on politics, science, literature and medical, agricultural and household hints brought him such prestige that he could list Washington, Franklin, Jefferson and other prominent figures among his subscribers. In January 1788 one of his articles offered "Directions to conduct a newspaper dispute, according to the most approved method now in practice." The sardonic suggestions graphically illustrate the nature of much of the period's printed correspondence:

"Supply yourself with all political, polemical, controversial, and hypercritical authors. . . . If you quote any . . . be sure to omit the sign of the quotation. It will then carry all the marks of originality. If you insert the sign . . . at the bottom . . . write in Italics: *according to the best of my recollection,* and as your recollection cannot be supposed infallible, you may with a good face (by changing an affirmative into a negative term, and vice-versa) pervert the sense of the author in favour of your argument. Thus, truth becomes a lie by prefixing the little negative *un,* and in a thousand other ways. . . . Authors generally write in a train . . . in quotation you may easily turn any author to your use, if you are careful to take out a link . . . I will warrant you, no one will give himself the pain to follow you to the passage quoted. If your piece is of a public nature . . . place at the top a long frontispiece in Latin, but be sure not to translate it. Surcharge your piece well with the names of Coke, Sydney, Locke, Hale and Blackstone; talk of Lycurgus, Solon and Draco, as though you had been their contemporaries . . . If you find yourself growing obscure, thrust in a laconic sentence from the classics. . . . At the conclusion, do not disgrace your piece with a signature in any modern language; let it rest on a Grecian or Roman pillar; an Aristides, Epaminondas, Lycurgus, Solon, Hortentius, Sempronius, or Brutus.

If your dispute is of a private or personal nature arrange your books as directed in article first . . . here you will find an inexhaustible fund for slander and defamation.
Mingle in your ink three quarters gall; this being analogous to your mind, must act in concert with it. . . . After you have finished . . . and found it the dictates of passion, slander, and revenge, you may venture to write your introduction. In this assert, that the lies and misrepresentations of your antagonist have moved you to be impartial, and perhaps rigidly severe. If you have ever discovered any marks of benevolence, generosity, or public spirit, do not to forget to mention them; they will prepare your readers to swallow the whole gorge; and keep it down until they read your antagonist.

Newspaper readers, amid all the villifications, may have read with relief that Elizabeth Miller "living in Arch-street opposite the Church Burying-ground" offered $20 reward for "a redish brown COW, with short legs and middling large body . . . with brown hair round her eyes" that had strayed from her yard. The Overseers of the Poor announced that they had received "divers complaints. . . . Of the great damage sustained by individuals from Hogs suffered to run at large . . ." James Crumbie, "a stay maker in Second Street, opposite the Golden Fleece" posted a $100 reward for the capture of the thief who stole "nine yards of Irish ticken, about nine yards of best white calimanco" and some other items. However, he assured "the Ladies" he had enough materials on hand to take care of their needs.

But the even, gentle tone of the advertisements was often broken by angry blasts. George Felcker was outraged because

> some villain did paste up, or cause to be pasted up, in the public market of this city, a libellous paper in which he made a scandalous use of my name. As these are the effects of some malicious dirty Tory, of whom I have good cause of suspicion These are . . . to inform the scoundrel, that should I discover him he may expect to have little favor shewn him, but he shall be treated as his crime deserves. And I do hereby offer a reward of Forty Dollars to any person who will discover the perpetrator . . . N.B. I hereby also call upon the author of the said scandalous libel to make known his name.

The journalistic storm reached its most violent heights during Washington's first administration as President, and was precipitated by the French Revolution. As the Nation's capital, the city was drawn into the distant dispute by an admixture of the French population and ancient sympathies. Washington, used to the shining role of the universally loved soldier-statesman, found his own Administration sharply split. Hamilton, his Secretary of the Treasury, along with Vice-President John Adams, were strongly pro-monarchy, while Secretary of State Jefferson was on the side of the French revolutionaries, although he hoped no harm would befall Louis XVI and Marie Antoinette.

Philadelphia had nine substantial newspapers—Dunlap having strengthened his by taking in William Claypoole as a partner. Jefferson decided it should have a tenth—one that would reflect his views, so he put Freneau on his payroll at the State Department and made him publisher of the *National Gazette*. The decision broke Benjamin Franklin Bache's heart. He wanted nothing more than to emulate his grandfather as a successful publisher, and was struggling with a little newspaper he hoped would gain Jefferson's support and sympathy. Still his years in France had led him to identify with the oppressed peasants, and Jefferson's choice would not alter his attitude. Washington, determined to keep the country neutral, thus became a target for the Francophiles.

Unfortunately for Washington, the stiff protocol that attended his weekly receptions gave rise to the rumor that a local monarchy was in the making. Anti-Federalist papers openly attacked the exclusiveness and the formality, and the President became decidedly edgy. A glazier summoned to fix a broken pane in the Presidential mansion, felt the wrath directly. He had pinched the bottom of a maid taking him upstairs to fix the window. Washington heard her squeal and rushed out of his room, half-lathered from an interrupted shave—demanded to know what happened, and kicked the glazier down the steps, ordering his secretary to throw the man into the street.

Jefferson, whose *National Gazette* was especially irritating Washington, innocently jotted down the President's reaction to adverse press comments:

> The President was much inflamed, got into one of those passions when he cannot command himself, ran on much on the personal abuse which had been bestowed on him, defied any man on earth to produce one single act of his since he had been in govmt which was not done on the purest motives, that he had never repented but once the having slipped the moment of resigning his office, & that was every moment since, that by god he had rather be in his grave than in his present situation. That he had rather be on his farm than to be made emperer of the world and yet they were charging him with wanting to be king. That that rascal Freneau sent him 3 of his papers every day, as if he thought he would become the distributor of his papers, that he could see in this nothing but an impudent design to insult him. He ended in this high tone. . . .

Washington talked about it with Jefferson:

> He was evidently sore & warm, and I took his intention to be that I should interpose in some way with Freneau, perhaps withdraw his appointment of translating clerk to my office. But I will not do it. His paper has saved our constitution which was galloping fast into monarchy & has been checked by no means so powerfully as by that paper.

Later, when Jefferson's identity with the *National Gazette* became clear to Washington, the Secretary of State denied that he in any way influenced its editorial policies—and Washington took him at his word.

1793 started with a balloon ascension. People stretched out on their backs in the Walnut Street Prison Yard in the mild January sunshine and watched the French-piloted, multi-colored sphere rise into the clear sky and float across to New Jersey. It gave added impetus to enthusiasm for the French. Philadelphians could pore avidly over the inflammatory speeches of Mirabeau and the revolutionists which Freneau and Bache published in their papers. Fenno's *United States Gazette,* spokesman for the conservative, propertied groups, with its pro-British, anti-French posture, heightened the contrast. Washington's stiff receptions became more and more like, what Philadelphians imagined the courts of Europe to be. Students put aside Vergil and picked up copies of Paine's writings. The Administration uneasily watched the establishment of Franco "Democratic Society" chapters springing up in villages and towns as well as in the large cities.

When Louis XVI was beheaded, toysellers found increased demands for model guillotines, and adults and children alike in Philadelphia amused themselves making imaginary victims out of bread and lopping off imaginary heads. "Louis Capet has lot his caput" became the whimsical jest. Washington grew angrier with the press. "We have some infamous Papers calculated for disturbing if not absolutely intended to disturb, the peace of the community." And Jefferson, almost with detached objectivity, said: "He is also extremely affected by the attacks made & kept up on him in the public papers. I think he feels these things more than any person I ever yet met with. . . ."

Washington was peppered in the Jeffersonian press. Bache called him "mischievous" "inefficient" "a farce of disinterestedness;" complainted of his "stately journeying through the American continent in search of personal incenese," a man "of little passions," "ostentatious professions of piety," "pusillanimous neglect", "want of merit," "insignificance" and "spurious fame." This was just a sample.

Directly across Second Street from Christ Church, Washington found a champion in the fat form of an ex-British sergeant-major. William Cobbett who, having taught himself to read and write at 19 when he was in the army, had been teaching Talleyrand basic English before opening his bookshop not far from Bache's establishment. The shop had attractive casement windows. In one Cobbett put all the portraits of kings and queens, including the deceased Louis XVI and Marie, that he could find, reserving the center spot for George of England. In another he put all the notorious criminals, and in the midst placed Joseph Priestley and Benjamin Franklin. For good measure he added the French minister, Fauchet, but relegated him to an obscure corner.

To cope with Bache's brutal, slashing prose, Washington had relied on the heavy polish of Hamilton and Fenno. Now in the eleventh hour of his Administration, came Cobbett, a master of tough, coarse invective. Cobbett refused financial help from the delighted Federalists. He was an independent journalist, pamphleteering under the name, "Peter Porcupine."

He catered to no one. He told the city's Irishmen they had been poorer than pigs in their native land. Frenchmen he simply told to go home. Americans were reminded they were sons of convicts, sent to these shores at the expense of His Majesty and by the grace of English juries. For Philadelphians, he had this tribute:

"... This All Pervading (Party) Spirit ..."

I am out of all patience with the Swinish Multitude of this place. Those fine-sounding words *Liberty* and *Equality* have hurt this place more than the British army and the yellow fever. . . . I cannot get along the streets for crowds of ragamuffins, tatterdemalions, and shabby freemen, strolling about idle, who, if they had masters, might be employed in something useful both to society and themselves. Go to the Statehouse or Congress Hall; the galleries are filled with a respectable group of idle oyster-men and lounging apprentices, superintending the proceedings of Government. Go to the Courthouse; it is crowded with vagrants who have nothing to do but study law. You cannot squeeze into an auction room for idle vagabonds, who are glad of something to stare at. Every rascal in the city who can steal half a dollar you will see in the chief seat at the theater. A funeral, a house on fire, a ship-launch, a speech, a birthday, or a quarrel in the streets, collects them in thousands . . . If I can rid the streets of these dirty swine, I shall be the best scavenger in the city. John Farmer tells his hogs that the Devil took possession of the swine long ago, and has not left them yet. The devil of lounging possesses the swine of Philadelphia. I wish the Gadarean devil would enter them, and conduct them into the Delaware.

People bought his tart tracts—some out of anger, some for amusement. To hurt Bache, he called Ben Franklin an atheist, a soundrel and a libertine whose motto was "Increase and multiply"—"an injunction that his great man had continually in his mind; and such was his zeal in the fulfillment of it, that he paid very little attention to time or place or person." As to his own lineage, Cobbett said:

Every one will, I hope, have the goodness to believe that my grandfather was no philosopher. Indeed he was not. He never made a lightning-rod nor bottled up a single quart of sun-shine in the whole course of his life. He was no almanach-maker, nor quack, nor soap-boiler, nor ambassador; nor printer's devil; neither was he a deist, and all his children were born in wedlock. The legacies he left were his scythe, his reaphook, and his flail; he bequeathed no old and irrecoverable debts to an hospital; he never cheated the poor during his life nor mocked them in his death . . . if his descendants cannot point to his statue over the door of a library, they have not the mortification to hear him accused daily of having been a whoremaster, an hypocrite, and an infidel.

Bache flayed Cobbett in the *Aurora*, distorting the truth almost as much as his protagonist. He said Cobbett was a deserter, had been flogged before the troops, did not pay his taxes, was an English spy and had sold himself to the Devil. He published an obscene and blasphemous pamphlet under Cobbett's name, which led to threats of burning the bookshop, breaking his windows, or giving him a thrashing.

But Cobbett was impervious, and nothing happened. He taunted, ridiculed and maligned Bache—and throughout 1796 the slugfest went on, with Cobbett emerging in 1797 with the most popular newspaper,

"*Porcupine's Gazette*" and prosperous bookstore in Philadelphia. He carried a regular feature in his *Gazette*, "French Barbarity"— describing in detail the massacres at Lyons, Paris, Vendee—the vicious drownings at Nantes, where young men and women were tied together in "Republican marriages" and thrown into the river—as well as the roastings alive that supplemented the guillotine. When Bache, in a moment of relaxation, published a story about a pig who was delighting Philadelphians because "He will read, spell, tell the Hour of the Day, distinguish colors, the number of persons present, etc. etc. . . ," Cobbett satirized the "Learned Pig's Departure."

> Yesterday, being Sunday, the Learned Pig took his departure for Trenton. He was conducted as far as Harrowgate by a select party of Sans-culottes, where, we are informed, they were regaled with a trough, filled with the choicest washings of the kitchen. The greatest hilarity prevailed during the entertainment, and a number of patriotic toasts were drunk. . . . 1. The French Republic, one and indivisible. 2. Thomas Jefferson, the historian of the Bull, and the man of the Swine. . . . 6. Ben Bache and bribery. 7. Thomas Mifflin, A. J. Dallas and Randolph, and success to all others who deal in meal . . . 9. Blair McClenachan, the first of hogs . . . 11. May the enemies of the swine never save their bacon! (The Pig having retired) 12. The Learned Pig—may each of us, his fellow-citizens, soon equal him in knowledge, as we already do in beastliness . . .

In 1796 Cobbett was the subject of a dozen pamphlets and a print, but none could match his vicious style, and all succeeded in increasing his circulation.

*   *   *   *   *

On July 14, 1797 Dr. Rush recorded in his commonplace book: "Went to see a learned pig . . ." Cobbett was unimpressed with Rush as he had been with the pig, and another outbreak of yellow fever gave him the opportunity to say so, and thus set in motion a chain of events that would lead to the Englishman's departure from Philadelphia to avoid paying a libel judgment. Cobbett was not alone in his criticism of Rush's "purge and bleed" treatments. Fenno in the *United States Gazette* used his own "Letters to the Editor" columns to vent his spleen on the "lunatic system" of medicine he charged Rush with practising. These, and letters from readers, were mild compared with Cobbett's trenchant comments, but Rush began suit against both editors. Fenno castigated the libel suit against him in a blistering editorial captioned, "Assault on the Liberty of the Press", and took the occasion to denounce Rush in even stronger terms. While this action was dropped, the suit against Cobbett was pressed to conclusion and resulted in a $5,000 verdict for Rush. Cobbett's property was sold to meet the judgment and costs, and the journalist moved to New York in 1799, and kept attacking Rush in pamphlets he labeled "The Rush Light." Then on June 1, 1800 he sailed for England, more writing, another libel action which led to more damages and a two-year prison term, and a place in English literature.

Philadelphia was hit hard by the depression of 1796-1797. Overexpansion, overspeculation and reckless purchases of land brought Robert Morris and sixty four merchants in debtor's prison. Supreme Court Justice James Wilson fled to avoid creditors, but was found in New Jersey, reading novels and drinking heavily, and was tossed unceremoniously into jail, destined to die in a southern rooming house in 1798. Another signer of the Declaration of Independence, Thomas FitzSimons went broke because a $160,000 loan he made to Morris was beyond collection. Morris' failure caused one hundred and fifty companies to fail in six weeks. Harder-headed men like Bingham, Girard and Thomas Willing, whose romance with land was kept in perspective, survived the crash, and life went on apace for them.

Talleyrand was still in town. On May 25, 1796, young Thomas Twining of the English tea family spotted him:

> . . . As I was walking up Chestnut Street this afternoon a tall gentleman in a blue coat, on the opposite side, was pointed out to me as Monsieur Talleyrand . . . I understood that the Bishop, for so he was called notwithstanding his blue coat, was not upon good terms with Mr. Bingham's family, or I should probably have met him amongst the other emigrants from France at Mrs. Bingham's parties.

But Talleyrand was getting ready to leave Philadelphia. His enemy Robespierre had been guillotined, and through the charms of Madame deStael, the bishop had been grudgingly removed from the proscribed list. So he was waiting for the Danish ship, *The New Enterprise,* to depart the city for Hamburg on June 13. Meanwhile he spent long hours with his friend Moreau de St. Mery at his bookshop on Walnut near Front, where the eminent French legal scholar sold prints and stationery—and contraceptives, the first in America.

Washington had decided not to run for a third term. To the constant carping of Bache had been added the venom of Thomas Paine—embittered at the delay of the President in getting him released from Luxembourg Prison where, for eight months, he lay under the shadow of the guillotine. Paine called Washington, "the patron of fraud . . . treacherous in private friendship . . . and a hypocrite in public life." Cobbett rallied to the President's defense:

> How Tom gets a living, or what brothel he inhabits I know not . . . Like Judas he will be remembered by posterity. Men will learn to express all that is base, malignant, treacherous, unnatural and blasphemous, by one single monosyllable—Paine.

Years later, Cobbett reconsidered Paine's career, and decided to build a shrine to his memory—going so far as to disinter Paine's body from its New Rochelle, N.Y., grave in the dead of night, and shipping it in an ordinary crate to England. There in 1792 Lord Erskine, defending Paine in a criminal action for seditious libel, had established in English law the precept Hamilton successfully argued in the *Zenger* case fifty-seven years before, and young William Bradford asserted in Philadelphia a century earlier. Cobbett tried in vain to interest his fellow Englishmen in a monument, and his proposal was met with laughter and derision. So he kept Paine's skeleton until his own death in 1835, and bequeathed it to his son. When the son went into bankruptcy the Lord Chancellor declined to list the late Paine as an asset. A day laborer kept the remains for a short time and then transferred them to a furniture dealer, from whence to where—no one knows.

Washington appreciated Cobbett. "Making allowances for the asperity of an Englishman," he observed, "for some of his strong and coarse expressions; and a want of official information of many facts; it is not a bad thing." On March 9, 1797, as he was about to leave office, he instructed Lear, his secretary: "Desire Peter *Porcupine's Gazette* to be sent to me (as a subscriber)."

His famous Farewell Address, with its cautions against foreign entanglements, was published in the *Pennsylvania Packet,* September 19, 1796. Bache pursued Washington right down to the moment of departure. On March 6, 1797 in the *Aurora* he rejoiced that

> the man who is the source of all the misfortunes of our country is this day reduced to a level with his fellow citizens, and is no longer possessed of power to multiply evils upon the United States. If ever there was a period for rejoicing, this is the moment. . . . When a retrospect has been taken of the Washington administration for eight years, it is a subject of the greatest astonishment that a single individual should have cankered the principles of republicism in an enlightened people just emerged from the gulf of despotism, and should have carried his designs against the public liberty so far as to have put in jeopardy its very existence. Such, however, are the facts, and with these staring us in the face, the day ought to be a JUBILEE in the United States."

". . . This All Pervading (Party) Spirit . . ."

A month later Bache took a walk along the docks at Southwark to inspect the frigate *United States* which was nearing completion in Humphrey's shipyard. It was not a propitious place for someone who had so violently attacked Washington, and he was given a beating by young Clement Humphreys. Captain John Barry, who was in the superintendent's shack at the time, came out just in time to see Bache running away.

The *Aurora* started off gently with President John Adams on March 4, 1797, partly because there was a bust of Franklin in the House of Representatives at Sixth and Chestnut where Adams gave his inaugural address—and partly because Jefferson suggested to Bache that Adams, with a bit of cultivation, might be brought over to the Republican philosophy. It was a brief illusion. Feeling that Adams was as much influenced as Washington had been by Hamilton's preferences for

MEMORIAL SERVICES FOR GEORGE WASHINGTON

Thursday, December 26, 1799 was another mild, foggy day as this symbolic cortege proceeded from Congress Hall to the Zion Lutheran Church at 4th and Cherry Streets, to hear Richard Henry Lee extol the late Washington as "first in war, first in peace and first in the hearts of his countrymen." The church, with the largest seating capacity in town, was chosen for that reason, and Lee, a congressman from Virginia was selected by a joint resolution to deliver his now famous eulogy. The ostensibly weeping mourner pictured at the right could just have easily been blowing his nose, for colds were prevalent—and more were caught that day, as people sloughed through mud to pay their respects. Never at a loss for a slogan, Dr. Rush solemnly called the colds "procession fever." It was a long service. Abigail Adams arrived at 11 A.M. and did not get back to the Presidential mansion until 4.20 P.M.

229

England over France, Bache gave wide publicity to a pamphlet which portrayed Hamilton as the seducer of an innocent Maria Reynolds, using some of the material gathered five years before by the Congressional committee in its discreet investigation. It now had been leaked to a free-lance writer, James T. Callender, whom Jefferson had cultivated, by a dismissed clerk of the House. Hamilton blamed Senator James Monroe, refused to accept his denial, and called him a liar. Monroe snapped, "You are a scoundrel." Hamilton replied, "I will meet you like a gentleman." "I am ready," Monroe answered, "get your pistols." The duel was averted by the pacification of the two by Senator Aaron Burr.

Bache traced the movements of Hamilton with glee. When Hamilton was preparing a definitive account of his relations with Maria Bache he gave a pre-publication forecast, "our ex-Secretary expects to be brought to bed of his pamphlet containing love-sick epistles." When it was released, Bache reported that in New York the pamphlet appeared in the morning "and at six o'clock in the evening the town rings with it." But "the women cry out against it as if its publication was high treason against the rights of women." Cobbett's *Gazette* sneered, "The white-livered, black-hearted thing Bache, that public pest and bane of decency."

Troubles in Ireland led many Irishmen to America, where their instinctive hatred of the British and appreciation for French aid to their own current revolution, made them natural allies for the Jeffersonians. An estimated 27,000 came through the port of Philadelphia between 1790 and 1800, and about one third settled there. Like the heavy influx in the years before the American Revolution the vast majority were Presbyterians from Ulster, Belfast and Londonderry. From 1797 to 1800, an estimated twenty percent of the new arrivals were Catholics.

As Secretary of the Hiberian Society for the Relief of Emigrants from Ireland, Matthew Carey designated two members to visit each inbound ship. Jeffersonians wined and dined them and offered toasts like "May the Irish harp be speedily torn from the British willow and made to vibrate to a revolutionary tune."

Until 1795 it was easy for an alien to become a United States citizen. The simple requirements of the first naturalization act of 1790 permitted any common law court to admit an applicant if he was of good character, lived in the country for two years and one year in the particular state. The Pennsylvania Constitution of 1790 was equally liberal. Any white freeman who resided in the Commonwealth for two years and paid state or county taxes assessed at least six months before an election could vote. By 1797 it was common practice for Jeffersonian Republicans in Philadelphia to pay some or all of the immigrant's taxes to control the city's vote. Stephen

Girard in 1798 did a bit of this kind of financing in an unsuccessful effort to get Israel Israel re-elected to the State Senate.

In the decade between 1790 and 1800 greater Philadelphia's population went from 44,096 to 61,559—13,240 of the increase were immigrants, and 7,415 were from Ireland.

The Federalists had been viewing the affinity between the Jeffersonians and the Irish with alarm. Recalling that Adams had won the presidency over Jefferson by three electoral votes in 1796, they projected their fears to what might happen in 1800. Harrison Gray Otis wrote to his pretty wife in Boston: "If some means are not adopted to prevent the indiscriminate admission of wild Irishmen & others to the right of suffrage, there will soon be an end to liberty & property." He amplified these sentiments in the House on July 1, 1797, defending a Federalist bill which proposed a $20 tax on certificates of admission. The Jeffersonians attacked the measure as a scheme to restrict immigration so as "to cut off an increasingly important source of Republican strength." Bache savagely attacked Otis, and happily reprinted a promise from the Boston *Chronicle* that the "wild Irish" of that city would never cast their votes for "Young Harry" again. The bill was defeated, but the respite for the Jeffersonians was brief. They were to be undone by that former Philadelphian, Talleyrand, now restored to power in France.

Philadelphia was anxiously awaiting word from the three envoys Adams had sent to France to iron out differences that brought the two countries to the brink of war. Throughout the last few months of 1797 and through January and February 1798 there was nothing but silence.

Talleyrand had been telling his Parisian friends that what had shocked him most in America and Philadelphia in particular was the greed for wealth. As foreign minister for the French Directory and confidante of the colorful, young Napoleon, Talleyrand made quite a thing about American avarice. Finding no inconsistency in his occasional role as bishop and his numerous mistresses, he found no difficulty in accumulating a personal fortune of $650,000 in "sweeteners" from countries which did not want to be invaded by Napoleon. Being a French patriot he got substantial "loans" for his nation to aid in its holy crusade against England.

Abigail Adams compared the three Americans in Paris to the three children in the fiery furnace—Shadrach, Meshach, and Abednego. She was not far wrong, for Talleyrand was using dancing girls, seductive ladies and Madame de Villette, Voltaire's "Belle and Bonne" to soften them. He even had Beaumarchais, author of "The Barber of Seville" and "Marriage of Figaro," gently but firmly tell them that the door to negotiation could only be opened by a $12½ million loan to France and a

231

$250,000 "sweetener" for the Bishop. This was sternly refused and the door remained closed.

The first communications from the trio in Paris, Charles Pinckney, John Marshall and Elbridge Gerry were delivered to the President's house on High Street in the evening of March 4, 1798. Several were in code, but one was in clear. It stated there was no hope that the envoys would be received and that a new decree directed the capture of all neutral ships carrying British goods. Adams sent copies of the uncoded dispatch to Congress, and subsequently reiterated requests for measures to protect American shipping and shores. Jefferson called it "the insane message," yet it split his democratic Republicans. But Congress had not seen the ciphered dispatches, and the Republicans thought Adams was suppressing them. Some were uneasy about demanding them, thinking there was a trick. Nonetheless, on April 2 the House voted the demand. Adams then laid the whole sordid story of extortion before them, together with the boasts of French influence in Congress and her military might.

First, Philadelphia, then the nation, was stunned. The city's merchants held a meeting and sent a letter to Adams thanking him "for his firm and steady conduct." The French cockade disappeared. Those who still dared to wear it risked having irate citizens tear it from their hats. The black cockades of the American Revolution became popular. Bache's *Aurora* denounced the whole thing as a Federalist plot, a betrayal of the American people, and an act of aggression against the French. He described Adams as "old, querulous, bald, blind, crippled, toothless." Abigail wrote, "Bache has the malice and falsehood of Satan and his vile partner the *Chronicle* (Boston) is equally as bad. An abused and insulted public cannot tolerate them much longer . . . they are so criminal that they ought to be presented by the grand jurors. . . . Nothing will have an effect until Congress pass a sedition bill. . . ."

A wave of public opinion supporting Adams swept through the city, and when 1,100 young Philadelphians solemnly marched, two by two, through crowd-lined streets to the Mansion, Adams received them in a uniform adapted to his role as Commander-In-Chief, with a sword buckled around his big belly. Adams took every occasion to infer the Jeffersonians put allegiance to France above America, and these aspersions widened the breach between them. Even Hamilton thought the President went too far:

> It is not for us, particularly for the government to breathe an irregular or violent spirit. . . . There are limits which must not be passed, and from my knowledge of the ardor of the President's mind . . . I begin to be apprehensive that he may run into indiscretion. . . . Some hint must be given, for we must make no mistakes.

Adams proclaimed May 9 as a day for "Public Humiliation, Fasting and Prayer Throughout the United States." Almost immediately he got an anonymous letter describing a French plot "to set fire to several different parts of Philadelphia" and "to massacre man, woman and child." A similar letter was found on a sidewalk. The Governor's office on May 4, 1798 announced:

> An alarm having been excited, by the rumor of some conspiracy to set the City on fire the Governor wrote a letter to the Mayor of the City, in order that every precaution might be taken to defeat so horrible an attempt, and suggested that a guard of constables to be placed at the Gun Powder Magazine would be proper; and that also a sufficient number of Peace Officers should patrole the Streets. . . .

Governor Mifflin promised "upon the application of the City or County Magistrates, to order a competent draft from the Militia if necessary in aid of the Civil Authority. . . ." To show that he meant business, on May 7 he ordered arms and ammunition furnished to General McPherson for the militia. On the 8th he again urged the Mayor to pay "particular attention . . . to the security of the gunpowder magazine, and suggested to him the propriety of establishing such a relief for a guard as will allow of six persons being constantly on watch."

On May 9, however, there was only one incident—thirty young Jeffersonians wearing tricolored cockades snatched black cockades from people in the State House yard, and a fracas ensued, with one arrest. Churches, synagogues and meeting houses were packed, as the clergymen preached against the evils of French atheism and the virtues of American patriotism.

Philadelphia's nerves did not need another jolt, but Cobbett provided it just the same. Less than a week after the fire scare he published a pamphlet wilder than the "Wild Irish" who were its target. A sinister conspiracy between France and "that restless, rebellious tribe, the emigrated United Irishmen" was unraveled in fright phrases. He gloomily described how Irish had infiltrated every department of government, and when the French invaded the American coast, they would rise up, overthrow the government and unleash a dragonized campaign of murder, rape and kidnapping. The pamphlet set off a chain reaction throughout the country, and inspired a Virginia editor to write, "Take care, take care, you sleepy southern fools. Your negroes will probably be your masters this day twelve month." Such editorials were coupled with news items: "An ill-looking fellow on horseback" from Philadelphia had been seen talking with some slaves, and the ruffian was a refugee from English justice in Ireland.

In Philadelphia swaggering toughs gathered under Jefferson's

233

windows at night to play "The Rogue's March." Amateur spies edged up to his table in taverns in obvious efforts to pick up pieces of his conversation. His mail was filled with bitter, accusing statements. At public dinners he was toasted to damnation: "John Adams—May he like Samson slay thousands of Frenchmen with the jaw bone of Jefferson."

Bache blanched at the military measures, and his *Aurora* called for a unit of "Republican Blues" committed to pro-French policies. The Governor, despite his ties with the Jeffersonians, quickly asserted he would not commission any officers for the Bache contingent.

The Adams Administration, which by now trusted no one, kept a close eye on Governor Mifflin. When John Marshall arrived in Philadelphia on June 18, three corps of cavalry "in full uniform" led a procession six miles out of the city to fall in behind his carriage and escort him into town. The Liberty Bell, destined to crack forty-one years later tolling Marshall's funeral, now led the bells of the churches in greeting an envoy who had defied France and survived its temptations. The same day Congress passed a new naturalization act requiring fourteen years' residence for citizenship. A week later it passed the Alien Act, empowering the President in war or at the threat of war to seize, secure or remove from the country all enemy aliens. "Threat of war" had to have the imminency of invasion—a definition which Federalists worried about for fear it excluded the resident French and the "Wild Irish." On July 14 the Sedition Act closed the loophole. It provided a maximum of five years imprisonment and $5000 fine for any person, citizen or alien who undertook to oppose or defeat any law of the United States or who

> shall threaten any officer of the United States Government with any damage to his character, person, or property, or attempt to procure any insurrection, plot, or unlawful assembly or unlawful combination.

The same penalties faced those found guilty

> of printing, writing or speaking in a scandalous or malicious way against the government of the United States, either house of Congress, or the President, with the purpose of bringing them into contempt, stirring up sedition, or aiding and abetting a foreign nation in hostile designs against the United States.

Truth was made a defense and the act was limited to two years.

To finance the military expenditures Congress rushed through two tax measures, one of which swiftly inspired a rebellion in Pennsylvania, reminiscent of the "Whiskey Rebellion" during Washington's administration. This, a property tax, called for assessment of lands, dwelling houses and enumeration of slaves. Assessors were directed to include, in appraising houses, "the number and dimensions of their windows." Thus the name "window tax."

More citizens in 1798 were upset by the "window tax" than the far-reaching Alien and Sedition Acts. There was nothing abstract about agents counting glass panes. Most of the anger occurred in the counties outside Philadelphia, where John Fries of Milford Township, Bucks County went around the countryside, with his dog "Whiskey" trotting by his side, urging the use of boiling water to discourage the tax assessors. This had great appeal to the housewives, and Fries supplemented their enthusiasm by forming a men's auxiliary of some fifty farmers, with muskets and pitchforks. They chased assessors from township to township. The United States Marshal succeeded in arresting some of the farmers in Northampton County, and Fries with 140 men went to Bethlehem, surrounded the tavern where they were held and freed the prisoners. The Federal Government sent a detachment under McPherson to apprehend Fries and his supporters. In the process they routed many innocent people and hauled off a number of suspects to Philadelphia. Fries who fled into a swamp was found when soldiers noticed "Whiskey" sniffing around in search of his master. He was arrested on charges of levying war against the United States.

The case brought out the top legal talent in Philadelphia, and Mr. Justice Iredell of the United States Supreme Court presiding as a circuit judge, pronounced it "the most awful and important that ever could arise in any country whatever." If it was not, the skilled attorneys, citing ponderous precedents, made it seem that way. Fries was convicted on May 9, 1799 and sentenced to death on May 14. His attorney succeeded in winning a new trial at Norristown on October 11 because of the yellow fever prevalent in Philadelphia. The trial was deferred because a jury could not be empaneled and shifted back to Philadelphia in April 1800. Fries was again convicted and appealed directly to President Adams on May 21, 1800 and got a full pardon for himself and his cohorts in the same plight.

The Administration did not wait for the Sedition Act to pass before proceeding against Bache. On June 16, 1798 he had printed a Talleyrand letter which had come into the State Department just two days before. Jefferson undoubtedly had slipped it to Bache. It indicated to the gullible Elbridge Gerry that if he remained in Paris, after Marshall and Pinckney left, Talleyrand would be glad to discuss the American-French relations. Jefferson felt that publication would cool things off. Cobbett damned Bache for treasonable correspondence with the enemy. William Rawle, United States attorney in Philadelphia did not think a charge of treason would stand up, but used the dubious common law to arrest Bache on June

235

28 for "libelling the President & the Executive Government in a manner tending to excite sedition, and opposition to the laws, by sundry publications and republications." Bache was released on $4,000 bail for trial in October.

The arrest just made Bache angrier. His attacks grew more violent. The Sedition Act had become law, and its sweeping language made Federalist congressmen complain their Republican opponents were violating it in debates on the floor of the House. Editors throughout the country excoriated the law as violating the First Amendment, but Federalist publishers found no fault. Even Washington, writing from Mount Vernon, thought the statute would have a salutary effect.

People soon discovered one did not have to publish a gazette to be within the scope of the law's prohibitions. When the President and his wife were passing through Newark on July 27, "The Association of Young Men" chanted "Behold the Chief who now commands . . ." and exuberantly fired a cannon in a 16-gun salute. A customer, emerging from a dram shop said to Luther Baldwin, "There goes the President and they are firing at his a--." "Luther", the *Newark Centinel of Freedom* reported, "a little merry, replies, that he did not care if they fired *thro* his a--: Then exclaims the dram seller, that is sedition—a considerable collection gathered—and the pretended federalists, being much disappointed that the president had not stopped that they might have the honor of kissing his hand, bent their malice on poor Luther, and the cry was, that he must be punished." Baldwin and his drinking companion were fined $150 and $50 respectively and thrown into jail until the fine was paid. The story was reprinted in *Aurora,* but the New York *Argus* asked:

> Can the most enthusiastic federalists and tories suppose that those who are opposed to them would feel any justification in firing at such a disguesting target as the --- of J.A. . . .

Bache had other problems. Some taverns were banning his newspaper, although his general readership was increasing through subscriptions. Through his long feud with the Federalists he kept up a running attack on Fenno and the *United States Gazette,* and more recently had jibed at Fenno's son, whom he described as "Fenno's young lady in breeches." On August 8, while walking down Fourth Street with a friend, Bache was pounced upon by the younger Fenno who scratched his face. Bache hit the assailant with his stick and they grappled, alternately banging each other's head against a brick wall. When they retreated, well-bloodied, Fenno's *Gazette* described the incident under a headline "VICTORY!"

"... This All Pervading (Party) Spirit ..."

There were bigger problems for Philadelphians. Yellow fever was raging again—the pathetic little yellow flags hung from houses of the sick and the dead, and yellow rope cordoned off streets where a number of people had been felled. The dread carts creaked on lonely processions to the graveyards. On September 1 the Philadelphia Health Department announced that safety should be found in flight to the banks of the Schuylkill.

The epidemic took its toll among the newspapers. Carey was forced to suspend publication—the editor of the *Philadelphia Gazette* tried to carry on after several of his staff died, and John Fenno's *Gazette of the United States* closed briefly after its publisher died of the fever. Bache was stricken on September 10, as he was writing about the 73 deaths in town that day. He had already written a piece that he had proof Adams lied when he said X, Y and Z were authentic French agents. They were cheap extortionists, he said, trying to make an easy dollar from the naive American negotiators. He died before midnight. Within an hour his wife, Margaret, who a week before had given birth to their fourth son, put out a special edition of the *Aurora*. It contained an eloquent tribute:

> The friends of civil liberty, and patrons of the *Aurora,* are informed that the Editor, BENJAMIN FRANKLIN BACHE, has fallen a victim to the plague that ravages this devoted city. In ordinary times, the loss of such a man would be a source of public sorrow. In these times, men who see, and think, and feel for their country and posterity can alone appreciate the loss; the loss of a man inflexible in virtue, unappalled by power or persecution, and who, in dying, knew no anxieties but what were excited by his apprehensions for his country—and for his young family.

> This calamity necessarily suspends the *Aurora*—but for a few days only. When such arrangements shall have been made as are necessary to ensure its wonted character of intelligence and energy, it will reappear under the direction of
>
> HIS WIDOW
(Philadelphia 11 IX 1798; one o'clock
in the morning)

Margaret Bache chose the assistant editor, William Duane, to succeed her husband. A tough, veteran newspaperman, born to Irish parents in New York, he spent his first fourteen years there and in Philadelphia before his mother took him to Ireland in 1774. He was editor of the Calcutta *Indian World* until his criticism of the East India Company led the English governor to send him back to London, where he covered Parliament for the *General Advertiser*. In 1796 he was back in

Philadelphia working with Bache. It took him only three months to get indicted, and he was particularly aggravated because he was something of an innocent bystander.

He had editorialized about the Alien Act, and was instrumental in urging aliens to send a petition to Congress for its repeal. With three newly-arrived Irishmen, Dr. James Reynolds, Robert Moore and Samuel Cuming, he went to St. Mary's Catholic Church on Sunday, February 9, 1799 and posted small signs:

> Natives of Ireland, who worship at this church . . . to remain in the yard after divine service until they have affixed their signatures to a memorial . . .

It was an old Irish custom to put notices outside the church, but the tone and purpose irritated Federalist Catholics when they came out of Mass. They ripped the signs down. Reynolds, Moore and Cuming patiently waited, with two long forms spread out on a flat tombstone. As several churchgoers were signing, a group pushed Reynolds, who promptly pulled a pistol. He was disarmed, knocked down and kicked and the petition session broke up.

Cobbett was tickled. This was the "United Irish Riot" he had been forecasting, and he waggled his pen at Philadelphians and said "the day is now come" when this "nefarious combination" favoring Irish independence would bring "terror and torment to America."

Duane and others were tried in a Philadelphia court on charges of "being evilly disposed persons . . . who wilfully and maliciously stirred up a seditious riot. . . ." The jury acquitted the defendants in thirty minutes. The verdict incensed the Adams administration and Cobbett. On June 24, 1799 Duane told his readers he had evidence of British influence in American politics and offered to produce a letter of President Adams. In 1792 Adams had made a comment to that effect. On July 30 Duane was arrested for seditious libel, but promised his subscribers that "Neither prosecution nor any other peril to which *bad* men" might expose him would swerve him. He was free on bail for an October trial. On August 3 he criticized the Federal troops, and a group of officers and men dragged him from his office and beat him. Another indictment was returned. But Duane held the trump card in the "authenticated" letter Adams had written when he was Vice President, and since it was bound to be offered in defense, as "truth," the judges were chary about embarrassing the President. The trial was deferred on both counts until June 11, 1800, and then conveniently forgotten. Duane announced on October 3 that the prosecution was "withdrawn by order of the President."

Washington's death in December 1799 distracted attention, and the

(Hist. & Museum Comm., Harrisburg; original in Hist. Society of Penna., Phila.)

THOMAS McKEAN
Brass knuckles in high places

Jeffersonian Republicans were exulting in the earlier victory in Pennsylvania's gubernatorial election when Chief Justice McKean the Republican candidate defeated U.S. Senator James Ross, Federalist, from Pittsburgh. Out of 70,679 votes cast, McKean won by a margin of 5,395.

It had been a dirty campaign, made dirtier by the press. Cobbett, in what was his valedictory, scathingly denounced McKean in a display of his worst invective. To undercut the German vote, Federalists spread a rumor that McKean was an Irish-born Catholic. Cobbett had no problem linking him with the "United Irishmen" and word was passed he wanted to import "Twenty Thousand United Irishmen" into the country because he said they were men who understood "true liberty and the Rights of Man." He was called "a vile old wretch"; "a vain old man"; an "overbearing and aristocratical" judge. And Federalists in Lancaster spread a rumor, a few days before the election, that McKean had died.

Duane and the *Aurora* led the journalistic fight against Ross, saying, among other things he stood "for standing armies, Loans at Eight per centum . . . High public salaries, Increase of Public Debt, Heavy taxes, Excise, Imposts, House tax, poll tax, window tax, hearth tax, Cattle and horse tax, land tax, Alien Bills and Sedition or Gag Bills to cram everything down your throats."

But, as a political center, Philadelphia was on the wane. It lost its status as capital of the State when the government moved to Lancaster on December 3, 1799. Yellow fever was the villain, and the epidemic of 1798 was the last straw. In April 1799, after discussing other locations where legislators would be safe from the dread disease, Lancaster was chosen. It was not an expensive move from the taxpayer's standpoint. Chairs, tables, desks, carpets and stoves were hauled away from the State House over a two-week period, at a total cost of $135.

More serious from a status standpoint was the moving of the Nation's capital in 1801 to the new "Federal city."

The city clung tenaciously throughout 1800 to its final fling, laughing over rumors spread by Jeffersonians about Adams, for this was the year of the presidential election. One story had Adams planning to marry one of his sons to a daughter of George III and starting an American dynasty that would reunite with Great Britain. Washington, before his death, heard of this—had hastened to Adams, dressed in a white uniform, to plead against it. But Adams would not listen. Washington then came back in a black uniform, renewed his arguments in vain. The third time he appeared in his Revolutionary uniform with drawn sword, and threatened to run Adams through if he did not abandon the idea. Only then, it was said, did Adams give up his ambition to be King.

Still another rumor recited that Adams sent Pinckney to England in a

United States frigate for four pretty girls as mistresses—Pinckney to select two for the President and two for himself. When the tall tale reached Adams he laughed: "If this be true General Pinckney has kept them all for himself and cheated me out of my two."

Talleyrand advised the French directory to abandon any thought of war with the United States and this took the edge off the tension which had lasted for two years. The Federalists were angry with Adams for sending a nomination for Ambassador to France over before the election, feeling they had lost a cohesive issue. Had he kept the pot stirred up they felt they might win.

Jefferson and Burr tied in electoral votes, 73 each, with Adams getting 65, Pinckney 64. Under the United States Constitution the election was plunged into the Federalist-controlled House of Representatives.

Governor McKean was frantic lest anyone but Jefferson be selected. He assured Jefferson, a few days before the anticipated tie that if "bad men" dared "traitorously to destroy, or embarrass our general Government and the Union of the States, I shall conceive it my duty to oppose them at every hazard of life and fortune; for I should deem it less inglorious to submit to foreign than domestic tyranny."

How far McKean was prepared to go came to light after Jefferson won. He told the new President in 1801:

A proclamation was framed by myself, enjoining obedience on all officers civilian military and the citizens of this State to you as President and Mr. Burr as Vice-President, in case you should so agree . . . ; a Resolution was also prepared for our House of Representatives to adopt, approving the proclamation and pledging themselves to support it, and an instrument to be signed by the eleven Senators, in case we could not prevail with one of the party in opposition, which would have made a majority in the Senate, as Mr. Potts, belonging to them has left the House (Senate is meant) thro' indisposition; he is lately dead. The militia would have been warned to be ready, arms for upwards of twenty thousand were secured, brass field-pieces, etc. etc. and an order would have been issued for the arresting and bringing to justice every member of Congress and other persons found in Pennsyla. who should have been concerned in the treason. And, I am persuaded, a verdict would have been given against them, even if the Jury had been returned by a Marshall.

When the news of Jefferson's election reached Philadelphia from the "Federal City" the price of whiskey and gin shot up 50% "since nine o'clock this morning." The *Gazette of the United States* reported the scene through its tears, complaining: "The bells have been ringing, guns firing, dogs barking, cats mewing, children crying and Jacobins getting drunk." Someone counted three hundred drunks. Barbers joked that shaves for Federalists would cost more because of their long faces. Abigail wondered why the chimes in Christ Church steeple pealed so merrily to hail the election of "an infidel." So did John Ward Fenno. He had put it bluntly in the *Gazette* during the campaign:

THE GRAND QUESTION STATED

At the present solemn moment the only question to be asked by every American, laying his hand on his heart, is "Shall I continue in allegiance to

GOD—AND A RELIGIOUS PRESIDENT

or impiously declare for

JEFFERSON—AND NO GOD!!!

But Philadelphians were casehardened to "scare" headlines, and Fenno soon vanished from the journalistic scene. Cobbett had gone to New York to continue his tirade against Rush. Duane was left unchallenged. But Duane had lost the advantage of "on the spot" coverage, since the President and Congress had gone off to the swampland along the Potomac.

No one noticed that the cowherd, who, for years appeared in the alleys near Second and Dock Street was also gone. He had been a long, familiar sight. But the growing city was closing out the grazing grounds.

Even before the Adams' left to spend the remaining days of his administration in the yet uncompleted White House, the Presidential Mansion on High Street was being converted into a hotel—and it was as a registered guest that Abigail spent her last days in Philadelphia. She had acquired a belated affection for the town and the people. "There is something always melancholy in the idea of leaving a place for the last time," she said, "It is like burying a friend."

References

"... IN THIS MIRROR ..."

Despite the clamor of Penn's constituents in the "three lower counties", and their gradual establishment as Delaware, Philadelphians throughout the 18th century regarded their neighbor as themselves. A number of prominent political figures and merchants figure in the history of both places, and John Munroe's article "The Philadelawareans" in The Pennsylvania Magazine of History and Biography (hereafter cited as PMHB) LXIX (1945), 128-149 offers fascinating details.

Anyone searching for Philadelphia's antecedents has to pick his way through much of Delaware's. Christopher Ward's *Dutch and Swedes on the Delaware 1609-64* (Philadelphia 1930) provides a readable, but sometimes inaccurate account. He subsequently capsulized it in *New Sweden on the Delaware* (Philadelphia 1938) for Wilmington's tricentennial celebration. Amandus Johnson's *The Swedish Settlements on the Delaware, 2 v.* (New York 1911) remains the standard to which most scholars repair. Israel Acrelius *A History of New Sweden* was the pioneer effort in 1759, and the Historical Society of Pennsylvania translated it from Swedish in 1874. It has much charm, as one might expect from a minister who took time to count the various kinds of drinks served in colonial taverns. Acrelius is frequently as wide-eyed as the carved cherubs in Old Swedes' Church, a refreshing change from pseudo-sophisticated historians. Documents of the Dutch and Swedes relating to what ultimately became Pennsylvania can be found in the magnificent labyrinth of the *Pennsylvania Archives* whose 138 volumes were published at various times between 1852 and 1949 in nine series. The 19th century editors seemed to print materials as they picked them up, so that seemingly unrelated sections and topics are put between the covers of one volume. Much of the material I have used came from the Second Series, v. 5. Albert Cook Myer's *Narratives of Early Pennsylvania, West New Jersey and Delaware 1630-1707* (New York 1912) contains selected documents and reports prefaced with crisp, scholarly introductions. The Finns can be found in Evert Alexander Louhi's *The Delaware Finns* (New York 1925) and John Wuorinen's, *The Finns on the Delaware 1638-1655* (New York 1938). Queen Christina periodically attracts biographers and in the pre-X movies, was glamorized by Garbo.

"... I AM NOT SUCH A MAN ..."

Forgotten though he may be by the average Pennsylvanian, William Penn intrigues a fair share of academicians as well as an occasional biographer. Arthur Pound's *The Penns of Pennsylvania and England* (New York, 1932) gives an easy-reading overview of the whole family, yet one of the best is Thomas Clarkson's *Memoirs of the Private and Public Life of William Penn* published in London in 1849. Mabel Brailsford's *The Making of William Penn* (New York 1939) concentrates on his early life, but is valuable for those interested in his formative years, particularly his education. Sydney G. Fisher, a 19th-century Philadelphia historian of stature did his usual solid job in *The True William Penn* (Philadelphia 1900), which was reissued as *William Penn* in 1932 for the 250th anniversary of Penn's arrival in America. Penn is fairly well delineated by various anniversaries, and writers are usually inspired by the realization that a half-century commemoration of this or that event merits a fresh look. His tercentenary in 1944 led the Commonwealth of Pennsylvania to publish the significantly titled *Remember William Penn 1644-1944,* which, in addition to a cornucopia of illustrations, neatly intersperses generous slices of Penn's writings with sound historical sketches of various phases of his career. *The Witness of William Penn* by Frederick B. Tolles and E. Gordon Alderfer (New York 1957) is an anthology with succinct, sharp prefaces. Both these last-cited works contain the pamphlet *The People's Ancient and Just Liberties Asserted,* a verbatim transcript of the Penn-Mead trial in which the antics of the defendants bear a startling similarity to the Chicago 7 case three centuries later, whatever differences may exist on the merits of the respective causes. Lawyers will like William R. Shepherd's *History of Proprietary Government in Pennsylvania* (New York 1896) for its technical analysis of the problems Penn faced with his Province. As might be expected Penn's social and political theories have been mulled over by scores of learned professors with varying degrees of intelligence. Those interested in the Indians of the period should write the State Historical and Museum Commission, Harrisburg, Pa., for a list of their publications, a number of which reflect detailed archaelogical finds Commission experts have made. The best overall general survey will be found in their *Indians in Pennsylvania,* by Paul A. W. Wallace (Harrisburg 1961)—a pleasant, readable and knowledgeable account by one of the leading authorities in the field. The Archives Division of the Museum has extensive material on Penn. The Historical Society of Pennsyl-

References

vania, 1300 Locust Street, Philadelphia, has the greatest collection of Penn memorabilia, including the wampum belt reputedly used in the celebrated treaty of Shackamaxon. It is now engaged in a project to publish all known Penn papers. For further details see Nicholas B. Wainwright, "The Penn Collection," PMHB, v. 87 (1963) 393-419 and Caroline Robbins, "The Papers of William Penn," PMHB v. 93 (1969) 3-12. Pennsbury Manor, the restored manor house—reconstructed would be a better word—shows some of the grandeur Penn relished.

THE MODEL CITY

Hannah Benner Roach's "The Planting of Philadelphia, A Seventeenth Century Real Estate Development" in *PMHB*, v. 92 (1968), pp. 3-47 and 143-195 is the most definitive study yet published on the topic, and her painstaking research illuminates heretofore dark corners. Carl Bridenbaugh's classic, *Cities in the Wilderness 1626-1742* (New York 1938) and its equally classic sequel, *Cities in Revolt 1743-1776* (New York 1955) (both now available in paperback) furnish interesting comparative studies of five cities, Philadelphia, Boston, New York, Newport and Charles Town. T. J. Wertenbaker's *The Founding of American Civilization, The Middle Colonies* (New York 1938) traces trends through architecture and is unique in treatment. Grant Miles Simon's chapter on "Houses and Early Life in Philadelphia" in *Historic Philadelphia* (American Philosophical Society, Phila. 1953) gives an interesting account, although I differ with his statement that "Philadelphia never had the look of a frontier town." In the very earliest stages when timber preceded brick by a few years, it could hardly avoided such an appearance. But admittedly the period was very brief, and since neither Mr. Simon nor I were present, his guess is as good as mine. Many visitors to the city during the formative years recorded their impressions. Peter Kalm's travels in North America 1748-1751, published in Stockholm in 1753-61 as *En Resa til Norra Amerika* were translated into English in London in 1770 and a 1937 edition byA. B. Benson (2 vol. New York) is now most frequently used.

The earliest comments are skillfully gathered together in Myer's *Narratives* described above. Several are in the vein of promotional tracts which Penn could and did use—Gabriel Thomas, for instance, hoped to ingratiate himself with the founder by turning out his in 1681, but by 1702 Thomas was accusing Penn of reducing him "to great proverty by . . . unjust dealings" and Penn described him as "so beggarly and base . . . that I am sorry to finde time lost upon him." Notwithstanding occasional flights of fancy, there is much sound stuff in these early accounts. Penn Mutual Life Insurance Company, happily conscious of its historic location on the site of the old Walnut Street Prison just opposite Independence Hall, has made invaluable contributions to furthering the knowledge of citizens and tourists, through several excellent pamphlets and publications. Carrol Frey's, "Philadelphia's Washington Square" which they issued in 1952 is illustrative, as is their more elaborate

Life and Times in Colonial Philadelphia

"The Independence Square Neighborhood" which they put out in conjunction with the 1926 Sesquicentennial. The Company's 24-page pamphlet, "Your Friend, William Penn" (1944) is a pleasant piece designed for casual readers and contains excellent pictures of items in their own collection related to Penn, including his Latin Bible. The port of Philadelphia is served by a monthly publication of the Delaware River Port Authority, "The DRPA Log," a lively journal which deserves far greater circulation and appreciation. Arthur L. Jensen *The Maritime Commerce of Philadelphia* (Madison, Wis. 1963) and Mary A. Hanna, *Trade of the Delaware District before the Revolution* (Madison, Wis. 1917) are but two scholarly works which show the keen interest of historians throughout the United States in the colonial Philadelphia scene; cf. James G. Lydon's "Philadelphia's Commercial Expansion 1720-1739" in PMHB, v. 91, pp. 401-418 (1967). *The Philadelphia-Baltimore Trade Rivalry 1780-1860* by James W. Livingood (Pa. Historical & Museum Commission, Harrisburg 1947) traces the inevitable result of Philadelphia's short-sightedness on thwarting legislative attention to trade routes through better highways into and out of the growing city. Throughout the 8th Series of the *Pennsylvania Archives* dealing with Votes and Proceedings of the Pennsylvania House of Representatives from December 4, 1682-September 1776, there are numerous incidents of complaints against the condition of the city streets.

"... KEEP THY SHOP ..."

Franklin's efforts on the fire-fighting front and his role in the formation of fire insurance companies is a particular source of pride to The Philadelphia Contributionship. Nicholas B. Wainwright's *A Philadelphia Story: The Philadelphia Contributionship for the Insurance of Houses ...* published by the company in 1952 discusses it in detail. The book formed the basis for his article "Philadelphia's Eighteenth-Century Fire Insurance Companies" in the Philosophical Society's *Historic Philadelphia,* referred to above. J. A. Fowler's *History of Insurance in Philadelphia for Two Centuries* (Phila. 1888) is an overview.

The Insurance Company of North America maintains an excellent museum in its offices at 16th and Parkway, including an extensive collection of fire-marks, ship models and artifacts associated with its marine coverage, and paintings. It all is graphically set forth in M. J. McCosker, *The Historical Collection of Insurance Company of North America* (Phila. 1967) The corporate history is recorded in Marquis James' *Biography of a Business* (New York 1942). Philadelphia furniture-makers and silversmith get authoritative attention in a variety of issues of ANTIQUES magazine. "Wallpapers used in 19th century America" by Catherine L. Frangiamore in the December 1972 issue touches the 18th century background. The attempt to manufacture porcelain in Philadelphia is detailed in Graham Hood's *Bonnin and Morris of Philadelphia 1770-1772* (Chapel Hill, 1972). Generally see The American Heritage *Colonial Antiques* (New York 1967) One of the best general ac-

246

References

counts is J. J. Stoudt's *Early Pennsylvania Arts and Crafts* (New York 1964) and for the more obscure artists and artisans, Carl and Jessica Bridenbaugh's *Rebels and Gentlemen* (New York 1942). See also C. Bridenbaugh's *The Colonial Craftsman* (Chicago 1966 ed.). Winterthur in New Castle County, Delaware, has the finest mint collection of 18th century Americana, and the sweep of its exhibits is set forth in J. A. H. Sweeney's *Winterthur Illustrated* (Winterthur 1963). *John and William Bartram* by Ernest Earnest (Phila. 1940) is still the best general biography of the father and son botanists. Raymond P. Stearns' encylopedic *Science in the British Colonies of America* (Urbana 1970) is essential for the serious student. On the early shops in Philadelphia Joseph Jackson's *Market Street, Philadelphia* (Phila. 1926) gets a bit lost in traffic at times but is valuable, as are all of Jackson's writings about the city. Watson, J. F. *Annals of Philadelphia* (3 v. Philadelphia 1926), with the third volume being additions and amendments by Samuel Hazard circa 1876, is indispensable. Born in Philadelphia in 1779, Watson collected trivia like old buttons, and since much of his knowledge was first-hand, his material is invaluable. At times he relies too much on his own observation, as in the case of carpets and wallpaper which he fixes at later dates than definitive research discloses. *Byways and Boulevards in and about Historic Philadelphia* by Brandt and Gummere (Philadelphia 1925) listed 33 firms founded pre-1800 which were still operative, the oldest being Francis Perot's Sons Malting Company (1687). All four insurance companies: Philadelphia Contributionship (1752); Mutual Assurance Co. (1784); Insurance Company of North America (1794) and The Insurance Company of the State of Pennsylvania (1794) are among those still flourishing. Two publishing houses, Lea and Febiger (1785) and J. B. Lippincott (1792) are on the distinguished list. A reconstituted sketch of Peale's "Transparent Triumphal Arch" can be seen in C. C. Sellers *Charles Willson Peale* (New York 1969) p. 195. This handsome volume by the leading authority on Peale is rich in detail and illustrations touching Peale's life, including the sketch of Franklin and the chambermaid. Gouverneur Morris' reaction can be found in Harold Swiggett's *The Extraordinary Mr. Morris* (New York 1952). Anne S. Genter, Sewickley, Pa., generously shared her extensive knowledge of 18th-century Philadelphia furniture and furnishings.

"...DEATH'S PALE ARMY..."

Medical history is always intriguing. F. R. Packard's *The Pennsylvania Hospital of Philadelphia* (Phila. 1938) is a pleasant description of its history, written by a physician. A mimeographed "brief history" by the hospital's P.R. Office (1959) is a fine summary. Dr. Packard is a bit skittish about the handling of Girard's wife's pregnancy, and Harry Emerson Wilde's biography of Girard, *Lonely Midas* (New York 1943) gives added details.

The Pennsylvania Hospital is the subject of an article by Dr. Edward B. Krumbhaar in *Historic Philadelphia*, pp. 237-244

Life and Times in Colonial Philadelphia

Benjamin Rush who, like most of us, was pretty opinionated, has two good biographers: Nathan G. Goodman's *Benjamin Rush* (Phila. 1934) is already something of a classic, and David F. Hawke's *Benjamin Rush* (Indianapolis & New York 1971); and L. H. Butterfield edited *Letters of Benjamin Rush* (Princeton 1951), 2 volumes for the American Philosophical Society. Dr. Whitfield J. Bell, Jr., the executive director of the Society, wrote *John Morgan, Continental Doctor* (Phila. 1965)

Franklin, involved in so many things, never lacks for biographers. I still prefer Carl Van Doren's (New York 1941), but for how much Franklin wrote about medical items and matters, the *Papers of Benjamin Franklin* (Yale University, 1959—) currently in the fifteenth volume, are indispensable. The Bridenbaugh's *Rebels and Gentlemen* gives a compassionate account of the medical community to 1776, marveling at their progress, as perhaps we should, but my own reaction is that if the Edinburgh-London trained Philadelphians had been less snobbish and concerned themselves with learning the basic blood content of the human body, patients would have benefitted far more than listening to the ponderous Latin terms—a feat at which Rush was at his obnoxious best. The newspapers of the time offer first-hand information about the "quacks" and their cures—and some of the advertisements resemble those seen in our own sophisticated age. Yellow fever is discussed in its many ramifications in Dr. Carlos Finlay's paper in the Jefferson Medical College Alumni Bulletin, summer 1971 and reprinted in the Congressional Record, January 19, 1972, pp. E-167 et seq. The best account of its impact on Philadelphia in 1793 is J. H. Powell's *Bring Out Your Dead* (Phila. 1949). Some of the countless pamphlets issued at the time are mentioned in the footnotes to volume 2 of Butterfield's, *Letters of Benjamin Rush* which also gives admirable, brief biographies of some of the physicians who did not warrant a book unto themselves. Virtually every biography of every prominent citizen in town at the time gives their actions and reactions during the crisis—Hamilton contracted it, but Washington, Jefferson and others got out of town before it was too late. Those concerned with earlier accounts of medicine in colonial Philadelphia will find a list in Bining, Brunhouse and Wilkinson *Writers on Pennsylvania History* (Pa. Historical & Museum Commission 1946) pp. 106-109. To show that politics was never far away from the medical scene, see "Politics, Parties and Pestilence: Epidemic Yellow Fever in Philadelphia and the Rise of the First Party System" by Martin S. Pernick, in 29 William & Mary Quarterly (October 1972), pp. 559-586. The redoubtable Elizabeth Drinker's experiences can be found in Henry D. Biddle, ed. *Extracts from the Journal of Elizabeth Drinker* (Philadelphia 1889).

"... A SYREN'S PART ..."

Charles Durang's *The Philadelphia Stage ... 1749 to 1855*, 6 vol. (Phila. 1868) is, by sheer weight alone, the standard work. Thomas C. Pollock's *The Philadelphia Theatre in the Eighteenth Century* (1933. Phila.) is a modern survey, and Arthur Hobson Quinn, "The Theatre and The Drama in Old Philadelphia" in *Historic Philadelphia*, pp. 313-317 offers a casual glance. I picked my way through a number of sources for my brief offering, including Watson, and Charles P. Keith's *Chronicles of Pennsylvania, 1688-1748* (Phila. 1917) and some unlikely books turned up little nuggets. *Rebels and Gentlemen* gives some interesting vignettes but its cut-off date of 1776, makes it stop on the edge of the brightest years. The battle between the theater and Pennsylvania authorities is described in William S. Dye's article in 55 PMHB (1931) 333-372; the British theatrical experience during the occupation in 6 Am. Literature, (1935), 381-388, a brief article by Fred L. Pattee, as well as in J. T. Flexner's account of Andre's activities in *The Traitor and the Spy* (New York 1953). Wayne's devotion to the theatre is recounted in H. E. Wildes' *Anthony Wayne* (New York 1941). Lewis Hallam, Jr., "The Father of the American Theatre" gets reverential space in Joseph Jackson's excellent *Literary Landmarks of Philadelphia* (Phila. 1939), where his various residences are traced in the city and eventually to the unmarked grave in St. Peter's churchyard.

THE CHARMS THAT SOOTHED

H. D. Eberlein's and C. VanDyke Hubbard's "Music in the Early Federal Era" in 69 PMHB (1945) 103-127 provided me with the lines from Salem's "pue" and other interesting data about the period. As they note, "Much of the music performed at . . . concerts at the New Theatre is to be found in the Music Collection of the Historical Society of Pennsylvania." *Church Music and Musical Life in Pennsylvania in the Eighteenth Century* (Natl. Soc. Colonial Dames, Phila. 1926-27, 2 vols.) is a good source work, and Oscar G. T. Sonneck's *Francis Hopkinson . . . and James Lyon* (Washington, D.C. 1905) offers a detailed portrait of Hopkinson as a musician along with a treasure trove of data about the musical scene in Philadelphia between 1728 and 1760. Edward E. Hipsher "Music in Philadelphia" is scattered through v. 2 (1937), v. 3 (1938) and v. 4 (1939-40) of Pa. Arts and Sciences. Eberlein and Hubbard, "The American 'Vauxhall' of the Federal Era," 68 PMHB (1944) 150-174 is a companion piece to the first citation. *Rebels and Gentlemen* explores the theme to 1776.

"THE LINE OF BEAUTY"

West, Stuart and Peale, get brief but excellent biographies in J. T. Flexner's *America's Old Masters* (1967 ed. New York—paperback). Sellers *Charles Willson Peale*, mentioned above, is without peer, but equally indispensable is his extraordinary catalogue, *Portraits and Miniatures by Charles Willson Peale* (Am. Phil. Soc. Phila. 1952) which, by any standard, must be one of the finest of its kind. Sellers gives brief biographies of the hundreds of subjects who sat for Peale. In its annual November issue *Antiques* features painters and paintings, and in 1971 carried a full-page color reproduction of Robert Feke's "Mrs. Charles Willing" as well as others in the Winterthur collection, and two black and whites of John Wollaston in the Mount Vernon collection. November 1972 has an article by Nicholas B. Wainwright, "Early American Paintings at the Historical Society of Pennsylvania" with splendid color copies of Wollaston's "William Plumsted," West's "Jane Galloway" and black and whites of the Peales, father and sons, of Franklin, Washington and Frederick Graff (1774-1847) who was superintendent of the Philadelphia waterworks at Center Square. Hesselius and John Meng are represented. Copley's "Thomas and Sarah Mifflin" and Joseph Wright's "George Washington" (said by Washington to be the most accurate portrait) are in full-page color. *Rebels and Gentlemen* is very good in the pre-1776 phase, and Stoudt's *Early Pennsylvania Arts and Crafts* offers a fine overview. Philadelphians and visitors who have not yet discovered the Historical Society of Pennsylvania, 1300 Locust Street, the Academy of Fine Arts and the Philadelphia Museum of Art as well as the American Philosophical Society have rich treats in store. *Philadelphia Guide* (pub. by Philadelphia Magazine) has details on visiting hours for these and other art and cultural places in town. William Williams is the subject of a piece by William Sawitzky in the 1937 volume of ANTIQUES, and his "Imaginary Landscape", painted in 1772 is reproduced in color in the November 1972, ANTIQUES, from the original in the Newark Museum, where the 18th century collection includes other Philadelphia artists, Wollaston and the younger Hesselius among them. Edward J. Nygren, "The First Art Schools at the Pennsylvania Academy of the Fine Arts", 95 PMHB 221 (1971) provides the sequel to the Peale adventure in art education. As with West, the Historical Society of Pennsylvania, has many Peale manuscripts, and some letters of Stuart, which is about all that either the Massachusetts and New York Historical Societies, the other leading repositories can boast. Stuart, however, was seen through the eyes of Philadelphians with a variety of reactions, as the text indicates.

INTERIOR LIGHT AND EXTERIOR DARKNESS

An English country vicar early in this century began a sermon: "Oh, Lord, as Thou has doubtless read in this morning's TIMES . . ." Denominational writers often think in the same vein, so one must approach warily clergymen recounting the history of their own creeds. Next to political writing it is apt to be the most partisan. But *Historic Philadelphia* has, notwithstanding, a fairly well-balanced account of 18th century churches in town, but much remains to be written, particularly about the Jews who contributed so much to the Philadelphia story. The faithful were closely tied in with politics, and ministers, subtly or bluntly, were used by politicians to spread gospels other than Christ's. Robert Proud, the first to produce a somewhat detached *History of Pennsylvania* in 1797 (2 v. Philadelphia) manages to avoid this fact by choosing a cut-off date before the churches got heatedly involved. A Quaker, Proud, an enlongated dour schoolmaster receives biographical recognition in

References

J. H. Powell's "Robert Proud, Pennsylvania's First Historian", *Pennsylvania History* XIII (1946), pp. 95 et seq., and J. A. Neuenschwander's "Robert Proud: A Chronicle of Scholarly Failure" in 92 PMHB 494 (1968). Theodore Thayer's *The Growth of Democracy 1740-1776* (Harrisburg, 1953) shows something of the intensity with which denominations, as such, become vital political factors and forces. The Quakers, having begun the "Holy Experiment", come in for a major share of scholarly attention. "Conscience, the Quaker Community, and the French and Indian War" by Jack D. Marietta, 95 PMHB (1971) p. 3 et seq. is illustrative. "The Political Dilemma of the Quakers in Pennsylvania 1681-1748", by Hermann Wellenreuther, 94 PMHB (1970) p. 135 et seq. is another. "Conscience, War and Politics" by Ralph L. Ketcham in 20 William & Mary Qtrly. (1963) 416-439 is still another. D. Rothermund's *The Layman's Progress: Religious and Political Experience in Colonial Pennsylvania, 1740-1770* (Phila. 1961) gives a good survey of the whole. "The Crisis of the Churches in the Middle Colonies 1720-1750" by Martin E. Lodge, 95 PMHB (1971) pp. 195 et seq., shows how George Whitefield shook things up, and W. H. Kenney, 3d shows his techniques in "George Whitefield, Dissenter Priest of the Great Awakening" in 26 William & Mary Qtrly. (1969) pp. 75 et seq. Franklin and Whitefield are best observed in vols. 2-3 of *The Papers of Benjamin Franklin* (1960) and in Van Doren's *Benjamin Franklin*. William Smith, Anglican clergyman and politician-provost of the fledgling University of Pennsylvania, is the subject of a biography by A. F. Gegenheimer (Phila. 1943). Henry Melchior Muhlenberg's opinion of his flocks and Philadelphia can be found in *Notebook of a Colonial Clergyman* (Tappert and Doberstein, ed. Phila. 1959) This is a condensation of Muhlenberg's three weighty journals. *The Muhlenbergs of Pennsylvania* by Paul A. W. Wallace (Phila. 1950) puts the pastor and his sons in perspective. Since Philadelphia has several excellent church-related historical societies, a wealth of information is available to those who want to pursue this phase in detail. The cults have not received their just due, and await their historian. A few general treatments are available—the best of which is of no value to afficiandos of colonial Pennsylvania, and the others too vague for our purposes. So apart from the Kelpius group which is fairly well documented, the freethinkers whom Muhlenberg and others encountered—along with Jemima Wilkinson—beckon some lively scholar. Edward C. Carter II's "A 'Wild Irishman' Under Every Federalist's Bed . . ." in 94 PMHB (1970) pp. 331 et seq. points up unfounded fears some Protestant sects had about the incursion of Irish Catholics from 1789 through 1806. The concern was ostensibly more political than religious, but as the text indicates uneasiness was prevalent, and while the French populace allayed some worries, they increased others. The Presbyterians were more vehement in the western part of the State than in Philadelphia, but made their presence felt. Hubertus Cumming's *Scot Breed* (Pittsburgh 1964) is excellent to catch the mood along the Susquehanna and the eastern counties in this period. Watson's *Annals of Philadelphia* gives some poignant and humorous incidents of churches and churchmen in the city, although he refuses to laugh at the culprits who put a sturgeon in a pulpit on Wednesday and made it impossible to conduct services the following Sunday.

TAVERNS IN THE TOWN

I have found no satisfactory book on Philadelphia taverns, or, for that matter, American colonial taverns. It is traditional to fly to Alice Morse Earle's 1900 *Stage-Coach & Tavern Days* (New York—now available in paperback, 1969 reprint) or Elsie Lathrop's *Early American Inns and Taverns* (New York 1926), but neither is much help here. Letters and diaries provided much of the material in this chapter, and Watson lent a hand, but one of the items on my agenda is to write a full-fledged study of tavern life in the colonial greater Philadelphia. Meanwhile Robert Earle Graham's article, "The Taverns of Colonial Philadelphia" in *Historic Philadelphia*, pp. 318-325 is of interest.

REFLECTIONS ON COURTSHIP AND MARRIAGE

The last time anyone bothered to take a comprehensive look at manners and morals in colonial Philadelphia was at the turn of the present century—hardly a suitable time for the kind of look that should have been taken. The contemporaries who lived through it did a much better job, although the 19th century was so shocked at Franklin they ran his writings through a filter. Most of the stuff written about the era, therefore, was a concoction of moonlight and roses, and those who want to see it at the bottom of a teacup can examine the list in *Writings in Pennsylvania History*. Another literary ambition of mine is to do justice to our forebears in this respect, so this chapter embodies just some of the things that I have found fascinating. Thomas R. Meehan's "Not Made Out of Levity," . . ." 92 PMHB (1968) 441 contains an interesting review of some of the early divorce cases, and Claude G. Bower's *Jefferson and Hamilton* (Boston and New York 1925) sniffs the excitement of the Republican Court better than anything I have seen. R. C. Albert's *The Golden Voyage—The Life and Times of William Bingham* (Boston 1969) gives a well-documented portrait of a boorish man with a splendid wife, thereby rescuing Anne Willing Bingham from inadequate hands along with her dull consort, and providing us with the best view of the Bingham's and their mansion and some of their guests. A brave and able performance. Burton Alva Konkle's *Benjamin Chew* (Phila. 1932) has the most complete account of the Meschianza since he reprints Andre's descriptive letter to Peggy Chew, and includes reproductions of Andre's sketches. Carl Van Doren's *Secret History of the American Revolution* (New York 1941) concerns itself with much of the Philadelphia background for Burr, Peggy Shippen and Andre in the definitive account of the conspiracy—which Flexner supplements in his *The Traitor and the Spy* (1953). One, however, cannot point to any volume in print which does the job in this aspect of Philadelphia life. It requires rummaging through letters and journals, occasionally catching pecksniffs like Watson off the pedestal, and picking up fragments that he and other moralistic writers jotted down without possibly understanding the meaning of what they quoted—a case in point being the ad put into the Philadelphia papers by two eager young British officers searching for a maid. I never tire of recommending George F. Scheer's and Hugh F. Rankin's *Rebels & Redcoats* (1957—New York) as the outstanding work on the human side of the American Revolution, and the most vivid picture of what the period was like. Equally I am astounded that Professor John Alden voices some reservations that Mrs. Joshua Loring was, in fact, the mistress of Sir William Howe—as most certainly contemporary observers believed. Howe would have been chagrined at the slight, but Alden at least was sufficiently interested in the Lorings to tell what happened to them in the post-war years, and his *History of the American Revolution* (New York 1969) is a good general account, notwithstanding this bit of naivete. His *General Charles Lee* (Louisiana 1951) fills a void. Anne Bezanson's *Prices and Inflation during the American Revolution: Pennsylvania, 1770-1790* (Phila. 1951) and Eugenie Leonard's "Paper as a Critical Commodity During the American Revolution" 74 PMHB (1950) pp. 488 et seq., touch household problems too easily overlooked. John C. Miller's *Triumph of Freedom 1775-1783* (Boston 1948) is both readable and scholarly, and since Miller was once teaching at Bryn Mawr, his accounts of Philadelphia society during the war have a bit more of the location "feel" than Alden's, although the two complement, rather than duplicate. In the full canvas of the Revolution any such treatment of a given sector must be necessarily limited. The most graphic account of the Revolution—largely because of word-pictures is Bruce Lancaster's, *From Lexington to Liberty* (New York 1943) and he supplied the narrative for *The American Heritage Book of the American Revolution* (New York 1958). Edmund Cody Burnett's *The Continental Congress* (New York 1941) will last a long time before it is superseded in depicting congressmen in Philadelphia, at work and play.

TEMPER OF THE TIMES

J. P. Brissot De Warville, describing his *New Travels in the United States* . . . during 1788 observed: "There is no other city on this continent where as much printing is done as in Philadelphia. There are a great many printing presses, gazettes, and bookstores in the city, and likewise a large number of paper mills in the state. Pennsylvania is truly the great emporium of the United States." (1964 ed. Harvard). No better mirror of the period exists than in newspapers, particularly after Franklin began operations. Many 18th century gazettes are available through microfilm. In 1969 the Pennsylvania Library Association aided researchers considerably by publishing *Pennsylvania Newspapers: A Bibliography and Union List* (Ruth Salisbury, ed. Pittsburgh). From the early struggles of William Bradford to about 1765, the press battled for survival against politicians—thereafter the role was reversed. Bradford has yet to get a sound biography—Franklin's saturate the scene, and since he was endlessly fascinating, the happy procession goes on. One of the neglected books is John C. Oswald's *Benjamin Franklin, Printer* (New York 1917) wherein the great man is surveyed from a printer's standpoint. Bernard Fay *The Two Franklins* (Boston 1933) brings Franklin and his newspaperman grandson Benjamin Bache together, and provides good background for Bache's bitter battles against the Federalist press. Oddly, "the fourth estate" has still to provide a definitive work on early Pennsylvania journalists. A spate of general histories are scattered on the shelves, but James Melvin Lee's *History of American Journalism* (New York, revised ed. 1923) remains one of the best for the period under study. Edith M. Bartow's *News and These United States* (New York 1952) is a fast moving summary better adapted to the casual reader than the specialist or serious student. Carl Bridenbaugh in the various books already cited gives adequate attention to printers, and is the author of "The Press and the Book in Eighteenth Century Philadelphia", 65 PMHB (1941) 1-30. An earlier piece in the magazine is John W. Wallace, "Early Printing in Philadelphia", 4 PMHB (1880) 432-445. Jackson's *Literary Landmarks of Philadelphia*, cited earlier, gives brief biographies and addresses for writers who achieved any stature. In this connection Herzberg's *The Reader's Encyclopedia of American Literature* (New York 1962) is an excellent complement, particularly in measuring the contributions of 18th century writers.

In addition to Brissot's eye witness account of Philadelphia, the earlier visit of Marquis De Chastellux in 1780 is recorded in *Travels in North America* (1963 ed. North Carolina, 2 vol.) Chastellux was more sophisticated and cynical than the virtuous Brissot, and the latter spends a good part of his time challenging Chastellux's observations. Letters of individuals, as distinguished from official correspondence, abound with personal reactions. *Harrison Gray Otis* . . . is fortunate to have the most honored historian of our times as a descendant and biographer, Samuel Eliot Morison (Boston 1969), and publication of the papers of Jefferson, Hamilton, Adams, Madison, Mason and other articulate and candid forefathers, in the massive projects now underway, supplement Franklin's projected fifty volume series which is proceeding at too leisurely a pace for anxious writers. Washington, like Franklin, has a plentitude of biographers. Volumes 4, 5, and 6 of Douglass Southall Freeman's monumental *George Washington* (New York 1951-1954), like their subject, are not given to frivolity, and the massive details are marshaled into an official portrait. Flexner's trilogy is more felicitous in style, but like all who dare follow Freeman, must be measured against the marble of the latter's solid achievement. Washington might have preferred to think of himself as Flexner does, but his objectivity would force him to acknowledge Freeman. The *Writings of Washington*, 39 vol. (Washington, D.C. 1932—J. Fitzpatrick, ed.) was thought to be the enduring compilation, but the Bicentennial-1976 has spurred historians to one that promises even greater definition.

Leonard W. Levy's *Legacy of Suppression* (Harvard 1960) is the best one volume survey of freedom and speech and press in early American history currently available for general readers, but lawyers are more likely to be lured by forbidding titles like my article in the Temple Law Quarterly 1941 (with then Dean, John C. Hervey) "Some Constitutional Aspects of Statutory Regulation of Libels on Government." I still cringe before that title, although Dean Hervey deemed it essential to appeal to our fellow lawyers—and the text, once past the forbidding title, redeems it in some measure. The *Index to Legal Periodicals*—a brave, monthly calendar of all writings on legal subjects—will demonstrate how many lawyers have written on the theme. Zechariah Chafee, Jr., was the great legal crusader in this area, and his *Free Speech in the United States* (Harvard 1948) remains a classic, although the numerous cases before the United States Supreme Court involving the First Amendment in recent years render anything earlier that is not wholly antiquarian, virtually obsolete.

Philip Davidson's *Propaganda and the American Revolution* (Chapel Hill 1941) is vital to any complete study of the years 1763-1783, and Bernard Bailyn's *Pamphlets of the American Revolution 1750-1776* (Harvard 1965, v. 1, 1750-1765) carried such an extensive and important foreword that he was prevailed upon to elaborate upon it and publish it separately as *The Ideological Origins of the American Revolution* (Harvard 1967) and won the Pulitzer Prize in History.

William R. Riddell's "Libel on the Assembly: a Pre-revolutionary Episode" in 52 PMHB (1928), pp. 176-192; 249-279, and 342-360, and Sidney I. Pomerantz, "The Patriot Newspaper and the American Revolution" in Richard B. Morris, ed. *The Era of the American Revolution* (New York 1939) pp. 305-331 are of interest.

"... THIS ALL PERVADING (PARTY) SPIRIT ..."

The political struggles on the State level are most effectively treated in H. M. Tinkcom's *Republicans and Federalists in Pennsylvania* 1790-1801 (Harrisburg, 1950). James E. Pollard's *The Presidents and the Press* (New York 1947) shows how scholarship and style can be blended to make an engrossing and authoritative book. The Alien and Sedition Acts are examined in depth by James Morton Smith, *Freedom's Fetters* (Cornell 1956) and John C. Miller, *Crisis in Freedom* (Boston 1951). Page Smith's *John Adams* 2 v. (New York 1963) is the first good biography Adams has received, and is excellent on his years in Philadelphia. Bowers, *Jefferson and Hamilton* is indispensable.

Election violence is described in "The Philadelphia Election Riot of 1742" by Norman S. Cohen, 92 PMHB 306-319 (1968) which is challenged in some particulars by William T. Parsons, "The Bloody Election of 1742", 36 Penna. History (1968) 290-306. Charles Page Smith, *James Wilson* (Chapel Hill 956) is the first good biography of a long overlooked founding father, and gives a graphic account of Philadelphia political battles. Thomas McKean is soon to receive two biographies, one expected to come from J. M. Coleman whose "Thomas McKean and the Origin of an Independent Judiciary" appears in 34

Penna. History (1967) pp. 111-130, and G. S. Rowe, author of "Thomas McKean and the Coming of the Revolution" in 96 PMHB (1972) pp. 3-47. Meanwhile the only biography in print is Buchanan's *Life of the Hon. Thomas McKean* (Lancaster 1890). *George Logan of Philadelphia* (New York 1953) by Frederick Tolles gives us the biography of the grandson of James Logan, and a prominent figure in the political struggles of the late 18th century. Robert Gough's "Notes on the Pennsylvania Revolutionaries of 1776" 96 PMHB (1972) 89-104 provides a convenient analysis of their economic-political backgrounds helpful in appraising their later actions. Burton A. Konkle, who produced a number of distinguished biographies on 18th century Philadelphians is the author of *Joseph Hopkinson* (Phila. 1931), *Thomas Willing and the First American Financial System* (Phila. 1937) and *The Life of Andrew Hamilton* (Phila. 1941). His *Hopkinson* discusses "Rush v. Cobbett."

Of the three major Philadelphia newspapers, the *Inquirer* alone can trace its genealogy to the 18th century, through a series of "begats" worthy of Genesis. When the *Aurora* began to founder it merged with the *Franklin Gazette* in 1824, and was renamed the *Aurora and Pennsylvania Gazette* until in 1829, its editors decided to publish the *Pennsylvania Inquirer*. In 1829 it passed into the editorial hands of Jesper Harding, who merged it with the *Democrat Press*, and in 1830 took over the *Morning Journal*. It thus became the *Pennsylvania Inquirer and Morning Journal*. When it merged with the *National Gazette* in 1841, the masthead was again changed to reflect the *Pennsylvania Inquirer and National Gazette*. In 1859 it came back to Jesper Harding's son, William, and in 1860 took the name *Philadelphia Inquirer*. In 1934 it absorbed the *Public Ledger* which had been founded in 1836 with the slogan it would "worship no men, and be devoted to no parties." The *Evening Bulletin* started its journalistic odyssey as *Cumming's Telegraphic Bulletin* in 1847, changed its name to the Daily Evening Bulletin in 1856 and to its present name in 1870. The *Philadelphia Daily News*, was started in 1925 by William Scott Vare, long a political leader in the city.

✳   ✳   ✳   ✳   ✳

The best guidebook to Philadelphia currently in print is published by PHILADELPHIA magazine, and is edited by Nancy Love. It combines bright writing with crisp history in describing the various historic sites. Those who want to see Philadelphia in the broader perspective of Pennsylvania, can find it in S. K. Steven's *Pennsylvania—Birthplace of a Nation* (New York 1964) and his 4 volume *Pennsylvania—Heritage of a Commonwealth* (West Palm Beach, Fla. 1968) Dr. Stevens, former executive director of the Pennsylvania Historical & Museum Commission, has written extensively on various aspects of the State. For sheer fascination, S. W. Fletcher's *Pennsylvania Agriculture and Country Life*, 2 v. (Harrisburg 1950 and 1955) is highly recommended. A publication of the State Commission it is a virtual compendium of information on life in Pennsylvania from 1640 forward to 1940.